GNOSIS OF GUADALUPE
a mystical path of the Mother

About Tau Malachi

Tau Malachi is a modern mystic and serves as a messenger of the Holy One, or Enlightenment, in our generation, teaching deep mysteries of the Christian Kabbalah, and serving as a significant voice of Gnostic Christianity in our times. The teachings and message that he shares are ancient, and they are new, alive in the Spirit, and they are a progression, or evolution, of the revelation of the Divine, or Enlightened Being, the Christ.

He began his journey on the Gnostic Path when he was eight years old, though his experience in the Spirit began before that time in his life. From that seed of light, a holy tree has grown. In 1983, he founded a circle of the Sophian Gnostic Tradition, Sophia Fellowship, of which he is the presiding lineage-holder, and he has written many books, such as *Gnosis of the Cosmic Christ*. Since then, he has founded an international Gnostic church, Ecclesia Pistis Sophia (EPS), and has generated an online community, writing many teachings almost daily, and sharing them on the internet for ten years.

This book is an edited and revised expression of some of the teachings that he shares, the "wisdom treasury" that he holds in devotion to the Divine and Sacred Feminine.

About Elder Gideon

Elder Gideon is an apprentice to his *Tzaddik*, Tau Malachi, and has been a companion of the Sophia Fellowship for twenty years. Meeting Tau Malachi and this lineage sent his spiritual journey in Christian mysticism on a life path of art, language, and education he could never have imagined. His prior fine art training in the US and Italy is now focused solely upon visualizing the Christian Kabbalah of Sophian Tradition, through a sacred arts, mixed media collaborative called Sophia Guild. Social and restorative justice drives his pedagogy as a public high school English teacher of underserved youth of color. He is humbled by this, his first opportunity to co-author with his *Tzaddik*.

EPS Press

visit: www.sophian.org
email: EPS.Press@yahoo.com
write: 1530 pB Lane #S1619
Wichita Falls, Texas 76302

GNOSIS OF GUADALUPE
a mystical path of the Mother

Tau Malachi & Elder Gideon

Gnosis of Guadalupe: A Mystical Path of the Mother © 2016 by Tau Malachi and Elder Gideon. All rights reserved. No part of this book may be used or reproduced in any manner whatsoever, including Internet usage, without written permission from EPS Press, except in the case of brief quotations embodied in critical articles and reviews.

First Edition

First Printing, 2016

Cover and interior design: Marion Morgan and Upstream Design
Cover image: Virgin of Guadalupe circa 1700s, Anonymous

EPS Press is a registered trademark of Ecclesia Pistis Sophia

Scripture quotations contained herein are from the New Revised Standard Version Bible, copyright 1989 by the Division of Christian Education of the National Council of the Churches of Christ in the U.S.A., and are used by permission. All rights reserved.

Library of Congress Cataloging-in-Publication (Pending)

ISBN-13:
978-0692810958 (EPS Press)
ISBN-10:0692810951

EPS Press
A Division of Ecclesia Pistis Sophia
1530 pB Lane #S1619 Wichita Falls, Texas 76302
www.sophian.org

Printed in the United States of America

Other books by Tau Malachi

The Gnostic Gospel of St. Thomas

Living Gnosis

St. Mary Magdalene

Gnosis of the Cosmic Christ

Gnostic Healing

Acknowledgements

Many thanks to John Mini, author of The Aztec Virgin, who graciously gave us permission to use his inspired recording of Guadalupe's oral tradition transmitted to him in the late 1980's by Atzec elders. He explains in his introduction, "I have reproduced this material as accurately and faithfully as possible from those original teachings. Regrettably, I am so far unable to convey to you the subtlety, profundity and variety of metaphors that the true masters of this tradition possess. However, I can impart the memories and understanding I have been left with from the vast panorama of wisdom they presented to me. May it serve you. *Ma iuh mochihua.*" Our lineage is most grateful for your luminous work. Ma bless you.

Thanks to Gnostic Teacher Yonah of the Columbus Gathering in Ohio, for so smoothly facilitating the realization of this intention from forum to print. *Imma Gadol* bless you.

Thanks to Gnostic Teacher Anna of the Fredericksburg Gathering in Virginia, for so patiently editing these texts as an attentive midwife. Ma bless you.

Thanks to Marion Morgan and Upstream Design for this layout. May Ma bless your creativity into the future.

Contents

Introduction	1
Her Story	9
Insights into Her Revelation	21
Sacred Play in the Mother	179
Healing Arts in Mother	247
Mother & the Serpent	275
Appendix I: Kabbalistic Tree of Life	310
Appendix II: Giving and Receiving Practices	313
Glossary	321
Bibliography	332
Index	334

 Introduction

I am the Divine Mother of the Great Truth.
I am the Divine Mother of the Giver of Life.
I am the Divine Mother of the Human One.
I am the Divine Mother of the Distant and Near.
I am the Divine Mother of the Lord of Heaven and Earth.

The voice of Our Lady of Guadalupe bidding a humble prophet to meet Her one bitter, December morning nearly five hundred years ago continues to speak to prophets living today. The presiding lineage-holder of the Sophian Gnostic Tradition, Tau Malachi, has walked with Guadalupe since his youth in dreams, visions, and revelations of Her as a sign of the Second Coming of Christ in our times. Even after founding Sophia Fellowship in 1983, he withheld speaking of Her openly throughout the first two decades he taught and initiated companions. They neither noticed nor asked about the common, painted statue of Guadalupe on his main altar in the space where he gave teachings, Her skin toned by years of incense offerings from his private devotion to Her before Her voice bid that he speak.

Dynamic events of growth and change for Tau Malachi, the immediate community of his spiritual companions, and the growing, international influence of his lineage came in 2008 with powerful, recurring visions of Guadalupe. These inspired a greater outpouring of discourses with his companions about God the Mother-Bride from the oral tradition of Judeo-Christian mysticism he'd received from elders and Tau in the former generation of the lineage. It was when he discovered and began reading the voices of living, indigenous traditions gathered together in John Mini's *Aztec Virgin* (2000) that the dreams and revelations of his own communion with Guadalupe began to show him a path by which he could openly share his devotion to the Mother. It was time. In the space of about four months, between fall equinox and winter solstice, Tau Malachi transmitted over three-hundred pages of text, now collated and edited into the book you're holding.

The teachings of the Divine and Sacred Feminine presented

here cannot be found anywhere else: a Judeo-Christian mysticism of God the Mother-Bride woven in Our Lady of Guadalupe. Introducing these transmissions, Tau Malachi first wrote, "In our branch of the Sophian Tradition, within the circle of Sophia Fellowship, we have adopted Our Lady of Guadalupe as the principle representation of the Divine Mother, the emanation of God the Mother, for She is the manifestation to the people and land in which we live and bears a profound spiritual revelation for our times; likewise, in Her we find a prophecy of the Age of the Holy Spirit and the dawn of a Supernal Humanity." Synthesizing the oral tradition he received from his predecessors with indigenous oral traditions of Guadalupe, Tau Malachi has generated an entire mystical path anyone can enter and experience, a path that is universal and practical.

These teachings are written devotionally and with intentionally repeated emphases. Every chapter has subheadings that allow a natural pause for contemplation. Moreover, this text offers special seed meditations for deepening your interior life with creative, spiritual practices for skillfully living in service and devotion to the Mother. Whether one is inclined to prayer indoors with a shrine they tend or outdoors on a mountain, in a stone circle, by a river, or with a sacred fire, *Gnosis of Guadalupe* empowers all who are called as a child of God the Mother to sacred work for the people and land. The character of these Christian teachings and practices might be rightly called "shamanic," as they intend a spirituality that joins body and soul, heaven and earth, through a communion with nature in Christ, in Mother.

Virtually every cycle of one's life is present in the five chapters of this mystical path. Chapter 1 presents a rare, Aztec telling of Guadalupe's story quoted in full from John Mini's work with Aztec communities in Mexico City in 1988. We are indebted to his luminous work and wish to thank him for so kindly permitting us to use his translation. Chapter 2 expands upon the details of Guadalupe's appearances and teachings to San Juan Diego with Tau Malachi's commentary, meditations, and practices from Sophian tradition, ranging from work with dreams and Sacred Circles, to walks of power and creating flower bundles. Chapter 3 delves more deeply into all manner of shamanic ways of prayer, where Tau Malachi guides the practitioner in how to build and tend a shrine or sacred fire, self-purify with water or smudging ceremony, and consciously direct desire energy, or serpent power, through the seven interior stars. Chapter 4 offers simple practices for those who wish to engage in healing arts, for self or others, with ceremonial tools such as drums, rattles, or feathers, and in outdoor settings by fire or river or with the earth, trees, sun, or moon. Chapter 5 explores the spirituality innate to women's moon cycles and the integration of sexuality with mysticism as a sacred prayer of the body. Concluding appendices introduce readers who might be unfamiliar with the Kabbalistic Tree of Life as well as Giving and Receiving Practices. An extensive glossary defines key principles in Sophian Tradition. A list of works cited offers readers further references.

The intention of this book is to empower your prayer life and strengthen your spiritual purpose in God the Mother. Spiritual purpose comes from within one's direct encounter with enlightening knowledge, or gnosis. Tau Malachi speaks of the Gnostic experience as: 1) an experience of higher states of consciousness and intelligence, 2) an opening of consciousness to inner, metaphysical dimensions, and 3) direct spiritual and mystical experience of Christ and God, the fruition of which is conscious union with Christ in God. As Our Lady of Guadalupe transmitted such holy knowledge to San Juan Diego then, so She continues transmitting gnosis to living light bearers today.

Gnosis alone can transmute anxiety and alienation. The urgent needs of all living beings do not allow time for despair but require action. To rightly act with vision and purpose as a child of the Mother comes from confidence in Her presence in all circumstances, good and bad. May we trust that we are never alone, that She is ever with us, and that righteous deeds done in a darker time shine that much more brightly. This is the essence of Her revelation to St. Juan Diego in his age and to Tau Malachi in our own. Ours is the privilege of serving not only in uncertain times, but in new beginnings as well: the Age of the Holy Spirit, the Second Coming, the Sun of Flowering. *The Mother is all. All is the Mother.*

The Sophian Tradition

Long before evidence emerged of alternative Gospels of Yeshua Messiah, Mary Magdalene, and the Apostles, a small, secret society of "Sophians" practiced an enlightenment Gospel of Christ. While they worshipped alongside other traditional Christians in any typical European church of the eighteenth and nineteenth centuries, Sophians privately gathered around a much deeper, inner message of Messiah. For millennia, outer Christian religion preached Yeshua as fundamentally separate from our experience. Conceived in a virgin mother to be born Christ, he alone could redeem us from sin by his cross and resurrection to bring us back to our father in heaven. How all of this is true in principle, for Sophian Tradition, requires seeing Yeshua as more than the Redeemer: He is the Gnostic Revealer, a teacher of a path to enlightenment.

This Gnostic view, however, departs from centuries of dogma which taught that Yeshua was born Messiah. Yeshua and Messiah, while inseparable, are yet distinct. Consider how in a state of sin—ignorance—one experiences suffering and separation as though in a collective dream, unaware they are asleep. For Sophians, it was at Yeshua's initiation at the Jordan River when Christ entered and merged with him, awakening him in, and even from, this dream-like collective reality. This awakening, for Sophians, is what it means to be Gnostic. So integrated had Yeshua become with Christ that he could miraculously awaken others in and from the same dream of sickness, demons, and even death, by activating the greater reality of Christ indwelling them all the while. Salvation to Gnostics is awakening to the indwelling Christ and the experience of Christ or God Consciousness: an enlightenment experience.

It is by grace of the same Gnostic Revealer, the Living Yeshua, that Sophian Tradition publicly continues to generate an inner, living Gospel that is ancient and progressive. It is abundantly clear from the wealth of ancient Gnostic writings now available to all that there were diverse views of Christ and the Gospel from the very beginning. Among such alternative views are several Gnostic creation stories which feature the Creator of reality as maternal Sophia. Even more surprising are the many Gnostic Gospels which narrate Mary Magdalene as an inmost disciple to Yeshua, one seeming to embody something of the Christ in herself. What these varied early Christian texts propose is a principle of God the Mother as well as God the Daughter-Bride. From these, Sophian Tradition weaves teachings on the transcendence and immanence of the Divine and Sacred Feminine to preach a yet more revolutionary message: Magdalene embodied Christ, and was co-preacher and co-redeemer with Yeshua. Her authority as the First Apostle to behold and preach the Risen Messiah elevates the unique capacity in womanhood to receive and transmit gnosis. Sophians insist on Magdalene's co-equality with Yeshua as the healing of all that divides the soul from the body and the body from the earth. Had early church fathers not destroyed Gnostic conceptions of the Divine and Sacred Feminine, Sophians are convinced that Christianity could have gone in a very different direction.

Sophian Gnosticism furthers a balance of the feminine principle with the masculine by drawing on a Jewish, mystical perspective of scripture—the Kabbalah. Divine names for God are but the beginning of the wealth and new wonder hidden in plain sight in the common Bible. *Elohim*, for example, is one such Divine name that is a feminine noun with a masculine plural ending. While translated flatly in English as "God," a more literal understanding of *Elohim* is One-Becoming-Many. What's more, *Elohim*, which is often used to describe the aspect of God that is Mother, is the Divine name in Genesis speaking Creation into being. Masters of Kabbalah describe that aspect of *Elohim* that is immanent and most deeply involved in creation as God the Daughter-Bride who personifies the community of Israel. She who indwells and moves all, the *Shekinah*, is the explicitly feminine *Ruach Ha-Kodesh*—the Holy Spirit. With Kabbalah, Sophians preach a most unique and integral Gospel of God the Son in union with God the Holy Bride. To relate with creation as the word of the Mother, and with each and every living being as a spark of her Daughter, restores the Gospel to its primal power and purpose.

By direct experience of the enlightenment of Messiah, Sophian Tradition advances its unique weave of Gnosticism and Kabbalah in the way of the ancient prophets of Israel. Like these visionaries, who guarded as well as ushered in the coming of Messiah, a century of successive Sophian lineage-holders have embodied the Second Coming of Christ, sharing powerful spiritual teachings and practices for the realization of Christ or God Consciousness.

In Victorian England, Tau Miriam was the first of her kind to fully break through into Supernal Consciousness, or Christ Consciousness, and revolutionize her lineage into a Gospel of Christian Kabbalah and the Second Coming. Incorporating shamanic dimensions into its ceremonial art, she also clarified our teachings of interior stars (chakras) and transmitted an entire oral tradition of the life of Lady Mary Magdalene. Her disciple and successor, Tau Elijah, whom she charged to carry the lineage to the United States in the early twentieth century, also experienced the breakthrough into Supernal Consciousness at a young age. Evolving the Gospel and teachings of the Holy Kabbalah he received from her, he integrated diverse influences from his many friendships with indigenous masters into his Gospel of the Cosmic Christ. Later in life while in permanent retreat in the Lake Tahoe area, he met his young successor, Tau Malachi, who traveled with him extensively and who saw first-hand the way of a great prophet and wonder worker. Tau Malachi fully experienced the Supernal Realization in July of 1993 during a spiritual retreat in the Nevada desert and continues to essentialize and progress the teachings of the lineage he received through his writings, discourses, and broadcasts of his Gospel of the Second Coming based upon his own experience of Christ Consciousness.

The Holy Mother Spirit who moved the ancient prophets to act and speak of the coming Messianic Age is the same who moves Tau Malachi, a Gnostic Apostle living today. Like the Hebrew prophet of his namesake, Tau Malachi speaks from the end of an era for a time that is coming. Both the ancient prophet and the living Gnostic Apostle herald a Messianic Age far beyond the imagination of mainstream religious authorities and scholars. As the embodiment of Messiah in Yeshua was too extraordinary for Jews of his time, so the embodiment of Messiah in many will be for Christians of our time. See, both the First and Second Coming of Messiah challenge religious power that sustains a divide between what is human and what is Divine. It is for this reason that religious leaders claimed that spiritual gifts of wonders, prophecies, and divinely-inspired scriptures of the early church were for another time before ours. Yet all manner of spiritual gifts, wonders, and new revelations moving with a Gnostic Apostle such as Tau Malachi expose as false any of religion's claims that one can draw near but never unify completely with Messiah.

Conscious union with Messiah is precisely how Tau Malachi describes the Second Coming, not as the return of the historical Yeshua from the sky overhead, but in the Gnostic experience of the indwelling Christ within. While Tau Malachi's Gospel of embodiment is an affront to some, for his companions in lineage it is a living, responsive sanctuary, for he, as well as other living masters, demonstrates how each of us may embody the same Presence of Awareness, the same enlightenment. If not here, where? If not now, when? Here and now is the Mother. To live, move, and embody this enlightenment fulfills her intention for each and every one of her children.

Now, on with her story.

Her Story

In the midst of a time of great darkness in Mexico, Our Lady appeared, an emanation of the Woman of Light, God the Mother. After ten years of war, swords were sheathed, arrows were returned to their quivers, shields were laid down, and a tenuous peace had come to the land. Although there was peace, the evil of the Spanish Inquisition moved in the land like a great plague. Nevertheless, remembrance of the Giver of Life, the God with Roots, Teotl-Dios, had burst into flame, flower, bloom. In the year of Our Lord, 1531, on the ninth of December, there was a humble peasant whose name was Juan Diego. His home was in "the place near the forest," but in his spiritual essence he still belonged to the ancient ways, the wisdom of his people.

Early on a Saturday morning Juan Diego was on his way to attend to his spiritual essence and to the errands of the day; dawn was just breaking as he came to the Hill at Tepeyacac. From the top of the Holy Hill he heard singing like that of marvelous birds, as though a great choir of heavenly angels rejoicing, their voices bursting into bloom. It was as though the Holy Hill was responding to their melody, the Holy Hill that had long been sacred to the Earth Mother, holding her knowledge and power, the dwelling of her great wisdom.

Juan Diego stopped and became still, and he looked and listened, and he said to himself, "Am I really so fortunate that I deserve to hear this? Am I dreaming? Am I imagining this? I must awaken from this dream. Where Am I? Is this the place our great grandfathers spoke of, the wise old ones, the place where heaven and earth meet, the Land of Flowers, the Flower Earth Place, the Dwelling of Our Sustenance?"

He stood, looking towards the east, to the top of the Holy Hill, where he heard the heavenly music coming from. The song ended and silence broke out, a deep and profound silence. Then, from the midst of the silence, someone was calling to him, speaking his name, "Ihuantzin...Ihuan Diegotzin...," a calling out as though a mother to her child. As though a child in response to his mother, Juan Diego went to the one who was calling him. His heart was not troubled, he was not surprised or startled, but rather he was happy and felt great pleasure as he ascended the Holy Hill, eager to arrive at his destination.

When he arrived at the crest of the Holy Hill he found a celestial noble woman standing there, and he knew that she did not walk with her feet on the ground, and as he gazed upon her she called him to draw near, She-Who-Is-The-Mother-Of-All. When he drew near he was astonished by her radiance and glory, the radiance and glory of the Queen of Heaven, the Presence and Power of the Most High. Her clothes shone like the sun, and as that immeasurable brilliance shone on the rocks surrounding her, they sparkled like precious jewels and everything had voice. The entire ground on top of the Holy Hill became like a great rainbow of celestial glory in this Heaven Earth Place, and the trees, the Nopal cactus, and all of the medicinal herbs that grew there were like green obsidian, their leaves like the finest turquoise, their stalks and thorns like gold, and in the air was something like gold dust, luminous sparkling particles of light-breath; seeing this Juan Diego was filled with holy awe and wonder, and he threw himself down at the feet of the Holy Mother, worshiping in the Presence and Power of the Supreme.

The Holy Mother spoke to her child, saying, "Listen, my youngest child, precious Juan, where are you going?"

He said to the Celestial Lady, "Patroness, noblewoman, my daughter, my mother, my grandmother, I am on my way to your home, your dwelling, seeking the spiritual essence the sacred priests teach us."

She said to him, "Know, my youngest child, I am the Forever Whole and Perfect Maiden Saint Mary, Holy Mother of God, Holy Mother of the Giver of Life, Holy Mother of the Creator of the Human One, Holy Mother of the One-Who-Is-Distant-And-Near, Holy Mother of the Creator of Heaven and the Earth, Primordial Wisdom, the Great Grandmother of All.

"It is my wish for them to build a Holy Temple, a Dwelling Place, here upon this Sacred Mount, where I will give myself to the people all of my love, compassion, assistance, and protection, a place of Holy Sanctuary, an abode of Holy Light. I am the Compassionate Mother of you and your people here in this land, and of all other people who love me, call to me, search for me and confide in me. I will listen to their pain, their sorrow, and suffering, and hear their cries and pleas from their misery, and I will comfort them and heal them, bless them, and grant them boons, all in the Name of God, the True Light, that Holy Light I Am.

"So that my desire may come into being and be fulfilled, go to the bishop in his palace in Mexico City and speak with him, telling him that I am having you go to explain to him how I want a Holy Temple built here for me. Tell him every detail of what you have seen and heard and experienced here with me, tell him of what you know and understand, the wisdom given to you. I will be happy and very grateful, and you will be richly rewarded for your service to me. You will reach great and lofty attainments as compensation for your efforts to put my intention into motion. My youngest child, you have heard and know my wish, my heart's desire, now go and make it so. Do what I have asked you to do."

Juan Diego had risen up in her presence as they spoke together, but when she had said this he threw himself again at her feet, and he respectfully requested to be excused to go and carry out the sacred task she had given to him. When she granted him leave, he went immediately down the Holy Hill upon his sacred task, going by way of the causeway to Mexico City, to the place of the bishop's palace.

Juan Diego went straight to the bishop's palace, Right Reverend Juan De Zumárraga. He asked the bishop's servants to tell the bishop that he wanted to see him. After waiting a long time he was finally given an audience. He went in, bowed down, giving proper salutations to the bishop, and then he spoke the message of the Virgin to the bishop, recounting the entire experience to him and speaking to the bishop all that the Holy Maiden had sent him to speak.

When the bishop heard Juan Diego's story, however, he did not believe him and was not convinced. He sent Juan Diego away, telling him to return later so that they could continue their conversation. The bishop told him that in the meantime he would consider the matter thoroughly and have some word on it when he came again.

Juan Diego left the palace of the bishop deeply disturbed and in great grief, feeling that he had failed and was unsuccessful in his sacred mission. He went his way greatly troubled, going straight back to Tepeyacac, the Holy Hill of the Mother.

There he found the Glorious Celestial Maiden, the Heavenly Holy Woman, waiting for him, and he threw himself at her feet and said, "Patroness, special and holy person, noblewoman, my daughter, my mother, my grandmother, I went to the place you sent me to carry out your request. In spite of the great challenge of getting in to see the bishop, I was able to gain entrance and I gave him your message, just as you asked me to do, and at first he seemed receptive, listening to all that I said; but when he spoke, it seemed that he did not believe and was not convinced. It was clear that he thought I was making the entire thing up and that it did not come from you. I plead with you, Holy Mother, ask one of the noble born people, someone of position and standing who will be respected to go and deliver your message. I am just an ordinary person, a peasant. The bishop's palace is not my place, my daughter, my youngest child, special and holy person, Divine Mother. Please forgive me if I am burdening you or displeasing you in any way, Celestial Maiden."

The Holy Forever Whole and Perfect Maiden responded to him, saying, "Listen, my youngest child. The people I trust to carry my message and my presence, and to execute this intention, are many, but they are not the most powerful people. It is very important that you are the one to initiate this movement. My will and desire, and my presence, are to act through your hand, my word being placed into your mouth and your heart. I strongly appeal to you, my youngest child, and I order you: Go again to the bishop tomorrow. Recount my message to him once again and teach him for me, and help him understand my intention and my desire so that he will authorize the building of the Holy Temple I am asking for. Proclaim to him again that it truly is me, the Forever Whole and Perfect Maiden, Saint Mary, the Mother of Teotl-Dios, who sends you."

Juan Diego said to the Holy Mother, "Patroness, lovely lady, my daughter, my mother, my grandmother, may I not trouble you in any way. I will take your message to the place you have sent me with all my heart. No matter what happens, I will not leave it behind or abandon you. Even though the path is painful and difficult for me, I will manifest your desire. But they may not listen to me, or if they do, they may not believe. Regardless, I will return to you with the bishop's reply tomorrow when the sun passes into the west, going down into the Underworld. So my youngest child, my daughter, my mother, my grandmother, special and holy person, noblewoman, I go as you wish. May you be well."

Then, Juan Diego departed and went home.

The following day just before dawn, Juan Diego went to a place of the ancient way to attend to his spiritual essence, and he went to be counted at the mass and to go and visit the bishop. The mass was complete midmorning and when it was finished he went straight to the bishop's palace, seeking an audience.

He went into the bishop on his knees and weeping as he shared once again the message of the Queen of Space, the Sky-Dancing Maiden. He still did not know if the bishop would believe, or if he would understand that the Holy Virgin wanted her Temple built on the Holy Hill, the Heaven Earth Place. He told the bishop everything he saw and heard and experienced, all that he knew and understood, and told him that he truly believed and knew that the Celestial Maiden was the Holy Virgin, the Most Precious Holy Mother of the Spiritual Sun, Our Redeemer and Illuminator, the Christ, the Anointed of God. However, the bishop still did not believe and was not convinced. Nothing Juan Diego had said persuaded him in the least, but the bishop suspected that he was a heretic or had gone mad.

The bishop said that he could not build a temple on Juan Diego's word alone, but that he would need some sign, and Juan Diego inquired what sort of sign the bishop desired, and told the bishop that he would ask the Noble Celestial Maiden to produce it. Then, feeling some sense of sincerity in him, the bishop sent him away. Nevertheless, suspecting Juan Diego of heresy, the bishop sent trusted servants, officers of the Inquisition, to follow him and report where he went and who he met with. These servants were priests of a very dark evil.

As these men followed him down the causeway he crossed over the wooden bridge and they lost sight of him; they looked everywhere for him but could not find him. It was as though Juan Diego had vanished into thin air right before their eyes, and, unable to understand what had happened, they returned to the bishop and gave an evil report, saying that Juan Diego was a deceiver and was surely lying, intending to punish him so he could never enact a deception again.

The next day, Monday, Juan Diego did not go to the bishop's palace with the sign he requested because his uncle, Juan Bernadino, had become extremely ill and was nearing death. Although Juan Diego had fetched a doctor for his uncle, it was too late, so in the wee hours of the morning, while it was still dark, his uncle asked him to go for a priest to hear his confession and prepare him for his responsibility to death. He was certain that his time had come and he would not arise, from his deathbed.

In the darkness of Tuesday morning, Juan Diego set out to bring a priest from his spiritual home to see his uncle through the crossing over. When Juan was passing by the west slope of the Holy Hill on his way, he thought to himself, "If I continue along the same path the Celestial Maiden, the High Holy Woman, will surely see me and command me to go to the bishop with her sign, but if she does that, I will have to go and my uncle will die without the guidance of a priest of the Way. It is my duty and responsibility to honor my uncle, so I will go around the backside of the Sacred Mount, going around by a different path. I cannot leave my uncle waiting. There is no time for that." By going around the Sacred Mountain he thought She-Who-Sees-Everywhere would not see him.

So Juan Diego went around the eastern slope so as not to be seen and detained by the Sky-Dancing Maiden, the Queen of Infinite Space. Seeing him, she came down the Holy Hill to meet him from where she was watching.

She said, "My youngest child, my messenger, where are you going?"

This time he was disturbed, ashamed, startled, frightened!

He fell at her feet, knowing in her Eagle Woman, Snake Woman,

War Woman, Infernal Woman, the Woman of All Womanhood, the Great Mother. He prayed to her, speaking with her, saying, "My daughter, my mother, my grandmother, great grandmother, noblewoman, may you be happy! Did you wake up well? Are you in sound health, patroness, Sweet Princess? I am going to make some trouble for you. One of your humble servants, my uncle, is very ill and he is going to die soon. With haste I must go to your home in Mexico City to fetch a priest for him to hear his confession and prepare him, for he is about to face that for which he was born, his responsibility to death. When I have done what I must do, I will return to you and take your message, special and holy person, my daughter, my mother, my grandmother. I will come first thing tomorrow."

The Forever Whole and Perfect Maiden replied, "Understand and know, my youngest child, nothing should frighten or concern you. Do not worry. Do not be afraid of the sickness, or any other illness or hardship. Am I not right here who is your Mother? Are you not under the shadow of my wings, under my protection? Am I not the foundation of your being, your sustenance, your happiness, peace, and effortlessness? Are you not in the fold of my garment, I who am the Weaver-Of-All, the Weaver of the Web of Life? Do you need anything else? Do not allow anything to worry or disturb you anymore. Do not worry about your uncle's illness. He will not die; already he is healed and well, rejoicing in the dawn of a new day and the renewal of light and life, tending his spiritual essence."

As it turned out, it was discovered that Juan Bernadino rose, completely healed at that moment.

Juan Diego believed in the Great and Holy Mother, and he was comforted by the Weaving Mother's words. So then, he prayed and pleaded with her to give him a sign to take to the bishop, a gesture that would bring the bishop to believe in her. The Celestial Sky-Dancing Maiden, the Queen of Heaven, instructed Juan Diego, "My precious little child, go to the top of the Holy Hill where you saw me and where I spoke with you. You will behold different kinds of colorful flowers growing there. Go and gather them, and bring them down from the Holy Hill to me."

Juan Diego ascended the Sacred Mount and when he arrived at the top, in dawn's first light, he was in complete awe and wonder of the vast variety of Spanish-essence precious flowers that were there, all bursting forth in bloom with celestial dew upon them, all setting forth their sweet fragrance as the pure sweetness and beauty of the Holy Virgin, the emanation of her presence and power, and the sign of her prophecy set into his heart, now manifest before his eyes. He was very surprised and amazed, for it was in the depth of winter, the most cold and icy time of the year when nothing can grow, let alone bloom. It was a great and delightful wonder, one reflecting the grace of the Mother's blessing upon those who love her and draw close to her, entering into her loving embrace. The top of Tepeyacac was no place for such flowers, even in the springtime. It was totally overgrown with thorns and thistle, wild bushes, Nopal cactus, and mesquite. At that time of year, even medicinal herbs that grew there would have been destroyed by frost and the bitter cold, but there, where she touched down, in the Heaven Earth Place of her Divine Grace, the flowers were in full bloom, full glory.

This humble wise man, the servant of the Holy Mother, harvested every flower, every blossom, and he put them in his cloak—the warmth of the Precious Maiden filling him—and he carried the bundle back down the Holy Hill to the Celestial Maiden who was waiting for him at its base. She took the bundle in her arms, opened it and held the flowers, smiling upon him, and then she put them back into his cloak, restoring the bundle and passing it back to him. She said, "My youngest child, my messenger, these flowers are my blessing upon you and the people this day, and they are the bishop's proof so that he might believe. Take them to him. Tell him for me that he ought to set my desire and will into action, and that you, as my messenger, can be trusted. Unfold your bundle only in front of the bishop. Show him what you bring. Tell him exactly what has transpired between us this morning, bearing witness of everything you have beheld and heard, and speak to him of the healing of your uncle, and speak of the wonders that are yet to come, and remember the time that is coming and the time to come that I spoke about with you, abiding in the confidence of my blessing and grace. Inspire the bishop so that the Holy Temple I have invoked comes into being and is built immediately."

When the Most High Holy Woman told him what he was to do he went straightaway, as before, to the bishop's palace. He carried the sacred bundle with the utmost care, walking in beauty and holiness along the way, and delighting in the rich fragrances of the flowers of Our Lady. When he arrived at the palace the servants of the bishop came out to see him. He requested an audience with the bishop, but the servants ignored him, and when he did not go away, with ill intention they tried to cast upon him the evil eye, but to no avail. They became curious about the bundle he was carrying. He had been waiting for a very long time so patiently, with his head down, holding the bundle with great care, and speaking only if and when spoken to; so they came close, trying to sneak a peek. He recognized that he could not hide completely what he had, or else they would take it from him by force, so he allowed them some glimpse, and they were completely dumbstruck by the sight and fragrance of flowers in the midst of the dead of winter.

The servants attempted to take the flowers away from him. Three times they tried and failed, because every time they tried to grasp them, the flowers they saw would transform into the Divine Image of Our Lady somehow imprinted upon the cloak.

The servants went to the bishop and reported what they saw, and the bishop realized that Juan Diego had brought the sign he had requested, and ordered that Juan Diego be brought to him right away.

When Juan Diego went in, he bowed down as before and recounted everything to the Right Reverend. He said to the bishop, "Sir, my lord, Speaker for Your People, I have completed the sacred task you gave to me. I went to tell the special and holy person who is my patroness, the Celestial Maiden, Saint Mary, Precious Mother of Teotl-Dios, that you requested a sign, some kind of proof, in order to believe me about her call for the building of her Holy Temple on the Sacred Mount, the place where she asked you to build it. I told her I gave you my word that I would bring back a sign, a proof of her desire, the sacred task that you placed into my hands. She swiftly and happily honored your wish for a sign so her desire might be carried out.

"Today, in the dark womb of the morning, she told me to come and see you again. I requested a sign of her so you would believe. She acted immediately, honoring the request that you gave me.

"She sent me to the top of the Holy Hill where I had met with her before, and told me to pick the several kinds of Spanish flowers blooming up there. So I did. When I had done so, I brought them back to her and she received the bundle into her arms and took out the flowers, then she restored the bundle and passed it back to me, and told me to bring the bundle to you, and to open it only before you. Even though I realize that the top of the Hill at Tepeyacac is not a place for such flowers, and that it is all overgrown with what seems like weeds and other wild plants, my heart did not go from its place in her, I did not doubt. I ascended the Sacred Mount in complete faith and trust, and gathered in her precious treasure for you and for the people.

"When I arrived at the top of the Holy Hill, it was, indeed, the Place of Flowers, the Heaven Earth Place. There were several flowers of Spanish-essence glistening with celestial dew and I picked them in a sacred manner right away, giving the appropriate offering and respect. She asked me to give them to you from her to manifest her desire. I am doing it so that through them you can have the sign you wanted. Understand that my word and my mission are true. Here they are. Please, receive them!"

Juan Diego opened his white cloak, and, as the many lovely flowers fell to the floor, the precious representation of Our Lady, the Forever Whole and Perfect Maiden, appeared imprinted upon the cloth, just as it is to this very day at the place of her Sacred and Holy Temple at Tepeyacac. This is the Divine Image which has become known as Our Lady of Guadalupe.

Insights Into Her Revelation

On the Timeless in Time

Something must be said of the sacred story of Juan Diego and the revelation of Our Lady of Guadalupe, and of all sacred stories of power, whether they are stories of the Old Testament or New Testament, or of any other wisdom tradition. In orthodox and fundamental religion, when these stories are told they are stories of the past, of times long ago, but in mysticism they are not of the past, nor are they in linear space-time at all, but they are of the present, the non-linear Eternal Now. When we listen to such stories, we are not listening to an event of the past, but we are participating in the event happening now, always. Whether in dream and vision, or on a spiritual level, the story is a gate through which we enter into non-linear sacred space-time, the ongoing revelation of the Divine in the energetic or spiritual dimension.

Every time we are listening to the story being told, that sacred event is transpiring as if for the first time. Something of that Living Presence and Power is brought into space-time, and we are participants in the sacred event. If we are open and sensitive to the energy dimension, the spiritual dimension, we may very well taste, smell and feel, see, and hear, as though we are there. "There" is "here," because the story is the emanation of that Living Presence and Power. In the telling of that story, it is transpiring here and now, and we are its participants.

It has been said in the Kabbalah that when Moses stood on the Sacred Mountain, the souls of all believers throughout all time were gathered there; so also when Adonai Yeshua spoke the Sermon on the Mount and when the Risen Savior taught on the Mount of Olives, the souls of all believers throughout all time were present in that sacred space. So it is with the revelation of Our Lady, the Mother God, on Tepeyacac. All spirits and souls who will receive her revelation throughout all time were gathered there, and are gathered there, all in her Living Presence and Power. When her story is shared today, so this great luminous assembly is gathered in that place, all in her Living Presence and Power. This view, this awareness, is a very different way to listen and hear sacred stories and tales of power, being an active and dynamic invocation. When we listen and hear in this way, we embody and channel something of the Mother's Force into our time and place. Telling the story itself is an action of power in the same way as living this experience was for Juan Diego, bearing her word, presence, and power to the bishop and the people. This reflects what's happening when we are sharing teachings in the power of the moment in an oral tradition. We are in the experience, speaking from the experience, and it becomes an energetic transmission that serves to facilitate something of that experience with others according to their capacity to receive it. The sharing of teachings or stories in this way becomes a theurgic, or magical, action of initiation, a spiritual empowerment.

Naturally, the extent to which the energetic transmission occurs depends upon everyone gathered in that moment, and upon their combined level of awareness, for all who are present co-create the circuit through which the Living Presence and Power flows. This view, this awareness, is a practice in the Mystical Path of Guadalupe, for as we tell her story and speak of its various parts, we seek to be aware of the event in the energetic or spiritual dimension transpiring in this moment. As we're seeking to bring something of its Divine Presence and Power into our point of space-time, the story becomes an active invocation of blessings extending Divine Light into the world.

As we explore this story in more detail, we can also say that new dreams and visions continue to occur today; wonders continue to transpire, contrary to what some religious doctrines might say. The power of the Holy Spirit is not diminished and has not ceased to flow among us, but She remains the same throughout all space-time, the Spirit of the Infinite and Eternal, in full power and glory. If anything, in the formation of religious creeds and doctrines, and the hungry ghost syndrome of consumerism, many have simply forgotten how to look and see, and listen and hear in the Spirit, and many may believe, but have never received the Spirit so as to experience and know her power. Whenever you read a sacred story or tale of power, or you hear a sacred story or tale of power, remember to open your mind and heart to the Holy Spirit, the Mother Spirit. As you do, she will take you up into the experience, all as is good and beneficial for you.

The Womb of the Mother & the Spiritual Warrior

In the midst of a time of great darkness in Mexico, Our Lady appeared, an emanation of the Woman of Light, God the Mother. After ten years of war, swords were sheathed, arrows were returned to their quivers, and shields were laid down and a tenuous peace had come to the land. Although there was peace, the evil of the Spanish Inquisition moved in the land like a great plague. Nevertheless, remembrance of the Giver of Life, the God with Roots, Teotl-Dios, had burst into flame, flower, bloom. In the year of Our Lord, 1531, on the ninth of December, there was a humble peasant whose name was Juan Diego. His home was in "the place near the forest," but in his spiritual essence he still belonged to the ancient ways, the wisdom of his people.

The revelation of the Divine Mother, Our Lady of Guadalupe, transpires at the end of an era in Mexico, a tumultuous and dark time following the conquest of the Aztec and Toltec peoples by the Spanish. As the Holy Kabbalah teaches us, when such grievous tribulation moves in a land it is the manifestation of *Gevurah*-Judgment, which is to say that in some way, on some level, it reflects the energy, the shades and shadows, of the people and the land. In a word, it is the "karma" of the people and the land.

The Aztec civilization had declined, degrading into a warrior culture, a society oriented to dominion and conquest. While in this world, in the ignorance, there may be a place for the dance between war and peace, as we know in our own society, even in our own times, the tendency to swiftly go off to war, the lust for war, reflects a fundamental imbalance and sickness in a society, the bestial or violent inclination coming into dominion. Naturally, it produces what may be called a "karmic backlash" in the play of cause and effect. Generally speaking, such an imbalance and sickness in a society is reflected on all levels, material, psychic, and spiritual, as we know in the experience of our own society in the United States. This was also true of the Aztec society at the end of its era.

In any war, of course, two forms of the ignorance come into conflict with one another, and most often, in this world, determining which is the lesser form of ignorance is impossible. The mixture of politics, material power, and religion among the Spanish, and the horrors of the Office of the Inquisition in the Roman Church, represented a clear evil, a terrible sickness. Thus, the peoples of two societies dominated by such ignorance are, in effect, caught up in the conflict of two titanic forces, two archons, and they suffer greatly whether they are on the side of defeat or victory.

To idealize the Aztec society and culture at the end of its era, or to idealize the Europeans and their conquest of the Americas, would blind us to the true message and intention of Our Lady and her revelation, for speaking of herself as the "Mother of Teotl-Dios," she takes no sides. She comes for the sake of all of her children, all peoples, reminding them of their spiritual essence and the True God, the True Light, by whatever name they might know and understand the Divine. The truth is, her appearance is not exclusively an Aztec or Christian revelation. It is a revelation of Teotl-Dios transcending any given religion or wisdom tradition. It is given to the faithful of both peoples, Aztec and Spanish European Christians. Her revelation comes from Primordial Being, Primordial Wisdom.

If we look into such revelations, almost always they come amidst times of trial and tribulation, times of great conflict and challenge. A new paradigm appears possible only in times of radical transition and change when what is most needed is new guidance, insight, and direction. Influx emerges during times of what Sophian tradition personifies as the Dark Mother, through whom we are able to see and embrace the Bright Mother, bringing a new vision of our coming into being. So it is after great horror and a living nightmare that the revelation of Our Lady of Guadalupe-Tonantztin, the Forever Whole and Perfect Maiden, was recognized, received, and flowers to this very day.

Although she appears during a time of turmoil in Mexico, appearing for the sake of indigenous Mexicans and the conquering Spanish people, in truth she appears at the outset of a global tumult that continues to this day, a time of transition between great ages—or aeons—which literally spans hundreds of years. Although many modern so-called prophets have rushed to proclaim the dawn of a "New Age" or a "Golden Era," in truth, the appearance of Our Lady comes at the outset of a plunge into a Dark Age, a time of an evolutionary crisis as we transit between two great aeons, the old age and new age. We may say that she comes to usher in the new age or aeon, and we may say that in her revelation we have a vision of that aeon of light. We may even say that she teaches us how to enter and dwell in that new aeon in the present moment as individuals, even while the world or collective remains in the old aeon. Clearly, as we all can see, the world, humanity, has not entered into the new aeon as yet, but continues in the dominion of the same old ignorance.

Guadalupe is the herald of a new age or new aeon, a new understanding of Heaven and Earth, and she is the birther of a new Humanity. Her birth pangs continue. We are in the womb of the Mother, and the trials and tribulations we face are the tumult of birth, which also are the pains of her Holy Child being born. The pains of the Holy Mother and her Child are one and the same. The revelation of Mother God happens in the midst of a dark time; it happens in the midst of the darkness of winter near the winter solstice, and it arises out of the subtle light of predawn, just as night is giving way to the day. All of this suggests the womb of the Holy Mother and her conception, gestation and giving birth. Although she is the Forever Whole and Perfect Maiden, which is to say, the Virgin, she is pregnant and she is giving birth to the Child of Light, a Divine and Supernal Humanity.

As she reveals herself to us, she who is God the Mother, we and our world on the one hand are the Child to whom she is giving birth; on the other hand, we are called as her midwives, the conscious agents in the manifestation of her desire, the union of Heaven and Earth, the generation of a New Heaven and New Earth, and New Humanity. Just like Juan Diego, we are called to an active and dynamic surrender, to embody the Mother's Force, the Light from above, and with the reception of that Holy and Supernal Light, we are called to awaken, to actualize and realize the Fiery Intelligence, the power of the Holy Spirit in us.

Now, the Mother does not appear to a wealthy or noble person, or to a person of position and power in the world, but she appears to a peasant, a common person. In fact, in her revelation she specifically states that it is not those of high social, political, and economic standing, but common, ordinary people, the oppressed and the outcast—the same kind of people in the Gospels Yeshua Messiah calls upon to follow him—who will bear her message and her Divine Presence and Power.

Juan Diego, however ordinary his claims of himself, is not exactly an "ordinary" peasant, for according to the tradition he encounters the Virgin on his way to attend to his spiritual essence and sacred tasks, implying the spiritual life and practice of a disciplined and trained individual, a spiritually gifted practitioner, a seer and wonderworker, a shaman. Indeed, as the experience and vision unfolds, we are told that he was not surprised or startled, which must mean that he was familiar with the energy dimension and world of spirits, and implies that he is a "walker between worlds," a shaman. Likewise, given that he immediately takes up the sacred task that he is given by Mother, one that is, in fact, extremely dangerous, risking his very life, we know that he is a spiritual warrior, righteous and impeccable, having great discipline and resolve, a great force of will. He is a shaman-warrior, a great holy person whose name is Cuauhtlatoatzin: Honorable Speaking Eagle.

We all have the potential to be a holy person. With training and discipline, we can all learn the way of the spiritual warrior and shaman. Perhaps we are not all called to be a seer and wonderworker, or a shaman among our people, but we all can be true warriors and we all carry "medicine," something of the presence and power of Our Mother. We all have a divine purpose here, a mission in the Mother Spirit to accomplish. Indeed, if we are to take up the spiritual life and practice, and the labor of conscious evolution in the midst of dark and tumultuous times, we must be spiritual warriors. Both women and men alike must be warriors, for the power of the present ignorance, the present darkness, is very strong in this world and it takes the strength, courage, and the force of will or discipline of a warrior to live the Life Divine, embodying the Light-Presence and Light-Power. Virtually nothing in the world, in the dominion of the demiurge, will support or encourage us in the Divine Life, but quite the opposite is true. The powers that rule the unenlightened society will do everything to discourage us and to undermine our efforts. Truly, to make any real progress in our spiritual labor we will have to be a warrior in spirit, just as Juan Diego was. Look and see! Here is a person in the midst of extremely dark times who, nevertheless, remains faithful, attending to his spiritual essence and sacred tasks, even in the face of great persecution and at the risk of his very life. Honorable Speaking Eagle, indeed!

Now we might inquire what it might mean to attend to our spiritual essence and engage in sacred tasks; inquiring, we might find hints as to what this might mean encoded skillfully in the story. First, Juan Diego is out and about before dawn: He is in the great outdoors, walking on Earth Mother beneath Sky Father, walking in the Presence of Awareness, aware of all life as sacred, aware of all life as the emanation and manifestation of the Great Spirit, of Teotl. Walking in this way he is walking in communion with the Spirit and the Powers, looking and seeing, listening and hearing, intimately connected with the Divine, walking in the awareness of the Divine within and all around him. In this we may understand why he is not surprised or startled when Heaven and Earth meet and Mother God appears to him, for already he walks in the awareness of the Divine Presence and Power. Already he is walking with and in Teotl-Dios.

Pre-dawn and sunrise together are well known as a time of great power, corresponding to the direction east in the Sacred Circle. This is a time of renewal and regeneration, the night giving way to the light and life of a new day. If we wish to draw forth something of our spiritual essence and wish to charge our energetic being, prayer and meditation at dawn is ideal, and the most powerful place for this is in the great outdoors, directly exposing ourselves to the sky, the power of the elements and the light of the morning sun. Even if we do not know how to pray or meditate, just sitting, standing, or walking at this time will draw out something of our spiritual essence and will charge and regenerate our energetic being, our energetic body. Dawn is a natural time of renewal, recharging, and regeneration. As reflected by the songs of birds and stirring of creatures awakening, the spirits and the powers are happy at this time, rejoicing in the dawn of a new day.

There are, of course, many practices, many prayers, meditations, and rituals that might be performed. As an example, creating a simple Sacred Circle, we may call upon the Divine. We may call upon our Heavenly Father and Earthly Mother, and we may invoke the Divine powers into the Sacred Circle. Then, facing the east, we may uplift our arms and welcome the Light of the Spiritual Sun, and we may pray for blessings upon ourselves and the people, perhaps offering up some smudge or incense as we do. Then we might sit or stand in the circle, listening and hearing, looking and seeing, abiding in communion. Perhaps we might go on a walk, abiding in the Presence of Awareness, communing with the Spirit and Powers along the way.

The Sacred Circle is the Circle of Life, and it is the holy womb of the Mother. We are the Holy Child being born from her womb, the Spiritual Sun before us and within us. It is all good. All life is sacred as it is, for it is all the Holy Light of the Spiritual Sun!

In this we may have some idea of what attending to our spiritual essence means, but, as can be seen, there are many different forms of spiritual practice we may take up, the above representing an example of a very simple and direct way, one that is accessible to everybody.

Now tending to sacred tasks can also mean many things. It can be the gathering of medicinal herbs or sacred objects, and it can be various spiritual works for people, or various good works. In the case of a spiritual warrior, it is honoring and carrying out any commitment that they have made. In the Way of the Weave, as taught in our tradition, and this is integral to the Mystical Path of Guadalupe, a sacred task could be any duty or activity, apparently sacred or mundane, performed with the awareness of our innate connection with the Divine, giving expression to the Divine, aware of the sacred and the mundane as inseparable from one another, completely interwoven with one another—all divine, all sacred. This is the awareness with which we must walk in the world, serving God, the True Light, in all that we do, and letting the Light-Presence and Light-Power of the Spiritual Sun take up the action and accomplish it, whether on a physical and material level, or on the psychic or spiritual level.

Specifically, though, sacred tasks are spiritual works we take up for people and are things that the Divine Powers ask us to do, tasks of the Continuum. Such are actions of a warrior and are spiritual labors of a shaman. Thus, in that Juan Diego is on his way to attend to his spiritual essence and to perform sacred tasks, we know that he is a trained and disciplined person, a spiritual warrior and shaman. At times it has been said that Juan Diego was on an active vision quest for the people, or that he was setting out upon a vision quest and was swiftly taken up by the Great Spirit and Powers. In this we understand that it is through an active spiritual life and practice that we draw near to the Divine Mother and deepen our experience of her. It must also be said that the Mother is Divine Grace, and that as much as reaching out and touching the devout and the initiate, she often reaches out and touches very ordinary individuals who have little in the way of a spiritual life and practice, for she is, indeed, the Compassionate Mother, and she is always present with us, loving all equally.

The Ancient Ways

...his home was in the place near the forest, but in his spiritual essence he still belonged to the ancient ways, the wisdom of his people.

The word for "the place near the forest" in Nahuatl, the language of the Aztec and Toltec people in which the Mother God spoke with Juan Diego, has many connotations, as well outlined and discussed in *The Aztec Virgin*, by John Mini. Essentially, it implies loyalty to spiritual leadership of the Aztecs, hence faith in Aztec and Toltec spirituality—"the ancient ways, the wisdom of his people." Submitting to Catholicism, and attending mass outwardly, inwardly and in secret Juan Diego continues to believe and practice the ancient ways of the indigenous people of Mexico. As we have said, he is a "man of knowledge," a warrior and shaman, adept in Aztec spirituality.

This, of course, is very similar to the practice of Gnostic spirituality following the dawn of the orthodox dominion. Often, although outwardly appearing faithful to the orthodox hierarchy and to its religious creeds and doctrines, inwardly and in secret, Gnostics held true to their own beliefs and spiritual practices. In many respects their knowledge is very similar to that of the Aztec and Toltec people to whom the Mother God spoke, a deeper spirituality beyond mere religious belief. Such spirituality focused by direct, mystical experiences is profoundly magical, powerful, and spiritually effective.

We may say Juan Diego is a "Gnostic," a man of gnosis: direct, unmediated, enlightened knowing. Living shamanic traditions around the world transmit this enlightened knowing by way of the direct experience of their symbols and sounds. Juan Diego clearly experienced Aztec gnosis, a tradition of direct communion with the Divine Presence and Power. We know this because the Mother God reveals herself to him and through him. He is an integral, inseparable part of her message. Speaking of herself as the Mother of Teotl-Dios, a term for God in Nahuatl and Spanish, she is speaking of herself as both the Mother God of the Aztec and Toltec people and the Virgin Mother of Christ. She is making it very clear that her revelation is more complex than the way either Catholics or Mexican spiritualists might oversimplify.

Enlightened shamanism is particularly intriguing when Christians look deeply into the foundations of their Biblical ancestors. If we remove the flat or shallow stereotypes of the prophets and the Messiah engendered by orthodox Judaism and Christianity, and look into the Scriptures with the view of the prophets and the Messiah as shamans, and view their spirituality as a shamanic path, we may glean far greater wisdom from them and we may restore ourselves to a pure spirituality, shedding the husk of man-made religion and enter into the experience of direct spiritual revelation.

When we look into the actual spiritual practices of the ancient Israeli patriarchs and matriarchs, and we look into the spiritual practices of the ancient Israeli prophets, what we find is a form of shamanism among the ancient Hebrew people, one very similar to the spirituality of indigenous people around the world. What was unusual in the time of ancient Judaism was its emphasis upon the singularity of the Great Spirit, the Sacred Unity underlying all creation. If we look to Yohanan the Baptist and Adonai Yeshua, we find the shamanic thread continuing, a profoundly nature and earth oriented spirituality. As much as ushering in the Advent of the Messiah, the realization of Supernal consciousness, if we listen to their teachings and look into the spiritual practices Yohanan and Yeshua taught and enacted, they are restoring the original Hebrew spirituality, the ancient ways of the Hebrew seer and wonderworker, the Hebrew shaman.

In his ministry, Adonai Yeshua was noted for his public wonderworking, the greatest of which were exorcisms and healings. This is the classical role of a "medicine man" or shaman in a tribe. Likewise, when giving teachings or speaking about the Divine sovereignty, almost always Yeshua spoke in terms of the wisdom of nature and of the glory and power of Creator in nature, the typical way a shaman teaches. If we are to speak of the gnosis of the Messiah, as much as speaking of the enlightenment experience, the Supernal Realization, we must also speak of his wonderworking or healing practices, which is to say his shamanic spirituality.

Now, when we look into the creeds and doctrines of orthodox and fundamentalist Christianity—the outer and unspiritual church—we see nothing of the deeper spirituality that Yohanan and Yeshua taught, only the most superficial beliefs and ceremonies lacking the true and full power of the Holy Spirit. Rather than a faith joining heaven and earth as Yohanan and Yeshua taught us, we see the emphasis upon heaven and a remote God, and the denial of the Earth and the immanent presence and power of God. In place of a pure spirituality in which everyone has immediate access to the Spirit and the Powers, a religion relying on the mediation of priests was constructed, the same dominion of the Sadducees and Pharisees against which Yohanan and Yeshua both so sharply attacked. What we see is the same old ignorance having dominated the Christian stream of Light Transmission.

Essentially, under the dominion of orthodoxy in the outer and unspiritual church, for the most part, the active power of the Holy Spirit and the true gnosis of the Messiah has been lost. The deeper truth of a union of heaven and earth and a pure spirituality of direct access and self-realization has been completely distorted and obscured. Compare this phenomenon with what Adonai Yeshua taught in saying 39 of the Gospel of St. Thomas: *The Pharisees and the scholars have taken the keys of knowledge and have hidden them. They have not entered nor have they allowed those who want to enter to do so. As for you, be as sly as snakes and as simple as doves.* Here and there something of the Holy Spirit, the Mother Spirit, touches down and reveals herself, but that is the rare exception rather than the norm. In original Christianity, according to the New Testament, the norm was the experience of the Holy Spirit working wonders with, in, and through the people, a spirituality of direct experience and knowledge.

As a spiritual warrior and shaman of the Aztec-Toltec tradition, Juan Diego is intimately acquainted with a pure spirituality, one founded upon direct spiritual and mystical experience, a spirituality in which everyone has immediate access to the Spirit and Powers, and in which everyone experiences the revelation of the Spirit in dreams and visions and omens. Essentially, he holds something of the deeper spirituality, the knowledge, wisdom and power that was lost by the outer church: the golden thread of gnosis and the Light Transmission, the reception of the Holy Spirit. Revealing herself to Juan Diego, an Aztec medicine man, a man of knowledge, Guadalupe acts to restore the active power of the Spirit to the Christian stream and speaks of the need for a weaving of streams, a weaving of wisdom traditions. Weaving is our necessary labor towards the advent of a true new age, the age of the Holy Spirit, the Second Coming of the Anointed of God. In Toltec-Aztec tradition this new era is called the "Sixth Sun," the "Sun of Flowers" or "Sun of Flowering-Blooming."

Yohanan and Yeshua taught a spirituality of the union of heaven and earth, a spirituality of direct experience of the Spirit and Powers, and of the embodiment of the Divine Presence and Power. This knowledge and wisdom has been concealed from the people, the faithful, and over time has been lost by the spiritual leaders of the outer church. It has not been completely lost from all, however, for indigenous peoples around the world hold something of this spiritual knowledge and wisdom. Indigenous gnosis, combined with the most essential gnosis of "the Way" as described by the first generation of Christians (Acts 9:2, 24:14) can revive faith, hope, and love in our land through a spirituality of direct Spirit-connectedness. Thus, weaving the wisdom of the shamanic path with the wisdom of Supernal realization—self-realization in the Messiah—the knowledge of the Christian Way is restored.

The deep need for a spirituality of direct experience is very clear when we look into the play of the active power of the Holy Spirit in the original church compared to the churches of today. In the early church, we hear of a living Body of Christ composed of all members of the church filled with Spirit-Power, and of an active life in the Spirit. Today, for the most part, we see only a body of blind belief, devoid of soul and the Spirit, something conceptual, not experiential, and something dead, not vibrant and alive. In this regard there is a need for the healing and resurrection of the Body of Christ, the restoration of a pure spirituality founded upon direct experience. Speaking to Juan Diego, an Aztec shaman, the Holy Mother teaches this when she asks, "Am I not right here who is your Mother?"

It is very significant that the Holy Mother reveals herself to an indigenous person, a warrior and shaman, for he brings with him the wisdom of a heavenly and earthly spirituality, a complete weave and union of heaven and earth, the knowledge of God within and all around us, as well as beyond us. For in a shamanic path we seek to move in harmony with the natural order; we seek order, balance and harmony in our lives. Rather than an adversarial and consumeristic relationship with nature, we seek a harmonious and reciprocal relationship, a deep and abiding communion with the Divine in nature on earth, and in the spirit world in heaven. We walk with the awareness of the Sacred Unity underlying all, the inseparability of heaven and earth, and we walk with the awareness of the energy dimension, the spiritual dimension, within and behind all things. We know the Divine is speaking with us in all things, sacred and mundane, so that there is no longer a division between the sacred and mundane, but the whole of life is in the Spirit, in the Divine Light.

We know everyone and everything has power, power that comes from the Holy Spirit, the light and breath of the Creator, and we seek to draw out that power as we have need of it and are called to do so. Although, indeed, as a matter of skillful means for the gathering and acquisition of power, we may create and build sacred sites, sanctuaries, and temples, in truth we have no need of them. The whole earth is sacred and is our temple, and our bodies are sacred and are our temples. The great outdoors is our true and holy sanctuary when we walk in a sacred manner, walking on Earth with and in the *Holy Shekinah*, the Divine Presence and Power. Indeed, wherever we are, in whatever we are doing, we may worship God, who is pure spirit, pure energy-intelligence, worshiping in spirit and truth, in simple awareness. This is the Way, and it is All-Good.

The Holy Mother appears and reveals herself to remind us of the Way and restore us to the Way, the Life Divine in Her, the Earth Mother and Queen of Heaven. She reminds us of the need to balance and unite heaven and earth in our lives, and in ourselves.

The Holy Hill of Our Lady

Early on a Saturday morning Juan Diego was on his way to attend to his spiritual essence and to the errands of the day; dawn was just breaking as he came to the Hill at Tepeyacac. From the top of the Holy Hill he heard singing like that of marvelous birds, as though a great choir of heavenly angels rejoicing, their voices bursting into bloom. It was as though the Holy Hill was responding to their melody, the Holy Hill that had long been sacred to the Earth Mother, holding her knowledge and power, the dwelling of her great wisdom.

Saturday, of course, is the traditional day of the Jewish Shabbat and corresponds with the planet Shabbatai-Saturn, the *Sefirah Binah*-Understanding, and the Partzuf *Imma*, the Holy Mother, Queen of Heaven, Queen of Shabbat. From a Kabbalistic perspective, a revelation of the Holy Mother on Saturday indicates an influx of the Supernal Mother, the *Supernal Shekinah*, *Binah*, into *Malkut*-Kingdom, the *Lower Shekinah*. This, indeed, might be well described as a bursting forth into flower-bloom-flame in the world as the Light that is below is activated by the Light that is above. This is something we know very well in our experiences of Light Transmission, being blessed to look and see the energy dimension, to behold the light realm here in this world where everything is lit up.

Moments of Light Transmission may be visionary, but they may also assume other forms, such as an acute awareness of hearing sound-vibration, the sensation and experience of feeling energy currents and vibration in the body, and it may include experiences of direct knowing, pure radiant awareness, the recognition of the non-dual truth. Juan Diego's experience encompasses all aspects of the Light Transmission over the course of his three-day adventure with the Mother: sound-vibration, hearing, and then the opening of the interior sight.

The experience of the energy dimension or Light Transmission was familiar to Juan Diego, for in the story we are told that he was not disturbed, startled, or afraid, and we know in our own experience that, at the outset of the experience of the Light Transmission, fear is common. In the process of becoming a person of gnosis, there are four "enemies" to be overcome. The first enemy is fear. Once fear is overcome, the sojourner must overcome the clarity that dawns, which in effect blinds them; overcoming clarity, they come into power and must overcome its ordeal. Then, in the end, the final enemy is old age, and that, too, must be overcome. Although Juan Diego is called a "man of knowledge," and is a warrior and shaman, the truth is that a person can only be a man or woman of knowledge for a brief moment in this world, right at the time that they meet their responsibility to death. At the moment of their death, there is a transference of consciousness into the energy body, the body of light, so that the person of knowledge, gnosis, does not fall unconscious or experience "death" but remains completely awake, completely conscious, in the transition. In this sense, Juan Diego is not yet a man of knowledge, for he has not faced the time of old age and the hour of his death, the final enemy to overcome. According to the tradition, he has met and overcome the first three enemies—fear, clarity, and power—to become a true righteous warrior and shaman, a seer and wonderworker.

Four Enemies

Here we must speak about the Four Enemies, a teaching about the journey of the man or woman of knowledge-gnosis that comes from the Toltec tradition. This teaching is integral to the Mystical Path of Guadalupe, one that we find true in our experience of the Light Transmission and the opening of consciousness to the world of spirits and angels.

The first enemy is fear, and although some individuals in modern spirituality claim to have many experiences of the energetic dimension and spiritual world without fear, or claim that the fear of God is "not their personal truth," it betrays that their direct spiritual and mystical experiences, as yet, are likely imagined, something akin to a luminous fantasy or daydream, not true dreaming or vision, not a direct experience of the full force and power of the spiritual world. In such cases, the questions of Juan Diego at the outset of his experience would be very wise, especially the question, "Am I imagining this?"

Now it must be said that there is nothing wrong with luminous fantasy and daydream; such "creative visualization" is used early in the path and early in many practices. It is very good and useful, and there is wisdom in it, and we can develop our *kavvanah*-concentration and *devekut*-passion through it, acquiring some self-knowledge, some insight into ourselves and our energy. But fantasy and daydreams must not be confused with the early experiences of Light Transmission and early experiences of our consciousness opening to the energetic dimension and to the world of spirits and angels. At the outset of this direct experience, an experience that is very alien to us at first, fear is natural and normal, and it would be very strange, very abnormal, for a person not to experience fear. In all my years upon the path and in my decades of teaching and initiating in circle, I've never known anyone who did not have to face the challenge of fear as their consciousness opened to the energetic dimension and they faced the full force and power of the spiritual world, not one single person.

Essentially, in our early experiences it is like our world is turned upside down, and often it is like our very body is disintegrating and disappearing from the force of an intense vibration within it, as though we are going to die, or as though we are going crazy. Very often the discomfort is not only spiritual and mental-emotional, but it can also be physical. At the same time, we are coming into contact with the spirits and angels, and they are very powerful, very strange, very mysterious, and they are potentially very dangerous; they are not exactly cute, fluffy things, nor the easy-to-control conceptualizations so many imagine them to be. Some can be friendly, some very unfriendly, and many are very large and powerful beings, unimaginably powerful. To our ordinary human self they are very alien and initial conscious contacts tend to be confusing, upsetting, and frightening.

Along with the fear our initial awareness brings as we open to a completely new and "alien" world, so also, quite naturally, the fears we carry arise and must be faced. The opening of consciousness to the energetic dimension and world of spirits and angels tends to amplify and invoke the fears we carry. Granted, the extent of the fear that we face may vary from person to person, and depends on the degree to which we have prepared ourselves. If we embrace our fears before our direct experience begins, this challenge of fear may be significantly reduced. But always there is the challenge to overcome fear in our early experiences of the Light Transmission. That, and we also need to learn how to cultivate and refine appropriate desire energy, for this is a wild energy at the outset of the spiritual path.

Fear tends to distort and obstruct our initial experiences of Light Transmission. It tends to cause us to fall unconscious, or in one way or another to try to avert our gaze or stop the experience. Some individuals may never get over their fear, being dominated and conquered by it. Some even run from the path because of it. Others, however, embrace and overcome their fear, mastering it. If you look into our unenlightened societies and cultures, especially in these times, you will see very clearly that most ordinary people are dominated by fear and live their lives in a play of distorted desire-energy manifest as fear; you will also see that outside of direct spiritual and mystical experience, fear is the predominant enemy of humankind, the slayer of the mind, the slayer of the soul. Here it must be said, however, that being fearless, or having courage, is not necessarily the absence of fear. Fearlessness and courage give the ability to embrace fear and transform it, to use its energy to integrate and absorb it. This enemy must be overcome for true enjoyment in life, whether in the material or spiritual dimensions of life.

Now, for the many who overcome fear, the experience of clarity—the energetic dimension and world of spirits and angels—will unfold the next enemy or challenge. As clarity continues growing, increasing, and deepening, there is a very powerful and profound feeling of invulnerability and knowledge that comes, a feeling that one has "arrived," is "special," is "enlightened." A terrible pride and arrogance can set in, and it is like we have put blinders on. We may stop striving to learn and to grow. Being so "clear" and "illumined" ourselves, we may rush out to teach and illumine others prematurely, and we may believe that we have far more knowledge and power than we actually have. We may get stuck in this, dominated by this, and never really come to full knowledge and power. Even worse, we may be in for a great fall or shock to our system, one from which we might never fully recover, or that may lead to insanity, great harm to our energy being or soul, or even our death.

If you want to know how powerful and dangerous this enemy is, consider the many would-be gurus and cult leaders who become intoxicated with themselves, with their "clarity," and consider those who end in suicide and who espouse suicide with their followers, or other bizarre ideas for the "salvation of the soul" or "world." Or consider the radical religious fundamentalists in their "certainty" about the "true god" and "righteousness," and the violence they preach in the name of a god of "compassion," "love," and "mercy." These are the more radical examples of the second enemy, clarity, but then so also is the "new ager" who needs neither education, training, a teacher, nor tradition, but who already knows everything. Consider the psychic, who channels spirits of the dead, or deceiving spirits, believing that they know everything about life and the afterlife, espousing teachings that contradict every authentic wisdom tradition in the world. These are also examples of clarity dominating individuals. If and when we are overcome by clarity, the second enemy, we stop growing and learning, which is a spiritual death, and as our examples reflect, it can lead to great darkness, great evil. It is a terrible danger in the mystical journey.

Regardless of how great a clarity dawns, we must be willing to the continued flickering of clarity and confusion, and not allow ourselves to grasp at the clarity or become addicted to it. Flickering between clarity and confusion invokes true illumination. In a similar way, we must never give in to thoughts or feelings that we are "special" or "elite" in any way, but we must be among the people, with the people, and coupled with spiritual self-worth, we must cultivate spiritual humility, as we see with Juan Diego, this spiritual warrior and shaman who is a peasant, a commoner, a humble man.

When we overcome clarity, no longer grasping at it or becoming intoxicated by it, then we come to real power. We are able to gather and acquire much knowledge and power. Like clarity, power can be very intoxicating. Although we may have a lot of power at the outset, we do not have the knowledge, understanding, and wisdom to use our power very effectively. At first, we tend to use our power when it would be best not to use it, and tend not to use it when we ought to use it. We do not really know or understand what it means to have power or stand in our power, and so our power tends to go all over the place, and the power dominates us.

We have to learn how to use the power we acquire in a way that is good and beneficial to us, and to others, in a way that might actually fulfill our dreams and the dreams of others. We must learn how to direct our power to bring our knowledge, understanding and wisdom to fruition, how to bring our Supernal *Habad* to fruition. This is the enlightenment and liberation of the soul, the fulfillment of our destiny, our soul's purpose. If we acquire great knowledge and power, and can work all kinds of wonders and magic, as St. Paul instructs in 1 Corinithians 13, but we do not fulfill our soul's purpose—our destiny to love and serve others—then power is for nothing. If with knowledge and power the soul is not liberated from the dominion of the demiurge and archons, then we will continue in our bondage to the endless rounds of rebirth and death, and we cannot be of full and true benefit to our relations. In much the same way as clarity, power can be a trap in which we believe that we have "arrived" or that we are fully "enlightened," when in truth we still have much work to do, and our destiny is, as yet, not fulfilled in this life.

Now the struggle with fear, clarity and power is the work of an entire life span. By the time we have truly faced and overcome these three enemies, we are no longer so young and vibrant; our physical or material being is no longer at its peak. Memory and energy begin to decrease, as do various functions of the body. Aging is the fourth and final enemy. In the midst of aging we must hold and maintain the knowledge, understanding, wisdom, and power we have acquired, and with knowledge and power we must meet our responsibility to death, dying consciously as we have lived consciously. If we can pass through this great transition without falling unconscious, if we can engage the transference of consciousness at the time of death, in that brief instant there will be a full and true man or woman of knowledge, the dawn of true gnosis, a fully enlightened and liberated mind or soul-stream. Needless to say, although many of us seek to become a man or woman of knowledge, a person of gnosis or divine illumination, relatively few of us become a man of knowledge or woman of knowledge in full. Truly, it is a spiritual labor through many lives to become a person of gnosis, True Gnosis.

What all of this means, of course, facing the challenge of fear, clarity, power and old age, is something we must come to know on an experiential level, and through a process of trial and error, an evolutionary process. It is a journey, the journey of a human being in the circle of life, and through the journey of the Sacred Circle we acquire our education, receive our lessons, learn and grow, and come to our maturation and fruition. Even when we may seem to fail, even in the midst of what seems grave error, it is completely integral to our eventual success.

What we are talking about is the healing and reintegration of our energy being with our material being, and our ultimate reintegration with the Light Continuum, with *Yahweh*. This is the *tikkune* and realization of our soul, our true and natural being. The Mystical Path of Guadalupe represents something of a "Thunderbolt Path," a swift and sure way to this reintegration, this illumination. Ultimately, each of us will have to find and recognize these enemies in our own experience, and discover the way to overcome them. If we are willing, the Divine Mother will help us recognize and face them, and with her help we will be victorious. That is her promise to us.

All of these "enemies" are internal. Our real enemy is not outside of us, but is within us, and the great conflict the enemy produces must be resolved inwardly, within ourselves. The same is true of the Divine Light that is within us, which we must bring forth from within. This play of shadow and light must be resolved in us; this dualism must be brought into cessation. As you might have noticed, every sojourner upon the path, women and men alike, must be a spiritual warrior. The way of the warrior is integral to the Mystical Path of Guadalupe, what Sophians would call the "wisdom of the Templar."

Rapport with the Invisible

Now here we may say something about relating with what cannot be seen. There are spirit guides, spirit allies, totems, guardian angels, and spirit keepers or guardians of the directions; there are angels of our Heavenly Father and angels of our Earthly Mother. A shaman has a relationship with all of these, all kinds of spirits or hosts: *Tzavaot*. There are also ancestor spirits and spirits of holy beings of the past, and a shaman often experiences the visitation of the full range of the world of spirits in dream and vision. Here and there, however, there are great shamans, great seers, who go beyond the world of the spirits, passing into a direct communion with the Divine, no longer relying only on the spirits, the angels of our Heavenly Father and Earthly Mother, as intermediaries. Such a person is a shaman of great power. Juan Diego is one of these people of power and holiness in his experience of the Forever Whole and Perfect Maiden, for she is something more than the spirit of a holy woman of the past. She is the tactile emanation of God the Mother, the Great Mother.

The Kabbalah says that "a stirring below creates a stirring above," and so we hear of this holy man, this warrior and shaman, attending to his spiritual essence and sacred tasks. He is actively engaged in the spiritual life and practice, walking in the Spirit and Powers, and in so doing he is a co-creator of the revelation of the Divine Mother, acting to co-create the conditions necessary for such a Body of Vision to arise and manifest. In his spiritual life and practice he has become educated through direct experience, and he has exercised discipline, overcoming the enemies of fear, clarity, and power, and he has continued to learn and grow, continued in his aspiration, seeking a greater revelation than that of the spirit world and world of angels. He is, indeed, an impeccable spiritual warrior, a truly spiritual and holy person. Thus, the emanation of the Holy Mother can happen for him, and happening for him, she appears for everyone through him. But it is he who has made himself the "lightning rod" for the sake of his people, and all people, so that she might touch down and be made accessible to the people, all his relations. This is the true spiritual work of a shaman, a seer, and wonderworker.

In the Kabbalah, the soul is layered. The inmost, unique essence of a human being is *yechidah*, our divine spark. The glory of this spark is *hayyah*, our life-force. Manifesting in a spiritual image and likeness is *neshamah*, our divine nature. Juan Diego reaches into his Supernal soul through sacred tasks, through thoughts, speech, and actions expressing his true being, his Supernal soul. He actualizes, realizes, and embodies his holy *neshamah*. This very powerful emanation of the Divine Mother is his capacity to experience this very lofty grade of a divine, incarnate vision. Truly, he has realized that he is her holy child, a son of God, a son of Light. And so it is, that in effect, she becomes physical and materializes for him, and from a visionary experience he is able to bring forth something physical, material: the flowers and her image.

Quite profoundly, he is as the greater prophets of ancient times, and perhaps something more, like a great apostle, for beholding the Mother of the Messiah is to know and understand the Messiah, the one anointed with the Supernal Light of God, and necessarily in such knowledge and understanding, a person receives the Supernal chrism, the anointing, in full. One becomes what one sees in such a mystical experience, for this is something far more than a vision in dream or a vision beheld in the hazy, subjective mirror of prophecy. The gradation of Juan Diego's experience is the Supernal dimension bursting forth in flower-bloom-flame within the material dimension, a truly awesome and wonderful event, a tangible advent of the Mother Spirit.

In this we may know and understand the sacred task of a spiritual warrior, a spiritual person, is to bring in and hold the energy, light of the Spiritual Sun for the people, and embody the Divine Light; to live that Holy Light as only they can fulfills the purpose of their soul in this world. We may say that Juan Diego fulfills his soul's purpose in this world, becoming a man of knowledge in full at the time of his death. His name among his people in Nahuatl was Honorable Speaking Eagle—Cuauatlatoatzin. Only a Speaking Eagle could see *She-Who-Comes-From-the-Realm-of-Light-as-a-Burning-Eagle: Tlecuautlacuepeuh*. This is Guadalupe—Tonantzin. Praise be She!

Holy Hill

Now Tepeyacac, the holy hill or sacred mount upon which the Holy Mother appears, literally means "Mountain Nose," and it implies spiritual discernment, a quality, as we shall see, that is very important in the story, and one that is essential for any real spiritual development and evolution. A holy hill, of course, is often the place of divine revelation. Many great revelations have occurred to seers and prophets on sacred mountains, the top of a mountain representing the place where heaven and earth meet, where ordinary and non-ordinary realities mingle and merge. Likewise, ascending and descending mountains implies initiation—the mount of initiation—and implies ascent into higher or expanded states of consciousness and the panoramic vision that comes in higher states of consciousness.

This holy hill is very significant, for it is a hill that has long been sacred to the Mother God among the Aztecs and Toltecs, specifically the Earth Mother. During the era of the Aztec peoples, a temple to the Earth Woman, Coatlique, stood on the Sacred Mountain for hundreds of years until the conquest of the Aztecs by the Spanish. The name Coatlique is very intriguing, for it means "She-Of-The-Serpent-Skirts," and she is one of the primary aspects of the Mother God among the Aztecs. The Serpent, of course, alludes to a power in us that, when awakened, sublimated, and uplifted, leads to knowledge, power, and illumination. It also alludes to the vast tapestry of energy currents or cosmic forces that form the matrix of the earth, the galaxy and the entire universe, the matrix of creation.

The Earth Mother, however, is more than this Good Earth, for she is the great matrix, and the planet Earth is but a very small fraction of her. When we call upon our Heavenly Father and Earthly Mother, Sky Father and Earth Mother, we mean something more than the limited boundary of the Earth's atmosphere and the planet Earth itself. These are, indeed, manifestations of the presence and power of our Father-Mother, the Holy One, and so it was among the Aztecs and Toltecs. Indeed, the Earth

Mother is the awareness of the interdependence, the 'interbeing' of all that appears, in heaven and on earth. Earth Mother is *Elohim* in the Kabbalah, just as Sky Father is *Yahweh*, the eternal Continuum of being, energy, and light: the Great Spirit.

The sacred mount of the Earth Mother is where Our Lady of Guadalupe appears. She is the Queen of Heaven, Queen of Deep Space, and as much as the Queen of Heaven, she is Earth Woman, Earth Mother. She is the Heavenly Mother, Starry Wisdom, Grandmother, and she is the Earth Mother, our Holy Mother, encompassing all from the Supernal to the material dimensions, the Primordial Ground from which all arises, in which all exists, and to which all returns.

There are many aspects of the Great Mother, many forms, many faces. Some of them are mentioned in her story: Eagle Woman, Serpent Woman, War Woman, Infernal Woman, and "Mother of the Weave," or Spider Woman. We will discuss these aspects in our exploration of Guadalupe as an emanation of the Woman of Light later. There are many more aspects of course: Weeping Woman, Laughing Woman, Power Woman, Star Woman, Deer Woman, Turtle Woman. The list is endless.

Essentially, the revelation on Tepeyacac gives us a deeper and more panoramic vision of who Our Lady is: the Great Mother, Mother God, the Matrix of Being. There is something to be said of the Holy Mother called "Woman," as opposed to "Goddess," something very wise and insightful, worthy to be mentioned. This speaks to the gnosis of the Divine Mother, the gnosis of the Divine and Sacred Feminine. In the Divine Feminine we know and understand a complete interweaving of the sacred and mundane, the heavenly and earthly, a non-linear and non-hierarchal understanding of reality. Likewise, it speaks to the embodiment of divinity in women and in men, reflecting that the Divine Presence and Power can be embodied—incarnate—in human beings. It is our destiny to embody something of the Divine, as we see in Yeshua Messiah and other holy ones who have walked among us. The Divine World and this world interpenetrate one another, and in the peak of spiritual and mystical experiences, this interpenetration occurs in profound ways, becoming actualized and realized by the Presence of Awareness.

The revelation on a sacred mountain calls to mind an ancient Name of God, *El Shaddai*. While often translated as God Almighty with a completely masculine connotation, in Hebrew it also implies the feminine, for shad means "breast." Therefore, *El Shaddai* speaks of *God-the-Breasted-One*. When they are "my breasts," *shaddai* suggest nurturing energy currents of the Earth Mother flowing forth from the tops of hills and mountains, rather like the milk that flows from the breasts of mothers nursing their children. Along with *Elohim*, the Divine Name for God used in the story of creation, *Shaddai* is a holy name implying a very different understanding of the Divine among the ancient, nomadic Hebrews, who, long before the emergence of the patriarchal and monarchical eras of Judaism, embodied a distinctly "shamanic" form of spirituality. Profoundly, in the revelation at Tepeyacac there is a strong suggestion of God-the-Breasted-One, understanding *El Shaddai* also as Mother God, *Elohim*.

Lucidity of Destiny

Now, for Juan Diego, the experience of the revelation of the Mother begins with hearing birds bursting forth into song at dawn and the perception of the holy hill responding to their song. Birds breaking out into song at dawn and a sort of crystalline clarity in perception and energy is not unusual at sunrise, as we all know, but the experience of Juan Diego is different, exceptional, and he is aware of that. His experience of reality shifts radically, and he is aware of heaven and earth meeting in the moment in a very profound and powerful way. He is aware that these song birds, these 'birds of the air', are being taken up by the Divine Presence and Power, the angels of the Earthly Mother and angels of the Heavenly Father merging so that he hears in voices of the birds of the air below the choirs of the birds of the air in the heavens. Shifting in reality within this, he sees the holy hill responding, becoming lit up, radiant with life, light, and glory, the energy dimension, the light realm, becoming visible in that place.

Juan Diego is on a walk of power, and although we cannot say exactly what internal practices he is engaged in, coming to this place of power he is called by the Spirit and Powers to turn aside, to look and see, listen and hear, and to take up a spiritual work in this place. As a man of knowledge and power, a warrior and a shaman, open and sensitive to the Spirit and Powers, he responds to the call, to his duty, taking up the responsibility to ascend the Sacred Mountain of the Earth Mother, and there he meets his very lofty destiny, noble and holy.

When Juan Diego meets his destiny, it is undeniable to him. This is evident in his capacity to even perceive this event, having trained and disciplined himself as a spiritual warrior. He understands that he is to serve as a vision bringer for the people and so is highly receptive to the great vision that unfolds on the Holy Hill. If we pray to see more than what appears, we too must be willing to the work of disciplining ourselves. We must be open to an experiential education to meet and recognize our destiny. Recognizing our own unique destiny requires the reintegration of our energy being with our physical being, and a restoration to our natural self, our true being, our spiritual essence. With time and devotion, we can be open and sensitive to the Great Spirit and Powers.

Juan Diego was able to recognize and accept his destiny only because he was a trained and disciplined spiritual warrior, living in the truth of his spiritual essence Although this meeting with his destiny is very obvious to him, truly, it is only because he was prepared in continual purification. He could have continued on his way and passed right by, either unable or unwilling to recognize the moment. At the very outset it was not necessarily that obvious. After all, birds bursting forth into song and a certain clarity at dawn isn't always an extraordinary event. If he were not prepared, awakened, aware, he might never have encountered the Mother, and if he had not been willing, he might not have turned aside.

We all come to moments of destiny, and we all come to a most significant moment of destiny in life. Meeting our destiny, recognizing it and being willing to accept it, we may then fulfill our soul's purpose. If and when we do, it will be a great blessing upon us and upon all our relations, and we will pass into another cycle of evolution beyond the physical or material dimension, no longer requiring physical or material incarnation. To truly meet and fulfill our destiny, of course, means that we will have to face and overcome the Four Enemies, and it means that we must be true to ourselves, become truly ourselves, knowing and understanding our inmost heart's desire, and daring to fulfill that Holy Desire of the Divine Mother in us.

Naturally, as we see in this story, meeting our destiny is only the beginning. Once we meet our destiny, we must then enact and fulfill that mission, just as Juan Diego does. Now, Juan Diego is a poor peasant among a conquered people, but he holds true to himself and true to the Spirit. As a poor man, though, he is fortunate, for in his poverty he has the opportunity, the freedom, to consider what is truly valuable and to seek it, and to know and be himself. Having witnessed much death and horror in his lifetime, he is not so caught up in name and form. Having experienced the end of the era of his people, he is not so snared in personal history, and being poor, he is not so distracted by possessions, social position, or worldly power. He is nearer to himself, and nearer to the Spirit. He is clearer and freer than most of us.

Here we must say something: If we wish to meet and fulfill our destiny, we must be willing to have our world turned upside down, and willing to experience the death of our ego's dominion. We must be willing to go in the opposite direction of the currents in the unenlightened society and dominion of the demiurge, willing to live and to die in the Spirit. We must be willing to be truly who and what we are, dropping all pretenses, all falsehoods, all that is unreal, and seek the Real, willing to embrace Reality as It Is, God as God Is, and willing to embody and manifest the Real, the True Light. Was Our Lady of Guadalupe what Juan Diego might have expected? Very likely she was not. And so we may also say that our destiny is not what our ego might wish, or what we might expect, for although it is something to be accomplished in this world, truly, it is not of this world. It is something of Heaven and this Good Earth, quite apart from the dominion of the demiurge or things valued by the unenlightened society. In this story of the revelation of Mother God we are invited to seek our heart's desire and invited to meet and fulfill our destiny in her.

Although we cannot say what spiritual practices Juan Diego was engaged in on his walk of power, nevertheless we are told something of the internal practice that he takes up as his visionary experience unfolds, which does, in fact, give some insight into his continuum of spiritual practice along the way. Next, we can consider these practices, which are deeply connected to paying attention to our energy and to our dreams.

A Practice: Gazing & Climbing

Here we may share two spiritual practices alluded to in this story. If you want insight into the Great Spirit, the Great Silence, go out and gaze upon where the sky and earth meet, resting your mind in the space in-between, and commune with the Great Mystery, the Holy One of Being.

If you want to know the power of the Sacred Mountain, go and climb to the top of a mountain, and on its peak pray, meditate, and perform sacred ceremony, calling upon Father Sky and Earth Mother, the Holy One, and the directions, and invoke the great spirit of the mountain, the angel of Our Earthly Mother that is in the mountain. Invoking, commune and enter into an exchange of powers with the spirits of that place.

There is great power at the top of sacred mountains, and the force of the winds and the spirits are very intense there. When great force is needed for a spiritual work, it is a good place to go. Only you must be careful, because the spirits of some mountains are not friendly to human beings but are extremely fierce or wrathful, and peaks of these mountains can be can be like negative power zones. Only a very experienced adept or powerful shaman can make use of them, and only when they are called by the

Great Spirit and Powers to ascend the mountain for the people. Finding a friendly and gentle mountain is wise for the novice.

The Power of Dream & Awakening

Juan Diego stopped and became still, and he looked and listened, and he said to himself, "Am I really so fortunate that I deserve to hear this? Am I dreaming? Am I imagining this? I must awaken from this dream. Where Am I? Is this the place our great grandfathers spoke of, the wise old ones, the place where heaven and earth meet, the Land of Flowers, the Flower Earth Place, the Dwelling of Our Sustenance?"

When the visionary experience begins for Juan Diego he knows to center and ground himself, and he knows to inquire into the nature of his experience with rigorous honesty. He does not just assume that his vision is real or divine, but he exercises spiritual discernment, looking to see if it is fantasy, a play of self-deception and deceiving spirits, or an actual vision or revelation of the Spirit and Powers. In the mystical journey, the gnostic and shamanic path, this is very important: to know the context of our experiences and to have spiritual discernment, to be aware of where we are and what is happening, inwardly and outwardly. In what Juan Diego does at the outset of his experience and in the questions he asks, we find essential spiritual practices of the Mystical Path of Guadalupe.

Juan Diego stopped and became still, and he looked and listened.

At the outset of the Mystical Path we must learn to go within and live within. Going within, learning to silence the mind and quiet the vital, we must learn to be open and sensitive to the Spirit and Powers, learning to abide in the Presence of Awareness, open to the Divine Light from above, the Mother's Force. Receiving the Light from above, we seek to bring that Holy Light down into our mental, vital, and physical consciousness, and into the Earth Mother, healing our energetic being and reintegrating our energetic being with our physical being. We seek to become a channel of the Spiritual Sun, to hold that Divine Presence and Power for the people.

There is a great power in our belly, rooted in the base of our spine; it is a Fiery Intelligence, the serpent power, the Fire Snake. When we receive the Light from above, the Mother's Force, this great power is activated, awakened. There are all kinds of magical powers or spiritual gifts within this serpent power, but in and of itself it is not illumination or enlightenment. This power must be sublimated and uplifted, and ultimately brought into repose, cessation, in the interior brow or crown stars. When it is refined and uplifted, then it becomes a force or power for the illumination of the mind, consciousness, or soul, a force or power of freedom, the great liberation.

Now, we need do nothing to awaken this Fiery Intelligence, for it is awakened by the light from above, Divine Grace. Likewise, we need do nothing but take up an active and dynamic surrender to Divine Grace, living from within and following the impulse of the Light-Presence and Light-Power in us. For the Fiery Intelligence is sublimated and guided in ascent by the same light from above. When we surrender to Divine Grace, the Mother, this Light-Presence and Light-Power take up our person and life, this Fiery Intelligence that is in us.

In this process, of course, we are talking about becoming aware of our energetic being and paying attention to our energy. In truth, on an energetic level, we are a field of energy, filled with light, in a vast ocean of energy fields, light fields. In some way, in effect, when we incarnate, we tend to lose touch with our energetic being, and we tend to lose touch with the source of our being, the Great Spirit, the Divine. Thus, the first step on the Mystical or Gnostic Path is becoming aware of our energy and restoring our awareness of our innate Spirit-connection.

This requires that we learn to go within and live within, and learn to be open and sensitive, and that we learn how to pray, meditate, and perform sacred ceremony, attending to our spiritual essence and sacred tasks, actively living the spiritual life and taking up a continuum of daily spiritual practice. If we are willing to attend to our spiritual essence and sacred tasks, we will naturally become aware of our energetic being and our energetic being will begin to regenerate and heal itself, and it will reintegrate itself with our physical being, and quite spontaneously we will experience the influx of Light from above, the reception of the Holy Spirit. The Fiery Intelligence in us will awaken, all according to our present capacity and the will of the Supreme, the Great Spirit.

In this process we can also receive the help of a person of knowledge and power, a seer and wonderworker, a shaman. They are like a bundle of power, a channel and generator of power, transmitting spiritual power, facilitating conscious contact with our energetic being, and helping us to awaken the great power that is in us. They can speak teachings, train, initiate, and empower us with direct experience. In this way, they serve as a guide and sanctuary for us in the journey. There is no doubt that Juan Diego had a teacher, a guide, for truly, no one goes very far in the journey without one. The guide is an integral part of how the Spirit and Powers reach out to us and help us.

By guide, however, we are not speaking of some "guru" or cult leader. We are speaking of a spiritual friend, a sacred friend, an experienced traveler who can offer some help and guidance. They are not going to tell us what decisions to make nor take responsibility for our lives, but rather they are going to share teachings and practices with us, and perhaps facilitate some experiences with us. They will serve as a guide in our spiritual life and practice. What we do with what they share and with our lives is up to us. Essentially, they are going to encourage us to walk our own path in life, to be ourselves, and to meet and fulfill our destiny, while they are going to be walking their own path in life, meeting and fulfilling their own destiny. A guide or mentor is traveling in the same Spirit and as their sacred friend we are companions with them in the journey. Perhaps, if we become close friends, we might become an apprentice to them, learning much about the ways of the Spirit and Powers from them.

Going within and becoming alert, abiding in the Presence of Awareness, the first question Juan Diego asks is: "Am I so fortunate that I deserve to hear this?" This expresses the proper attitude and view in the Mystical Path of Guadalupe: an attitude of appreciation and gratitude, thankfulness for life and all it has to offer. This is a view of reality, life, as deeply mystical and magical, in which one gazes with eyes of holy awe and wonder, knowing that anything is possible, knowing that miracles, magic, great wonders, are possible, and that they are happening every day, all of the time. In this view, the whole of reality, sacred and mundane, is completely magical. It is a spiritual and mystical adventure, and everything is an expression, a manifestation, of the Spirit and the Powers. Everything is divine and sacred.

This is not simply a belief, however, it is a direct perception, experiential knowledge or gnosis, for as we begin to experience the energetic dimension, the spiritual world within and behind the reality of our experience, we become aware of our energetic being, and the energetic play of everything. Truly we know and understand that the reality of our experience, on all levels, is magical, is dream-like, that it is all a radiant display of mind, consciousness, or soul. Indeed, this material world itself, and all worlds of our experience, are dream-like, but rather than a personal or individual dream, they are like a collective dream, a collective radiant display of the energy of all beings that are in them. All creatures are co-creators with God, co-creators of the reality of their experience.

In this question there is an awareness that everything is a play of desire. All is desire-energy. Juan Diego's question teaches us that, in truth, the spiritual and mystical journey is all about staying on the cutting edge of our desires, cultivating and refining our desires to express and fulfill our true desire, our inmost heart's desire. This, in essence, is what it means to "sublimate the serpent power." On a fundamental level the Fire Snake is desire-energy, and sublimating and uplifting it means the cultivation and refinement of our desires. The repose or cessation of the Serpent means the fulfillment of our desires.

If you look to the rewards that Our Lady promises to Juan Diego in his service to her, and promises to us in our devotion to her, it is the fulfillment of his desires and our desires, earthly and heavenly. We have not been given life to withhold ourselves from it, but rather we are given life by the Great Spirit, by the Mother, to live life abundantly to the fullest possible extent. The ignorance of religion tries to rob us of the joy of life, just as it tries to steal the power of the Holy Spirit from us. But truly, the Creator intends us to live life and to enjoy life so long as we have it, to be who and what we are created to be, and to embody our unique individuality, our spiritual essence.

The first question Juan Diego asks also focuses upon hearing, the foremost interior sense through which the Spirit and Powers communicate with us, speaking in our hearts, illuminating our minds. The Spiritual Sun, as we know very well in the Christian stream, is the Living Word of God, spoken and heard. Juan Diego listens to the Living Word in the power of the moment, and so also must we. This is a good question to ask ourselves in virtually any situation. If and when the answer is "yes," then we can truly enjoy what's transpiring and receive the blessing that is in it, receiving it from God, the Great Spirit and Powers, receiving it from the Holy Mother, *Elohim, El Shaddai,* and knowing the Sky Father, *Yahweh,* in it. If and when our answer is "no," then we may ask, "Why not?" Perhaps there is something distorting or obstructing our reception of the blessing, the good, the Mother seeks to give to us, and we need to stay in the experience and let it heal us. That, or perhaps we should remove ourselves from the situation because it truly is not for us and maybe it will cause us harm. In either case, regardless of the answer, it is a very good question, one invoking discerning awareness, which is always wise. It is good to get into the habit of asking this question, and to give praise and thanks to the Divine Mother for all of the good and the blessings we receive, giving thanks for everything, spiritual and material.

The next question this wise man asks is, "Am I dreaming?" It is very sad, very unfortunate, that in our modern culture, our unenlightened society, we are not taught to dream, to have visions. Our children learn nothing about dreams and the true power of dreaming, and they are not taught how to awaken in dreams or how to awaken from the dream. Quite the opposite, we are told that dreams are "unreal" and have no value, that we should not dream or have visions. If we do, there is something "wrong" with us and we should ignore and disregard them. Yet our dreams are, in fact, very important, essential to our soul. Through dreams the Spirit and Powers communicate with us, and the energetic being, the deeper part of us, speaks to us. In dreams we actually enter into other dimensions, other realms, worlds and universes, and they are equally as "real" as this world.

It is very ironic that we are taught to revere and worship those who have had dreams and visions in the ancient past, but we are told not to honor our dreams and visions, as we are told that they are worthless. We are told that luminous dreams and visions, or prophecy, is a thing of the past, that the Living Spirit has stopped speaking to us, and we cannot have big dreams and visions today. Science and religion both preach this ignorance, saying that our dreams and visions are only fantasy, unreal. It is true, some dreams are personal subconscious ramblings, and are not big dreams or divine visions. But even these, however, have value, for they reflect something of the state of our lives, our mind and heart, and our own energy, and we can learn from them. All our dreams are not this, though. Many are something much more, and while everyone may not remember their dreams, nevertheless everyone dreams, and among their dreams there are big dreams or visions.

There is even value in daydreams, so long as we understand their context. Daydreaming is our non-linear problem solving and creative capacity, and it is important to cultivate that capacity and not allow it to atrophy and fall away. Many true visions begin with the play of fantasy and daydreaming, our envisioning becoming something more when the Spirit and Powers take it up. We must learn to pay attention to our dreams and learn how to dream consciously. Even more, we must learn how to awaken in our dreams, how to generate lucid dreams, and how to awaken from the dream, to master the dream, which is mastering desire.

Now, basically speaking, this question Juan Diego asks himself is typically the question arising at the outset of a lucid dream. It invokes the awareness, the remembrance, that we are asleep and dreaming. The moment we're aware that we are dreaming, our dream is transformed. We have become lucid. In essence, our dream becomes an out-of-body experience, something very different from subconscious rambling or an ordinary dream. In the same way that it is good to ask, "Am I so fortunate that I deserve to experience this?" in any situation, it is also good to make a habit of inquiring, "Am I dreaming?" frequently throughout the day. For as we know, what we do in our waking consciousness often shows up in our dreams. Asking this question often, it will arise in our dreams and may invoke a lucid dream.

At the same time, asking yourself this question frequently may invoke a state of heightened perception or clarity in a situation, or the perception of the true context of what's happening in the moment. Rather than living in reaction, we may generate the ability to consciously respond to what's happening, becoming aware of the energetic level of the exchange or experience. Likewise, in that all reality of our experience is dream-like, a radiant display of our own mind, consciousness, or soul, asking ourselves this question may invoke awareness of the dream-like nature of reality, direct perception of Reality as It Is.

When we are unconscious in dream, unaware that we are asleep and dreaming, we are, in effect, fated to be carried wherever the dream takes us, for better or for worse, whether bright or dark. The same is true in waking consciousness in this life when we lack the Presence of Awareness and are unconscious. Awakening in our dreams, and awaking in life, is essential, for we gain greater freedom and are no longer fated by habitual patterns of thought, emotion, and reactive behaviors of the past, no longer bound to the karmic continuum in the same way.

Along with this question, in rigorous honesty, Juan Diego also inquires of himself, "Am I imagining all of this?" He inquires if what he is experiencing is some sort of wish-fulfilling fantasy or daydream, for he knows that there is a difference between fantasy or daydream and true dreams and visions, and he wants to be clear, and know and understand the actual context of his experience. He is a very sober and discerning man. This, of course, is not to suggest that there is anything wrong with fantasy and daydreams, for there is great value and power in our imagination, amazing power actually. But we must know the difference between true dreams and visions, and our creative imagination; we must know and understand the context of our experience to receive it for what it is and respond correctly.

Juan Diego's sobriety, his discernment, is often lacking in the would-be mystics of modern spirituality, the new age, and pop-occultism, and many get intoxicated by a vivid fantasy life, being led astray by self-deceptions of vital sentiments and wishful thinking, or become deceived by "trickster spirits." Thus, this question is very important, generating the ability to discern between fantasy and truly inspired dreams and visions. His question also invokes clearer perception of the reality of our experience, for all too often we are projecting our egoistic desires and fears upon the reality of our experience so that our perception of reality is distorted and obstructed by our egoistic self-grasping. Consequently, most of the time we do not look and see Reality as It Is, let alone God as God Is, but rather we "see" only our subjective perception, or our "take" on things, and what we see is a gross distortion of the Real. If we make a habit of asking this question frequently, we may acquire greater discernment of the context of our experiences, as well as begin to break through our subjective projections upon the reality of our experience. It is a very good question to ask ourselves, assuming we are willing to learn the answer.

Having asked these important questions, this holy man then proclaims, "I must awaken from this dream!" He determines that a true dream or vision is underway, that it is something more than a fantasy or idle daydream, and he understands that he cannot let his ego grasp at the experience and taint it, but that he must allow the experience to unfold free from attachment or aversion. With this question, he invokes a state of non-attachment and non-aversion as reflected when it is said that he is not disturbed, startled or afraid. Likewise, he knows and understands that awakening in dream and in this life is only the beginning. Awakening in dream, mastering our dreams, we must awaken from the dream to the Real, to God, to the Divine. This implies his desire to become a true man of knowledge and the cultivation of the capacity for the transference of consciousness at the time of death. The merit of this practice over years in sleep and dream leads to the generation of this capacity at the time of our death.

Along with the three previous questions, making a habit of speaking this affirmation with true passion and awareness is also a good practice, a core practice of the Mystical Path of Guadalupe. Much could be said of the experience of awakening from the dream. It is the realization of our Supernal and Divine Being, our being as we are in God, the Infinite and Eternal. Truly, whatever might be said does not matter, and is only a concept in the mind until we experience this awakening, the knowledge of which must be gained through our own direct experience.

Following this affirmation of awakening, Juan Diego asks, "Where am I?" With this question he brings himself fully into the moment, letting go of projections of himself into the fantasies of the past and future to be present in his experience, present in what's happening, present in reality. Likewise, he is aware of the play of the winds or powers of the Sacred Circle—the directions—and he is invoking the awareness of the direction he is walking as this experience unfolds, invoking the deeper knowledge and understanding of the context of his experience on an energetic level. With this question, he is going to the center of the Sacred Circle, where the Great Spirit abides and the Powers gather; turning to the east, the place of insight and inspiration, renewal, regeneration, revelation, and Light Transmission, he is standing in his power, ready to be received and to receive, offering himself up to the Great Spirit in the form of the Holy Mother.

It is good to know where you are and to know what direction you are walking in, and to center yourself in the Divine. It is good to know where you are, whether in terms of your energy, your state of mind and heart and life, or in terms of your place in the world, and in space-time. So it is good to get into the habit of asking this question too, "Where am I?" Here is an open secret: Where you are, in this moment, this is where God is, God the Mother. Just as she asks Juan Diego, she asks you: "Am I not right here who is your Mother?"

Now, Juan Diego asks a final question of himself: "Is this the place our great grandfathers spoke of, the wise old ones, the place where heaven and earth meet, the Land of Flowers, the Flower Earth Place, the Dwelling of Our Sustenance?" This, of course, circles back to his first question and the awareness of the truly magical and mystical nature of life, or reality. But in this question is the awareness of the Divine sovereignty, the light realm, within and all around us, and the awareness of the Presence and Power of God within and all around us, that wherever we are, when we walk in beauty and holiness, that place is holy. It is the Heaven Earth Place, and we walk in the company of the Great Spirit and Powers, we walk with and in the Divine Mother. If we walk with the awareness of the Divine sovereignty spread out upon the earth, or with the awareness of the light realm within and all around us, and the awareness of the company of the *Holy Shekinah*, needless to say our life and our consciousness will be transformed. Our experience of life will be very different.

Here we may speak an open secret: The world is sacred as it is. All life is sacred. You are a sacred and holy being, and so are all beings, all your relations. All reality, the Great Matrix of Creation, is the emanation of the Divine, the Infinite—*Ain Sof*. "Is this the Heaven Earth Place?" Asking this question often will invoke this awareness, and perhaps it will invoke the direct perception that is true. Right where you are, as you are reading in this moment, the heavens and earth meet, heaven and earth are in union in you, the Speaking One, the Human Being!

Now, when we take up the spiritual life and cultivate a daily continuum of spiritual practice, attending to our spiritual essence and sacred tasks, naturally we are likely to begin to remember our dreams, experience more luminous dreams and visions, and experience lucid dreams. This spontaneously happens for many initiates and practitioners. Likewise, in the tradition many practices are taught for the generation of luminous dreams and lucid dreams; there are many "dream union" practices. Nevertheless, many people may have great difficulty remembering their dreams, let alone awakening in dream, so here we can share a very simple practice everyone can do to invoke the wisdom of their dreams and remembrance of their dreams, a practice so simple little children can do it, one that is very powerful and very effective.

A Practice: Building the Dream Altar

In your dreams you have access to an exhaustless and unimaginable resource of knowledge and power, infinite Divine Wisdom, but you must have a way to get that knowledge and power from the dreamtime to here. Truly, you can go anywhere and do anything in your dreams, and you can acquire any knowledge and power you seek from your dreams, the answer to any question you might have, and the empowerment to do anything you desire to do. You have total freedom to do as you wish and to manifest your heart's desire. The difficulty is, however, that we tend to lose our way in the dreamtime, or rather, we tend to lose touch with our energetic being and true self in the dreamtime, and so we lose most of the knowledge and power on our return journey into the body and incarnation.

It is just like being born. Unless we have wise guides to help us remember, helping us come in and stay on track from the outset of our incarnation, the vast energy and effort that it takes to learn how to do basic things and how to survive in this world swiftly leaves our true original purpose and intention behind. Once we lose this awareness, this knowledge and power of our soul, it becomes very hard to reacquire it. Often it becomes virtually impossible, the most difficult thing. There is a practice, though, by which we can form something of a bridge between our waking consciousness and the dreamtime, a practice taught in the Kabbalah and in several indigenous wisdom traditions in the Americas: building a dream altar.

This altar is not anything physical, but it is something you envision with your mind's eye, using your creative imagination. The dream world, of course, is beyond space-time, so even as you are reading this, hearing this, already you have built your dream altar. In fact, whether you know it or not, you have come here to read this and to receive these teachings because you were guided to do so by the Spirit and Powers in your dreams. Virtually everything of significance in your life is inspired and guided in this way! The spirits in other realms, worlds, and dimensions of the dreamtime constantly seek to form connections with this world through us by way of everything we inwardly think, feel, and imagine. Your dream altar is a "place" with which those connections can link.

It is very easy to build and use your dream altar. Just inquire of yourself, "What does my dream altar look like, what is on it, what's around it?" and look and see it in your mind's eye: There it is, that's your dream altar! Before you begin to actively use your dream altar, consider and contemplate what's on it, how it appears, and what's around it. Get to know it, and consider what it might have to say to you from the very outset. Be cautious not to change or rearrange it too much, not to impose an egoistic use of your imagination on it too much. The more you project onto it from your surface consciousness and egoistic self, the less receptive and effective your dream altar will be, so you want to be gentle with it and let the Spirit and Powers speak to you through it.

When you have become familiar with it, then you can begin to use it. You can take your problems, your questions, your desires, and place them on your dream altar before you go to sleep each night, and then you can check in with your dream altar at night or in the morning when you awaken from sleep to see if anything has been changed, removed, added or rearranged, looking to see, and listening to hear, what the Spirit and Powers are saying to you, and what your energetic being is revealing.

You may receive very direct answers to your questions, or you might be given sacred tasks to perform through which you will acquire your answers and your healing; the communication of the Spirit and Powers may come directly through your dream altar, or it might come as insight and inspiration at some point in your day. You might find that whatever concerns you had are simply resolved, without any apparent reason or effort from yourself, like "an answer to prayers." You will be astonished at the power of your dream altar, finding great wonders will transpire through it! Tend it well and be playful with it. Enjoy yourself and it will bring you many blessings over the years. Work with it and you will see.

A Practice: The Dream Warrior

There is something more to be said of dream and dreamtime here, for our desire to remember our dreams, to generate luminous dreams and lucid dreams is not only for the sake of acquiring knowledge and power for ourselves. There is, in truth, much more to dreaming than that. Essentially, we must understand that dreamtime is the spirit world. In dreams, we go into the spirit world, and just as the spirit world may influence and bring about changes in this world, we influence and bring about changes in the spirit world. The spirit world and dreamtime is largely the astral dimension, though some dreams venture into the more interior dimensions, mental, higher vital, causal, and spiritual dimensions. Here and there are powerful dreamers who venture into the Supernal dimension in their dreams, great adepts and masters, very holy and powerful people. Generally speaking, though, most dreams occur in the astral, whether the upper, middle, or lower astral dimensions. This is the primary dimension of the spirit world that intersects, influences, and is influenced by, the material dimension.

We know very well what is being done to this world, the earth, the environment and creatures in it. Humankind has a great sickness, like a cancerous growth or hole in the soul, which drives the insanity of a greedy and lustful consumerism, and a tendency to great violence. Because of this terrible sickness, we are destroying the earth, our environment, and our fellow creatures, our relations. It must be said that Earth Mother will act to restore a balance and to regenerate herself if we do not do so ourselves. In a personified manner of speaking, she is getting "angry," though really, it is our own energy in a state of disorder, imbalance, and disharmony—ignorance—that will be reflected to us by Earth Mother.

What does this have to do with dreamtime? Just as we are polluting and destroying the environment of this world, we are also polluting and destroying the environments of the worlds in dreamtime, of the spirit world. Essentially, most people take their negative energy with them into the dreamtime, and this has a strong impact on the dreamtime and the spirits. As the environments of their worlds are adversely affected, the spirits tend to get frustrated and upset, and they get angry and hostile. Likewise, very dark and hostile spirits are generated and brought into the dreamtime or astral, so there is a powerful shift in the balance of forces, spirits, in dreamtime.

Not only are people taking their negative energy into dreamtime, the sickness of greed, and such, but unaware of the equal reality of dreamtime and the spirit world, they do not know the power of the spirits they are contacting and are often negatively influenced by them, unconsciously compelled by fierce angry spirits, and by unclean and evil spirits. You may recall the many exorcisms that Adonai Yeshua performed in his time. Today the influence and influx of fierce, unclean, and dark spirits is far greater, literally tens of thousands of times greater than in the time of Adonai Yeshua.

Significantly, we are not only taking our negativity into dreamtime, but our technologies are intersecting the dreamtime. Our play with electricity and nuclear energy, radio and television waves, cell phone signals, virtual reality, and the internet reaches deeply into the dreamtime or spirit world. If we just consider the internet, and the greed, lust, and overall negativity that dominates it, we may consider its influence upon dreamtime and the spirit world, the astral dimension. In other words, our negative influence and effect upon dreamtime and the spirit world is rapidly increasing and coming to a head, just as our negative influence and effect upon this good earth and its environments is coming to a head.

There was a time when most people knew how to dream and understood the power of the dreamtime and spirit world, a time when there were not so many bad or shadowy dreams, when people did not sleep so deeply, but got more rest and tended to remember their dreams, and had more luminous and lucid dreams and more visions. But those times are long gone and now there are relatively few conscious dreamers in the great mass of humanity; dreamtime can be a much more volatile and hostile place, certainly at the level of the astral dimensions.

Even many religions and much of modern spirituality have an adverse effect upon the dreamtime and spirit world. So what ought to be helpful to the spirit world is instead more often harmful. This speaks to the great need for us to work with our dreams and master our dreams, the need for true spiritual warriors in dreamtime, knowledge-keepers, and energy guardians in dreamtime and the spirit world. There are relatively so few today who have a good knowledge of the dreamtime and the power to use it that a person who can act as a conscious agent of the Divine in dreamtime and this world is essential. We have great need of true seers, healers and wonderworkers, true masters of dreaming and the spirit worlds.

The dream practices in the Mystical Path of Guadalupe are not for ourselves alone; they are for everybody, all our relations, visible and invisible. We may say that the spirits in the spirit world need our help too, as do our relations here in this world. There is a need for light-bearers, healers, and peacemakers in dreamtime and the spirit worlds, as well as in this world. In this regard, perhaps you may be familiar with what the Kabbalah says about the *tikkune*—the healing—of our soul or our energy being: It is also the tikkune of the world, of spirits, angels, and even the Holy Sefirot. This is what we are talking about in terms of a "dream warrior," a spiritual warrior for the people and for the sake of heaven.

What is described here may sound very archaic and crazy to most average people, but really, what's archaic and crazy are the behaviors being enacted in ignorance of all of this, the way of the unenlightened society and culture called 'normal.' It is important that we know that through our spiritual work in dream and the inner dimensions, we can make a difference, just as surely as through our spiritual work in this life and the material dimension we can make a difference.

In the midst of very dark and challenging times, as you might imagine, our work in dream and the inner dimensions becomes even more important, for in the midst of an increase of fear and anger in such times, an even greater negative effect is imposed upon the astral, and there is an even greater influx of fierce, unclean, and evil spirits into the subtle environment of the earth. The active labor of spiritual warriors, dream warriors, becomes especially crucial.

In the Holy Mother we have a very special empowerment to this spiritual labor, so that in our spiritual work we are not alone, but the Living Presence and Power of the Holy Mother is with us, and when we take up the Divine Action, it is Divine Grace that completes and accomplishes it. This is an important time to labor in our waking life and dream life for a greater good. The vision of the Great Mother calls us to it and empowers us in it. May we hear and respond to the call of the Mother.

A Practice: Dream Union with the Great Mother

Aware of yourself as in the folds of the Great Mother's robe of infinite space, lie down to sleep. Going to sleep, remember yourself in the folds of the Mother's robe as a shining star.

Alternatively, abide on the mother's lap, laying your head down upon her lap, resting in her compassion and in her grace. Go to sleep and dream well.

Or, as you're going to sleep, envision a Spiritual Sun within and behind your heart and gather yourself into it. Then, above your head, envision the image of Our Lady, the image of the Great Mother. Envision yourself as light flowing into her heart womb, merging with her completely as you fall asleep. In this way, you will come to luminous and lucid dreams. May you awaken in the Mother in dreamtime; she will come to you.

For another method as you're going to sleep, envision a rose blooming on the top of your head, releasing your essence into the Great Mother. It is done.

Speaking Silence & The Sacred Circle

He stood, looking towards the east, to the top of the Holy Hill, where he heard the heavenly music coming from. The song ended and silence broke out—a deep and profound silence. Then, from the midst of the silence, someone was calling to him, speaking his name, "Ihuantzin...Ihuan Diegotzin...," a calling out as though a mother to her child. As though a child in response to his mother, Juan Diego went to the one who was calling him. His heart was not troubled, he was not surprised or startled, but rather he was happy and felt great pleasure as he ascended the Holy Hill, eager to arrive at his destination.

The knowledge of the Sacred Circle and the winds or directions is invoked at this point in the story. If Juan Diego is looking up at the sacred mountain to the east, he is standing in the west. The sacred mountain is the Sacred Circle; its peak is the center of the circle, and he is in the west, walking in the direction west, but he is now called by the Great Spirit and powers to walk the direction east, to go to the center of the circle. While the directions and Winds of the Sacred Circle are discussed in later chapters, here we can point out a couple of obvious teachings in this story.

West is the place of dying and death, and the integration of our life experience. West is also the place of dreams and visions, as well as the place of love and devotion. Juan Diego has endured a nightmare in his lifetime, the slaughter of innumerable people, the destruction of his society and culture, and even his wisdom lineage has come to a time of death, transition.

East is the place of conception and birth, new beginnings and initiation, and it is the place of healing and of spiritual discernment, spiritual knowledge. By being directed to walk east, Juan Diego is called to a new beginning, an initiation which heals and empowers him to receive new knowledge, weaving the wisdom of his people's tradition with another stream of wisdom, the Christian stream. As has been said, the revelation of Guadalupe is an upliftment and restoration of the Spirit and the Light within both streams, a calling forth of their spiritual essence from the Primordial Tradition.

Now, consider the adventure of Elijah, the Hebrew prophet, the shaman of *Yahweh*. Perhaps you will remember the story of his experience of revelation on the Sacred Mount, at the mouth of the cave, and his passage through various barriers in consciousness until God spoke to him from within *Hashmal*, not the tumult of vital sentiments and the chattering mind, but in sheer silence, speaking in a still small voice (1 Kings 19:12). And perhaps you may recall, the word of *Yahweh* came to him in a dark time when his own lineage was threatened by extinction. Like the revelation of the *Shekinah* of *Yahweh*, the Mother speaking with Elijah, so now the *Shekinah* of *Yahweh* speaks with Juan Diego from within *Hashmal*, a speaking silence.

She calls to Juan Diego with the most intimate knowledge that a Mother would have of her child, calling him by his name with utmost sweetness of love and affection. He responds with an immediate knowing of the voice of his Holy Mother, without being troubled, startled or afraid, going to her with the delight, the joy of a little child, free of himself in his love of her. Such is our experience of Mother God; when she calls to us we know her voice and presence, and we are not afraid, but we are filled with awe and wonder, and with a peace of perfect sanctuary and with great joy, bliss. When she calls us, and we are willing to answer, such is our experience with her, She-Who-Is-Our-Mother, the Mother of All.

Of course, to enter into her embrace we must be willing to abandon ourselves to her passionate love and to the vastness of her infinite spaciousness, radiance, and power. We must be willing to die and be reborn in her, and be willing to enter into union with her Living Presence and Power, letting her carry us wherever she will, all as ordained by the Supreme.

Such love of the Holy Mother as this must be cultivated, and although her embrace is perfect peace and pure joy, unimaginable bliss, the journey into the Mother is not necessarily an easy one. We know this in the experience of Juan Diego coming to this moment with the Mother. He has passed through great darkness and faced great challenges, and along the way he has had to meet with the enemies in his quest to be a spiritual warrior, shaman, and a person of knowledge. In the sacred task the Mother gives to him, he will have to face great danger, going into the heart of darkness itself, even into the abysmal depths of the underworld. As we know, however, the love of the Divine Mother sees him through, and cleaving to her, he abides in her Living Presence and Power, her blessing and protection.

The movement through vital and mental responses into silence reflects *kavvanah*, the concentration of the mind, and his rushing to the sound of his Mother's voice reflects *devekut*, the passionate cleaving of the heart in the love of the Divine. We must cultivate such concentration and cleaving if we are to hear and see our Divine Mother. Our capacity to concentrate and cleave is everything in the Way.

This speaks to the spiritual labor of preparation through prayer and meditation and sacred ceremony, and to the spiritual life through which we actualize and realize the soul of light that is in us. Specifically, it echoes the teachings on the refinement of desire energy, for only when we truly desire the Mother will she reveal herself to us in full, and only through passionate desire for her do we concentrate our energy and cleave to her, entering into union with her. Whenever we are ready, whenever we co-create the conditions necessary for the movement of Divine Grace, we find the Mother is with us and that her Great Force moves with, in, and through us. Such is the nature of the Supernal Grace of God, the Supreme—*Elyon*.

West is also the direction of the elemental force of water and the place of water ceremony for purification. We may say that spiritual preparation is all about self-purification, the restoration of ourselves to our innate wholeness and perfection, as in the very beginning of life. Juan Diego has, indeed, purified himself, as we see from his swift response to the voice of the Mother; he goes to her in the full vigor of his youth, although, no doubt, Juan Diego is a mature man. The place of our wholeness and perfection is in the Center of the Sacred Circle, where God dwells and where the Powers gather. Having prepared himself, the Mother draws him into what some Native American traditions would call the "Center of the Hoop."

A Practice: Exploring the Sacred Circle

There is a spiritual practice given here regarding water ceremony and exploring the Sacred Circle. If you want to know something about the directions and their powers, better than reading about them and thinking about them, as though concepts in our mind have anything to do with them, instead, go outdoors. Perform water ceremony, self-baptism, and go and create a Sacred Circle, calling upon Sky Father and Earth Mother. Invoke the Powers, walk the directions of the Sacred Circle and become acquainted with them in your own experience. Go and commune with the Mother and the Powers, the winds of the four directions.

When you become acquainted, then go walk in the direction west and stand in the west, and listen for the call of the Great Spirit, the Great Mother, and the Powers. When you are called, turn to the direction east and walk in that direction. Go to the center of the Sacred Circle, and abiding in the silence of the center, listen and hear, look and see, and let the Spirit and Powers speak to you. When the word of *Yahweh*—Sky Father—comes through *Elohim*—Heaven Earth Mother—cleave to your Mother, the *Holy Shekinah*. As you do this, remember to go within and live within, in the Spiritual Sun within and behind your heart. Perhaps you will receive something of the Holy Spirit, the Mother Spirit in this way.

The First Word of the Mother

When he arrived at the crest of the Holy Hill he found a celestial noble woman standing there, and he knew that she did not walk with her feet on the ground, and as he gazed upon her she called him to draw near, She-Who-Is-The-Mother-Of-All. When he drew near he was astonished by her radiance and glory, the radiance and glory of the Queen of Heaven, the Presence and Power of the Most High. Her clothes shone like the sun, and as that immeasurable brilliance shone on the rocks surrounding her, they sparkled like precious jewels and everything had voice. The entire ground on top of the Holy Hill became like a great rainbow of celestial glory in this Heaven Earth Place, and the trees, the Nopal cactus, and all of the medicinal herbs that grew there were like green obsidian, their leaves like the finest turquoise, their stalks and thorns like gold, and in the air was something like gold dust, luminous sparkling particles of light-breath. Seeing this, Juan Diego was filled with holy awe and wonder, and he threw himself down at the feet of the Holy Mother, worshiping in the Presence and Power of the Supreme.

The Holy Mother spoke to her child, saying, "Listen, my youngest child, precious Juan, where are you going?"

The very first word of the Mother to Juan Diego is "listen," and in the spiritual life this is our first lesson: to listen and hear the voice of our heart, our true being, the Mother Spirit and Powers. Unless we can listen and hear, we cannot experience direct communion with the Divine and we cannot know our own heart and soul, our true being.

To listen implies that we must be awake and alert, present in the moment, aware of what's happening, what's being spoken, and it implies that we must be silent, receptive, to hear what's being spoken and understand it. This silence or receptivity is not just an outward silence, but it must be an inward silence and stillness, as well; the mind's incessant chatter is brought to silence and the tumult of our vital and emotional being is brought to stillness. It is in this state of silent and still receptivity, releasing all attachment and aversion—all reaction—that we can listen and hear the Spirit and Powers, and listen and hear our heart and soul, our true being. Here we must say, our heart and soul, our true being, and the Spirit and Powers, are inseparable from one another. To know our true self, our true being, is to know and commune with the Spirit and Powers.

Now, when we listen and hear, and when we commune with the Great Spirit, what we encounter and experience is the Great Silence. There is no big booming voice of God from the heavens, but rather, there is a Speaking Silence—*Hashmal*—and the word of God, the Great Spirit, manifests as a still small voice in our heart as intuition and inspiration. Unless we are silent and still, no longer caught up in the chatter of the mind and tumult of the vital, emotional being, we cannot hear this word of God in our heart. If we think we do hear the "word of God," more often than not it is bound up in our egoistic desires and fears, a fanciful manifestation of wishful thinking of our own making. Learning to be silent, abiding in the Presence of Awareness, free from attachment and aversion, is essential to receiving and hearing the word of God, the Great Spirit, the Great Silence. Our silence touches upon the Great Silence, and in this way insight and illumination dawns. We must be willing to the deep and profound silence that God is.

Another way of saying this is that we must become empty of ourselves, letting go of all preconception, precondition, and expectation, everything we think we are and think we know, everything we think reality is and think God is. Our emptiness touches that Great No-Thingness that God is. In this way we are filled with the Holy Spirit, the Mother Spirit. The Mother says to Juan Diego, and to us, "Be empty so that I can fill you!"

Invoking a state of receptivity, the Mother speaks to Juan Diego in the most intimate and affectionate terms, calling him her "youngest" child and "precious" in her sight, her love shining upon him in her appearance, and in her glory and power, and in her words and her voice. In this way she receives and embraces him, and she receives and embraces us. Into his emptiness she pours the fullness of her light and love, and so also pours this into our emptiness when we become empty of ourselves and receptive to her.

Now, at the very outset she asks him an important question. In fact it is a question she will ask him twice in the process of her revelation to him: "Where are you going?"

She is asking you and me that question right now! What is she actually asking us? She is asking us about our energy. How are we using our energy? What are we doing with our lives? What are we doing with our energy? What are our hopes and dreams? What are our priorities? What's our orientation and direction in life?

When the Holy Mother asks this, she is often asking us: Why are you not here with me? Why are you unaware of me, unaware that I am with you? Why are you running around so busy and fraught with worry, when all the while everything you could ever possibly want or need is right here? Why do you believe that you are lacking something, or that you are unworthy or worthless, when you are whole and complete in me, perfect as you are, lacking nothing?

She is also calling our attention to the dual nature of our being in this life, the spiritual and material, and the dual nature of God in our experience in life, transcendent and immanent. She is inquiring about our preparedness for our responsibility to death, and our reintegration with God, the Light Continuum—*Yahweh*. She is inquiring whether or not we are prepared to meet our Maker, and she is asking us if we know and commune with the source of our being, the Great Spirit, the Great Silence, the Great Void.

Like the questions Juan Diego asks at the very outset of his experience, this is an important question for us to ask ourselves from time to time, completely open and willing to hear the answer. If we feel that we are on track, enjoying life, enjoying being, well and good, we ought to continue in the way we are going. But if not, then we ought to look at what we are doing and seek to make a change in direction, even a very radical change, if necessary. It is very important to be aware of our energy and to know what we are doing with our energy, and to know what direction we are going.

Naturally, this question is an interactive meditation manifesting a need or desire, which is oriented entirely by our awareness of intention. The Mother wishes her children to prosper and succeed, to be healthy and happy, to enjoy life and experience the fulfillment of their heart's desires. She wants perfect success for them, to be and become all that they can be, and to experience the fullness of life in her. If and when we are confused and unclear about how to succeed, she will teach us and guide us towards our success, and she will empower us, and help us succeed. We only need open ourselves to her and abide in her presence, and she will be swift to bless and help us.

This is very well reflected later in the story when she asks Juan

Diego the same question again. Opening himself to her and abiding in her presence, without even needing to ask her, his wish is fulfilled and his uncle is healed, brought back from the threshold of death, and she gives him the sign he has asked her for to take back to the unbelieving bishop.

Here we must say that this is most often the way it is with the Mother. When we honor her and are devoted to her, and we commune in her Living Presence and Power, without our even asking, she fulfills our wishes and grants us boons. We find ourselves in a natural and spontaneous flow of blessings, experiencing a synchronistic flow of good fortune. Indeed, even in reading or hearing the Mother's story, and turning your mind and heart to her, to think of her and feel her, already there is likely a flow of blessings beginning to transpire in your life; already you are being blessed by her Living Presence and Power. That's the way it is with Mother God. She gives freely all that is good for us, blessing us and granting us boons, both spiritual and material.

Here we may say, the powers and the spirits are very attracted to those who love and cleave to the Great Mother; they love those who love the Mother, and just as the Mother they are swift to lend their help and power to those devoted to her. She is in them and they are in her. So the spirits become our helpers and allies as our relations in her. Such is the unimaginable sweetness of the Holy Mother.

A Practice: Listening to the Great Silence

Go and sit somewhere and just be. Listen to the sound of your breath and beat of your heart, and rejoice in the life you have in the Mother. Go within, and go deeper still, but remain alert to what's happening, outwardly and inwardly. In silence, commune with the Great Silence, and listen and hear the word of God, the still small voice in your heart. God the Mother speaks to those who listen.

It is ideal to go into the great outdoors to do this, not-doing, just being. You can do this anywhere as well, at any time. *Be still and know that I am God* (Psalm 46:10). As David prayed in Psalm 131: 1-2, so may we:

O Lord, my heart is not lifted up,
  my eyes are not raised too high;
I do not occupy myself with things
  too great and too marvelous for me.
But I have calmed and quieted my soul,
  like a weaned child with its mother;
  my soul is like the weaned child that is with me.

Just be in the Mother. That's all there is to it!

The Dwelling of the Mother

He said to the Celestial Lady, "Patroness, noblewoman, my daughter, my mother, my grandmother, I am on my way to your home, your dwelling, seeking the spiritual essence the sacred priests teach us."

When the Divine Mother inquires of Juan Diego where he is going, this is his response to her. He speaks to her with the greatest respect and affection, calling her his "patroness" and "noble woman," and "daughter," "mother" and "grandmother." Patroness indicates the Holy Mother as provider and protector, our sustenance, and noblewoman speaks of the emanation of the Mother and of the embodiment of the Mother. It is she who comes down and who appears to us, and she who is embodied in womanhood, and especially in holy women, women who walk in beauty and holiness, and who stand in their truth and power.

Now daughter, mother, and grandmother, of course, speak of the three aspects of the Divine and Sacred Feminine: the youthful, the mature, and the elder wise in years. This is the Divine Mother as the Circle of Life, from conception to death and the afterlife: all of our experience of being, all expressions or dimensions of consciousness, all reality material and spiritual, the Great Matrix. At the same time, the Daughter indicates the Holy

Bride, the *Lower Shekinah*, which is our individual and personal experience of the Divine Mother, and individual emanations or manifestations of her. The Mother indicates the *Upper Shekinah*, her emanation or manifestation to all and as all, her cosmic or universal aspect as the Great Mother—*Imma Gadol*. Grandmother is her transcendent and primordial aspect, the Divine Feminine as the Ancient One, the primordial source and ground from which all arises. The Father, Mother, Son, and Bride are the Great Force and Matrix of Creation.

Addressing her with honor and respect, Juan Diego speaks the gnosis, the knowledge, understanding, and wisdom of the Great Mother—Mother God. He does so in the most essential and simple way possible, neither with creed, doctrine, nor theology, but as an utterance of his direct perception and experience of her, an experience that is multidimensional, supramental. Creeds, doctrines, and theologies take the place of direct experience and the gnosis, the knowing, that comes through direct experience. In the Mother we need no creed, doctrine, or theology, for we experience and know her directly. She reveals herself to us and illuminates us, and so also does her Holy Child, the Spiritual Sun, of which we are all emanations in our energetic being.

If there must be creeds, doctrines, and theologies because our mental and vital being cherishes such things, then let us know and understand that she is the Mother of them all. More specifically, whatever creed, doctrine, or theology we might cling to and identify ourselves with, even when that does not include Mother God, still, she is our Holy Mother, and whenever we wish to open our mind, heart, and life to her, she will reveal herself to us and illuminate us. Such is the nature of the Divine Mother, the Compassionate Mother. In a manner of speaking, it does not matter whether or not you believe in the Mother or know the Mother, for she believes in you and knows you, and eventually you will have her faith and knowledge. All are destined to awaken in the dream and to awaken from the dream, all in due season.

Now in the oral tradition among the Aztec elders, Juan Diego says that he is going to her "home in Mexico-Tlatelolco," which is to say her "home in the land, and in the people," and it indicates the Holy Mother as the Queen of the Land, the Princess of the People. She is with the people and the land, she is in the people and the land, and she is manifest as the people and the land, though at one and the same time she is beyond them, transcendent. She is indwelling and pervading all creation, and surrounding all creation, and yet transcending all creation. Truly, she is the Great Mother, cosmic and primordial.

Here, in our version of the story, Juan Diego speaks of her "home," her "dwelling," and we know that dwelling in Hebrew is *Makom*, a Divine Name which is also a Name of the Mother. The dwelling is wherever the Mother-*Elohim* is. Juan Diego is going to The Name, which is Her Name, and Her Name is Her Presence and Power, and it is Her Body, Her Emanation. The Mother dwells in herself, and the Mother dwells in all, and everywhere is Her Dwelling, Her Name.

We know and understand that a church building is not her dwelling, save in that she dwells everywhere, including the space encompassed by such buildings. She appears to ask that a Holy Temple, a dwelling place, be built in honor of her for the sake of the people, a place of the concentration of her Presence and Power, and the gathering of the Powers, so as yet there is no Holy Temple she has chosen as her Power Place.

Juan Diego is not speaking of a Catholic church building, but rather of a greater awareness of the *Holy Shekinah*, akin to what Adonai Yeshua taught the Samaritan woman at Jacob's Well (St. John 4), when he said that the time was coming and had come, when we would no longer need to go to the temple or sacred mountain to worship God, but we would worship God in spirit and truth, in all things, everywhere. We worship in our homes and in the great outdoors, for we are the living temple of the Living God—*Elohim Hayyim*. When he says this, of course, he is also saying that we need no religion, no creed, doctrine, or theology. We need only know and understand the Way, the direct spiritual communion with the Divine and embodiment of the Divine, a life lived with and in God, the True Light.

We may ponder the Mother asking that a temple be built at Tepeyacac, on the Holy Hill. This is for the sake of people in the midst of dark times, something you give to little children for their enjoyment and nurturance; it does not come with a creed or doctrine, however, nor a new religion. The revelation Guadalupe brings is both indigenous and it is Christian. Neither tradition can claim sole and exclusive dominion of her appearance. Being both indigenous, Christian, and beyond either of these, Guadalupe is cosmic, primordial, and universal: the revelation of the Great Mother God in the predawn of the age of the Holy Spirit, the Mother Spirit.

The temple is for younger siblings, the little ones, and it is a visible sign of her greater message. Older siblings, the mature, the wise, know and understand she dwells everywhere. They commune with her wherever they are, in everything, all of the time, in the waking world and dreamtime, and in the afterlife, and when they go to attend to their spiritual essence, usually they go into the great outdoors, for in the great outdoors they find profound inspiration and an effortless communion.

Naturally, in the land, on the earth, there are places of power, concentrations of power, and there are lines of power, flows or currents of power. Those who are wise know how to find and use these. Everything is a manifestation of energy, light, and all is as a vast field or ocean of energy and light, so everywhere there is power, for everything is power, an emanation of energy-intelligence.

There is, indeed, something of skillful means in going to places of power when called by the Spirit and the Powers, when there is a need; and there is, indeed, something of skillful means in creating altars and sanctuaries in places of power to gather and concentrate power, and for the sake of the generation and transmission of spiritual power. Creating such external points of focus may help us reintegrate our energetic and our physical being, and it is part of the play of the Divine Mother in the material dimension. Points of focus of the spiritual dimensions intersect in powerful ways with the material dimension, yet, we are not bound to such things, and in truth the greatest place of power is wherever the Human One of Light, the Spiritual Sun, is made manifest and embodied, wherever a realized human being is abiding, in movement or repose.

Now Juan Diego says that he is going on his way, "seeking the spiritual essence the sacred priests teach us," and given that the home or dwelling of the Mother is in the people and the land, if her home is not a Catholic church, then the sacred priests of whom Juan Diego is speaking are not necessarily the Catholic priests. Perhaps they could be, assuming that they knew the Sun of God in their own experience and how to draw upon the Light of the Spiritual Sun, the true spiritual essence. In Nahuatl the word for "sacred priest" indicates a person of power and knowledge, a person who holds energy, an energy keeper or spiritual guardian. This is a person filled with the Holy Spirit, the Light of the Spiritual Sun, who is a generator of energy embodying something of the Spiritual Sun for the people.

The spiritual essence Juan Diego is seeking is the Light and Fire of the Spiritual Sun, which in Hebrew is called *Ruach Ha-Kodesh*, the Spirit of Holiness. In a true and sacred priesthood there is no division between the sacred priests and the people. Priests are among the people, and rather than someone placing themselves in between the people and God, a true and sacred priest is a facilitator of direct spiritual and mystical experiences of God with the people, a midwife to the Mother Spirit giving birth to the Spiritual Sun in the people. They know and understand, and teach the way in which all people are sacred priests.

The role of priests among a people of priests is to follow a call from the Spirit and Powers to serve as specialized keepers of knowledge and power, and as teachers and guides, servants of all. We know Juan Diego is a spiritual warrior and a shaman, a holy man, so we know that he is among the sacred priests. But he is a very humble man and has no great claim to make of himself, so he speaks of his elders and his teachers rather than speaking of himself. Likewise he knows that in the Mother and in the Spiritual Sun, as we awaken, we are all in the sacred priesthood. The knowledge and understanding of the true spiritual essence is within each and every one of us. We merely need to restore the awareness of our energetic being.

Sunrise and sunset are powerful times for prayer and worship, just as noon and midnight are powerful times for spiritual works. We follow the Path of the Spiritual Sun through the day; in the very same way we do so throughout the seasons, following the Circle of Days and Circle of Years, walking the Sacred Circle of Life. Also, as we have indicated previously, going out in the morning to greet the Spiritual Sun and to draw upon the spiritual essence of the Sun of God is a central practice in the Mystical Path of Guadalupe. Her great power time is predawn, and her transmission of glory and power is in the Bright Morning Star and in the Rising Sun, the presence and power of the Risen Messiah—Hayyah Yeshua.

As we know in the Holy Kabbalah, Nogah is the planet Venus, the transmitter of the light of the star Sirius, and Nogah is the Herald and Opener of the Way in the path of the Spiritual Sun, taking its position with the rising and setting sun in due season, calling the spiritually-attuned to right worship according to the cycles of power. We know that *Shemesh*, the star that is our Sun, is the *Holy Sefirah Tiferet* in *Asiyah*, bringing in the *shefa*, *ruhaniyot*, and *mochin*—the energy, essence, and mind—of the Messiah into the physical plane. The spiritual energy of the Opener of the Way and the Anointed of God are tandem as the Bright Morning Star and the Sun. We draw upon this combined power—spiritual, psychic, and material—when we go out and greet the Sun in its rising.

It has been said by the masters of the tradition, "Those who know how to meet the Mother and Sun in the morning, and who know how to draw the spiritual essence of the Sun from within them, will know life abundant, prosperity, success, health, and happiness. They will abide in the sacred priesthood as light-bearers, healers and peacemakers among the people."

The Sun of God, Adonai Yeshua, has spoken, saying, *You who have seen me have seen the Father* (St. John 14:9). As the invisible atmosphere is made visible by the Rising Sun, the Sky Father being revealed in the Spiritual Sun, so too with the Rising Sun we see and know Earth Mother, and all her angels. Likewise, when the

Sun sets, passing into the otherworld, we behold the Queen of Heaven and Grandmother Deep Space, and something of the Cosmic and Primordial Mother is revealed. All the while, in everything, we know the dance of the Holy Bride with us, for she is our individual and personal experience of all of this: the Grandmother, the Father, the Mother and the Spiritual Sun. The Bride is our experience of the Light of the Spiritual Sun, the Holy Spirit. This is our experience of the Path of the Sun and Moon, and the Great Milky Way, standing on Earth Mother beneath Sky Father, the awareness of which is in the Bride, the Mother and Grandmother: She who gives birth to the Spiritual Sun and reveals the Living Father, the Great and Invisible Spirit.

We are all experiencing this. Though many of us might be unconscious, if we want to wake up, we can go look and see and become aware of the play of the Spiritual Sun and *Shekinah*, the Holy Child and Mother-Bride within and all around us. As we have shared, a simple way is to go out and greet the Rising Sun. There are many other ways. If you will go within and go out to greet the Sun of God, standing on Earth Mother, beneath Sky Father, at or near dawn, the Holy Spirit will teach you many ways of union with the Sun and Mother, and she will show you many secret mysteries we cannot write or speak, but may be known and understood only through direct spiritual and mystical experience. Each soul must learn to listen and hear, and look and see for itself, for only in this is there salvation, illumination and freedom.

A Practice: Communion With the Sun of God

When you go out to greet the Sun of God envision yourself self-radiant with glory like the Sun of God rising before you and commune in the presence of God, the True Light. This is enough.

If you wish to bring in, anchor and hold the Light of the Spiritual Sun for the people and the land, then envision the Rays of the Spiritual Sun all drawn with, in and through you, and channel that Holy Light into the Good Earth, and let it ray out from you to all your relations, blessing and healing them. This is enough.

If you wish to know Sky Father, the Great Spirit, envision the whole earth and you as the Light of the Spiritual Sun, and envision that the whole earth dissolves into fluid flowing light and merges with you, and then envision your union with the Sun of God in the same way. Abiding in union with the Sun of God, envision yourself as the Sun of God merging with Father Sky, and disappear like a rainbow vanishing in the sky. This is enough.

Of predawn we shall say, know this as the Mother's Womb, and know the Light of the Spiritual Sun as the Mother's Force. Let that Holy Light kindle the Fire Snake in you, and let that Fiery Intelligence be uplifted to the Spiritual Sun of God when you greet the Sun. This is our offering in the gnostic worship of the Sun of God, and it is good.

To this may be added the consecration of bread and wine as the Holy Light and Fire of the Spiritual Sun. Partaking of it, you abide in the Light-Presence and Light-Power of the Sun of God. As you partake of it, offer yourself up as a blessing and nourishment for all your relations, and let your light shine throughout the day, remembering that as an emanation of the Spiritual Sun you are the light and life of the world.

In this you have another way of greeting the Sun at dawn, the Sun emerging from the Holy Womb of the Mother, her great glory and power shining upon you.

Gnosis of Mother God, the Great Mother

She said to him, "Know, my youngest child, I am the Forever Whole and Perfect Maiden Saint Mary, Holy Mother of God, Holy Mother of the Giver of Life, Holy Mother of the Creator of the Human One, Holy Mother of the One-Who-Is-Distant-And-Near, Holy Mother of the Creator of Heaven and the Earth, Primordial Wisdom, the Great Grandmother of All.

The Holy Mother speaks to us who she is, and her words form an essential contemplation and meditation in the Mystical Path of Guadalupe. Likewise, as she reveals who she is, and throughout the story, we are given Divine Names of the Holy Mother, which empower us to invoke and call upon her. Each of us can contemplate what she says, and meditate upon it, and we can call upon her by the Holy Names she has given us, and thus experience and know her directly.

Before anything is said about these Divine Names, before there is any teaching or commentary given, it is important that you know that the most essential knowledge and understanding of what the Mother says and the Holy Names she gives will come through your own contemplation and meditation, and through your own prayers calling upon her Divine Names. What you glean in your own experience of the Mother is what she speaks to you, and it is what is most important to you and your journey, your path, in this life. It is good and it is wise to gather knowledge from the insights and experience of others, for we have much to gain from one another. But it is very important that we recognize, honor, and respect the knowledge, understanding, and wisdom—the *Habad*—the Mother gives to us, and that we do not fall into the delusion of lack, as though our own knowledge, understanding, and wisdom is any less than anyone else's.

It must also be said that most of our *Habad* of the Mother is something more experiential, something on a more feeling and intuitive level, than anything intellectual. We know her in our experience and in our awareness, we feel her and intuit her presence, power, and her mysteries, and much of what we know is knowledge of the heart, things we cannot speak or explain. So the greater part of what we know and understand of her cannot be spoken or written, but anyone willing to enter into her embrace may experience and know the Mother.

This is what the Mystical Path of Guadalupe is all about: Being with and in Mother, and Mother being with and in us, knowing her in everything and everyone, and most especially within ourselves. Take the time to contemplate and meditate upon each Holy Name, and pray with the Holy Names of the Mother, and see and hear what the Mother Spirit speaks in your heart and in your own experience. This is the revelation of Mother to you, a revelation that is individual, unique, and personal.

The Mother calls her child by name, and she teaches her children her Names. She invokes a very close, personal relationship. To every child she teaches special Names, Names she only speaks to that child. If you ask the Mother, she will reveal secret Names to you and words of power that are only for you to use.

Before you read and listen any further, perhaps you might want to go and contemplate and meditate upon this part of the story yourself, and call upon her Names yourself. Go and envision her before you, as before Juan Diego, and chant the Name of *Imma Gadol* as you bow down before her and offer yourself to her, and as you rise up, gaze upon her and listen to what she says, listen to these Names she speaks, and let her reveal herself to you. If you give yourself to Mother, she will give herself to you. She will give you everything good. When you have done this, then perhaps, if you are inclined, come back and continue to read and listen to this sacred discourse of the Mother.

The Divine Names of the Mother

The Father and Mother are inseparable from one another: *Abba* and *Imma*, the Holy One. *El Elyon*, God Most High, the Supreme, emanates as *Eheieh*. *Eheieh* emanates as *Yahweh Elohim*, the Father-Mother, *Abba* and *Imma*. *El Elyon*, God Most High, is the primordial transcendence of all masculine and feminine aspects of Supreme Being. From *El Elyon* emanates all Names, the first of which is *Eheieh*, "I Am" or "I Shall Be," of infinite, exhaustless potential. The force and generator of this infinite potential is distinguished as *Abba*, the Father. As a man after conceiving a child is reposed and transcendent, so is *Yahweh*—"That which was, is, and forever shall be"—pure being. The form and appearance of this potential is made actual by *Imma*, the Mother. As women change with the gestation and birth of a child, so does *Elohim*—"One as many"—the infinite display of diversity. The unity, the being, is *Yahweh*; the diversity, the becoming, is *Elohim*. Together, *Yahweh Elohim*, the LORD God, is the mystery of the Mother revealing unity through diversity.

The first Holy Name the Mother speaks to Juan Diego is "I Am," *Eheieh*, which implies *El Elyon*, the Supreme, and which arises in creation as *Yahweh Elohim*, Father and Mother, the Holy One. The Holy One is Father and Mother, but here it is as Mother God that the Holy One emanates and manifests. *Imma*, the Mother, is *Elohim*, and all is in her, male and female, light and darkness, life and death. She is all that is revealed of the Divine, all that is known and understood of the Divine, and she is all that appears, all creation, and yet, though immanent, she is transcendent, the Great and Holy Mother, *Gadol Va-Kodesh Imma*.

She is the Holy One, the Divine as an integral Sacred Unity, and yet she becomes many, having many aspects, many emanations. Although she has many aspects, many emanations, many faces and forms, she remains always herself, always the Holy One, the Sacred Unity. While she is a constant continuum of change, of transformation, in her essence and nature she never changes, and although emanating as all, her infinite potential of emanation, creation, formation and making is exhaustless, for she is the supreme, the infinite, and eternal, the Holy One of Being, primordial being.

Her first Holy Name as *Imma Elohim*, Mother God, is the Forever Whole and Perfect Maiden, the Holy Bride and Virgin Mother. She is the Bride and she is the Mother, but whether as Bride or as Mother, she is Forever Whole and Perfect, the Virgin. She is pure and she is herself, Primordial Wisdom, Mother Clear Light, and Daughter Clear Light inseparable from one another, the Mother of Enlightenment: Illuminatrix. Our Lady of Guadalupe is the Mother and the Bride, the *Upper* and *Lower Shekinah*, *Binah* and *Malkut*; she proclaims to us that she is "Saint Mary," Mother Miriam, but she is also the Magdalene, the Holy Bride who is the divine consort of the Spiritual Sun, the *Shekinah* of the Messiah.

When she calls herself the Forever Whole and Perfect Maiden Saint Mary, she is not the Virgin Mary in the way the Catholic Church would conceive of her. Rather, it is Mother Miriam understood as an enlightened being, a holy and illumined woman, and yet more, as the emanation and embodiment of Mother God giving birth to the Spiritual Sun of God. In a word, she is the "Goddess," God the Mother, *El Imma*. In the theologies of orthodoxy, of course, Mother Mary is, in effect, a sexless woman: an image of the Divine and Sacred Feminine stripped of her power, her dynamism, her fertility, and her sensual, sexual, and earthy qualities. Her womanhood and her true Divinity is stolen from her. This is not Mother Mary in the revelation of Our Lady of Guadalupe! No, indeed, although she is the Virgin Mother, she is completely active and dynamic in every possible way in the full power and glory of Womanhood and Divinity. She is also ever the Virgin, meaning completely transcendent and unchanged in her Divine Essence and Nature, always remaining That-Which-She-Is in Herself and in all.

The second Divine Name of the Mother is the Holy Mother of God, or the Mother of the True God. On one hand, this is Mother Miriam as the Mother of the Messiah, the Spiritual Sun of God; on the other hand, this is the Mother giving birth to the Father, Grandmother Wisdom, Grandmother God, the Ancient One, the Primordial One. She is the Mother of all Divinity, if such a thing may be said. She is the Holy Womb in which God, the True Light, the Divine, is conceived. Yet the conception of God is no conception, and the birth of God is no birth; it is the pure emanation of God from within Godself, becoming Father, Mother, Son, and Bride. That which conceives and gives birth to God, the Mother of the True God, however, is rightly called Grandmother. If we wish to contemplate this in our experience, we may consider Sky Father and Earth Mother, and we may consider Mother Deep Space beyond Sky Father and Earth Mother, she who becomes Sky Father and Earth Mother in our experience. She is, indeed, Grandmother to us, Mother Deep Space.

The Divine Names Mother of the Giver of Life and Mother of the Creator of the Human One extend this awareness of Our Lady of Guadalupe as the Great Mother, the Cosmic and Primordial Mother. The Giver of Life is the Spiritual Sun, the Messiah, and the Creator of the Human One—the Speaking One—is the Father and Mother, all of this arising from the Primordial Womb of God, Primordial Wisdom, Grandmother Wisdom.

The Divine Name of the Mother of the One-Who-Is-Distant-And-Near speaks the great and supreme mystery of her as the Mother of herself, as the Mother of the Mother: Self-generating, Self-begetting, Self-emanating Primordial Being, without beginning, without end.

The Divine Name of the Holy Mother of the Creator of Heaven and Earth indicates she is the *Shekinah* of the Supreme, which is the Supreme itself, and so she is called Primordial Wisdom, Sophia, and she is called the Great Grandmother of All. Great Grandmother is the Essence of the Divine, which is known only by God in Godself, True Godhead.

This is neither the "Virgin Mary" of Roman Catholics nor Eastern Orthodoxy. No, indeed, she is much more than the very limited and restricted conception of the Divine and Sacred Feminine in orthodoxy; she is God the Mother, God as Mother, and truly the Mother of God, above and below, in heaven and on earth: the Great Mother. Most good Christians reading their Scriptures never consider what it means when Yeshua Messiah speaks in the Name of the Father, *Abba*, the Living Father, the Heavenly Father, Sky Father. To speak in the Name of the Father assumes and implies the Mother, for there can be no Father without Mother, and the Heavenly Father directly speaks of the Earth Mother and Heavenly Mother.

If God is Father, then God is also Mother. It can be no other way. If God is Father and Mother, then God is beyond Father or Mother. It can be no other way. If God is Father and Mother, the Father is transcendent and the Mother is immanent. Though inseparable from the Father, she is transcendent and immanent. As the immanent presence and power of God, the immanent Divinity, she is everything revealed, known, and understood of God and Godhead, the All-In-All.

This is the great and holy mystery that Our Lady of Guadalupe is revealing to us: the truth of God as Mother, Mother God. Worshiping the Mother we worship God, the True Light.

A Practice: Union with Our Lady

Do you want to know Our Lady? Then make a shrine to her and pray to her, and call upon her Holy Names; invoke her, and so, as she has asked, you will see: "Am I not right here who is your Mother?" You will know her presence with you wherever you are, wherever you go. Likewise, if you pay attention to your dreams, seeking luminous dream and lucid dream, and you worship Our Lady with passion, cleaving to her and desiring her, she will appear in your dreams, and she may give you a vision of herself, coming to you as to many others since the days of Juan Diego. If you want to know her more intimately, then envision yourself in your body of light, the Spiritual Sun within and behind your heart, and see a ray of light shooting forth from the Spiritual Sun within you, magically appearing in the space before you as the Noble Celestial Woman, Our Lady of Guadalupe.

Open your mind and heart to her; pray to her and commune with her, and as you do, see her smiling upon you and blessing you with rays and streams of Divine Light from her Emanation Body. Now, Sophians know her as an emanation described in Revelation chapter 12 as the Woman of Light—*Imma Or Ain Sof*, the Mother of Infinite Light—and so the chant of the Woman of Light is also her chant: *Ha-Isha Ha-Elyona, Imma Israel*. This is the sacred chant we take up as we meditate upon her, which means, "Most High Woman, Mother of the elect." Alternatively: *Ha-Isha Ha-Elyona, Gadol Imma* can be used, this latter being a sacred chant that she gave generations ago to Sophian lineage-holders by direct revelation in dream and vision. There is also an energetic power chant that she has given to us: *Ya Ya, Ya Imma, Ya Ha*.

Taking up one of her chants, when the chant is brought to an end, envision the Divine Image of Our Lady becoming fluid, flowing light. Envision that Holy Light, the Mother's Force, streaming to the top of your head and pouring down through your head and heart into your belly. Feel it awaken the Fire Snake in your belly, and let that holy fire be uplifted to the top of your head as an offering to Father Sky and Grandmother Deep Space, passing into union with the Queen of Heaven, the Celestial Maiden. Her Mind is your mind; her Sacred Heart is your heart; her Divine Body is your body. You embody her Living Presence and Power; it is within and all around you. You are hers and she is yours, now and forever.

As you walk in the world, walk in her Heaven Earth Place, seeing all as her dwelling and body. All sound-vibration you hear, hear as her sweet and heavenly voice, and hear her word in it; every thought and emotion arising in your mind, receive as the innate radiance of her Holy Wisdom, arising in her, abiding in her, and going into her, running and returning to its source in her. In this you will be sealed in covenant with the Great Mother, your soul bound and unified with her, Mother Truth-Light, *Imma Amet-Or*.

When it is time, and when you are able and willing, rather than see her dissolving and merging with you, you may envision your dissolution going into her. This is called the Perfection of Union. In this there is full and true knowledge of her, full reintegration with God, the True Light. The promise of Hayyah Yeshua at the outset in the Gospel of St. Thomas is fulfilled in this way, and so also the prophecy of the vision of the Woman of Light and her Holy Child in the Revelation of St. John. You will not experience death but will be taken up in divine rapture, passing into the Supernal Abode through the Grace of the Holy Mother. *Hallelu Imma*! Praise the Mother!

This is the practice of Union with Our Lady of Guadalupe. Many blessings and boons come to those who take it up, and swiftly they come to know the Holy Light and Fire of the Mother in them, the Light and Fire of the Spiritual Sun, the Anointed of God. *Hallelu Yah*! Praise the Father-Mother! Amen.

The Holy Temple of the Great Mother

"It is my wish for them to build a Holy Temple, a Dwelling Place, here upon this Sacred Mount, where I will give myself to the people, all of my love, compassion, assistance, and protection, a place of Holy Sanctuary, an abode of Holy Light. I am the Compassionate Mother of you and your people here in this land, and of all other

people who love me, call to me, search for me and confide in me. I will listen to their pain, their sorrow and suffering, and hear their cries and pleas from their misery, and I will comfort them and heal them, bless them and grant them boons, all in the Name of God, the True Light, that Holy Light I Am."

The *Makom*, Dwelling, of the Mother is everywhere. We may say that the whole of this Good Earth is her Dwelling, and yet more, the entire galaxy and universe, all creation. We may say that her Holy Temple is the great outdoors, and that it is our lives and our bodies. Naturally, then, we cannot help but wonder at the desire of the Holy Mother to have a temple built in her honor, and we must question what this means.

The entire thrust of her revelation to Juan Diego is that a temple should be built upon Tepeyacac, a temple dedicated to the Holy Mother as a sacred space for the worship of God as the Mother. She herself provided her Divine Image to be enshrined there, the temple and her image being a material manifestation of her Living Presence and Power, one very tangible for the people. Does the Mother need a temple on a sacred mountain? No, in fact, she does not. But the people have need of it, her little children need and want it, something material to remind them of the spiritual and energetic, and to serve as a talisman of an energetic spiritual transmission. Her temple is a great beacon of the Divine Mother in the world. Although eclipsed by the dominion of an earthly ruler or archon, in truth it is more than Catholic. Her temple is a place of healing and Light Transmission in space-time, which is the Holy Mother, the Cosmic and Primordial Mother.

In the time of Juan Diego the people desperately needed such a place, a tangible symbol of hope and healing, the presence and power of the Mother God. Today, perhaps even more so, the people have a deep need for such a holy place of the Divine and Sacred Feminine. In the midst of the evolutionary crisis we face, the Divine and Sacred Feminine must be restored in our spiritual lives. It is through the restoration of the Divine and Sacred Feminine that there is hope for our healing and survival, and for the dawn of the age of the Holy Spirit, the Second Coming of the

Sun of God, the fruition of Divine Illumination in humanity.

The Mother does not need a temple, but it is a matter of skillful means for the people, for us. In truth we do not need a temple to worship the Mother, but in the material dimension the creation of temples, sanctuaries, and shrines is skillful, for they are places of power and the gathering of the Powers for spiritual work and worship. Often such places help us become more attuned and receptive to the Spirit and Powers, so we are able to have deeper and more penetrating spiritual experiences, empowering our spiritual lives. While we should not become bound to such things, as to some idol, believing that without them we cannot experience the Spirit and Powers, or worship God, nevertheless in the material dimension they are skillful means and are very good for us. They uplift and empower us, and invoke holy remembrance of the Divine I Am.

Now, the Mother calls Juan Diego as a messenger of her desire for a Holy Temple on the sacred mountain; she calls for the building of her temple. But in this call there is another call to all of us who are devotees of the Divine Mother, a call to a practice central to the Mystical Path of Guadalupe: the building of shrines to her in our homes, in our places of business, in our land, all as points in space-time of the emanation of her Presence and Power. It is like a vast constellation of stars, or like a great matrix of the Divine Light, and wherever a holy sanctuary or shrine is built to her, there is a concentration of her power, and the Divine Powers and luminous spirits gather there. Whether great or small, when a shrine is built to the Divine Mother it is the same. It is an emanation of her Holy Temple on top of Tepeyacac into another space made sacred and holy to her.

When a person becomes a devotee of our Lady of Guadalupe, and takes up the Mystical Path of Guadalupe, it is only natural that they should wish to build a shrine to her, a place to focus prayer and energy, and a reminder that she is ever near, ever present with us. It must be said, however, that the Holy Mother does not stay in her temple, or in her sanctuary or shrine, but rather, she goes with her devotees wherever they go, in life, in dream and in death. Yet, in going with them, she also waits for them in her special holy places, just as she waited for Juan Diego on top of the sacred mountain, calling him to herself.

Aside from the building of the temple, the Mother appears to give herself to us: To give us her love and compassion, assistance, and protection, to provide us with sanctuary, a place in the Divine Light. She offers us a most intimate and personal relationship with her, intimate knowledge and experience of her, and more than anything she offers us healing and blessings and boons, which is to say the fulfillment of our heart's desires, our true desires. In offering herself to us in this way, and giving us another Holy Name for her, the Compassionate Mother, she shatters and dispels the evil *klippah* of religion that preaches a judgmental and wrathful god, a false god, revealing the true nature of the Divine as loving, compassionate, and merciful, something deeply nourishing and nurturing, the fulfillment of our dreams.

This is the revelation of the True God, the True Light, and of a pure spirituality—not religion—a spirituality of direct experience and knowledge, illumination and freedom. The spirituality the Mother reveals is, in fact, what Adonai Yeshua taught us. Unfortunately, what Yeshua taught seems to have precious little to do with what has come to be called "Christianity" or the religion preaching the "Gospel of Christ." The Mother reveals to us the true meaning of the Gospel of Love. Her response to Juan Diego when he tries to sneak past her later in the story reflects this very well, for it is with love and compassion that she meets him, not judgment or wrath.

Now this speaks to another practice in the Mystical Path of Guadalupe: To embrace all our relations with respect, with tolerance and understanding, with love and compassion, understanding all life and the world as sacred, just as they are. It is walking with an open heart and mind, being gentle to ourselves and to one another, letting go of judgments, as Adonai Yeshua taught us to do. We do not need to taint everything with moral judgments and the like, but rather, love can be our measure and teacher of what is right for us to do. In pursuing our heart's desires, and seeking to help fulfill the desires of others, we will experience the blessings and boons of the Mother. When we draw near to her, making ourselves like the Mother, naturally her Living Presence and Power flows through us and through our life. The essential practice is this: Be as the Mother to all of your relations. If you walk as a woman, be as the Holy Mother: loving, compassionate, merciful, and kind.

The Mother comes to relieve the sorrow and suffering of the people. This, then, becomes a key practice on Her Path. Once again, the Holy Mother invokes the Divine Name of *Eheieh*, and she speaks a great and holy mystery as she does this, for saying she is the Holy Light, she tells us she is Pure Energy. This becomes a very deep contemplation to us in the Mystical Path of Guadalupe, for the very nature of the path is an awareness of our energetic being, its healing and reintegration, and awareness of the energetic dimension, the spiritual dimension. Our energy being and the energy dimension is as the Emanation Body of the Mother. As the material dimension is inseparable from the energy dimension, so too is this physical or material world and our physical or material being. The seeds of a non-dual realization, the realization of Supernal or Supramental Consciousness, is in the message of the Mother, the Divine I Am.

The Mother has made us a promise, and she will fulfill it if we have faith in her and cleave to her, loving her and all our relations as we love ourselves.

Sending Her Messenger, the Vision Bringer

"So that my desire may come into being and be fulfilled, go to the bishop in his palace in Mexico City and speak with him, telling him that I am having you go to explain to him how I want a Holy Temple built here for me. Tell him every detail of what you have seen and heard and experienced here with me, tell him of what you know and understand, the wisdom given to you. I will be happy and very grateful, and you will be richly rewarded for your service to me. You will reach great and lofty attainments as compensation for your efforts to put my intention into motion. My youngest child, you have heard and know my wish, my heart's desire, now go and make it so. Do what I have asked you to do."

Juan Diego is called as the messenger or vision bringer of the Mother. Such luminous visions are not only for the one who sees them, but they are for the people, and the seer is called as a vision bringer to the people, a messenger or prophet. Needless to say, this is a very great honor and blessing, and it is a very sacred and holy task, one requiring great faith and intelligence, and great strength and courage. It is a great honor and blessing, but it is also a great challenge, for as a spiritual messenger, a vision bringer or prophet, one can face extreme persecution in this world, and at times even the possibility of physical violence and death, as we see in the story of Yeshua Messiah who is beaten and put to death, but who is raised from death by God.

In the case of Juan Diego the threat of being tortured and murdered is very real. The bishop to whom he is sent is among the heads of the Spanish Inquisition in Mexico and near his palace are places of imprisonment, torture, and death. He has been responsible for the deaths of many people by unimaginable brutality and horrific means, such as burning alive. Essentially, the bishop is an embodiment of great darkness and evil, and being sent to his palace is like being sent to the abodes of the underworld and hell with a message of God, the True Light. Truly, Juan Diego is being given an enormous challenge, the task of a spiritual warrior, an impeccable warrior. This is no small thing the Mother is asking Juan Diego to do. She is literally asking him to risk his very life to bring the vision—her message—to the people.

In the Kabbalah we are told that until we are able to share and give what we receive from the Spirit and Powers, we have not received and integrated it in full. Receiving spiritual influx, a vision, knowledge, and power, we must share and give what we receive, and only then it is ours, an integral part of our energetic being, our soul. The spiritual knowledge and power we are given is for action in this world and the inner dimensions; it is empowerment as a conscious agent of the Divine, a light-bearer, healer, and peacemaker. Whatever is revealed to us through direct spiritual and mystical experience, we must actualize and realize and embody in our lives. This is the measure of the truth or reality of our spiritual and mystical experiences, the degree to which they change us, and the degree to which we actualize our experience through action, through word, and deed.

Now truly, in effect, this world, the unenlightened society and culture, is hostile to the Light Transmission. Even among many of the faithful and supposed spiritual leaders of religion, there is hostility towards the Spirit and those who experience the Light Transmission: authentic mystics, seers, and wonderworkers. Although religion venerates mystics of the past, it tends to persecute living mystics or prophets. Religious leaders of the blind, deaf, and dumb, who themselves cannot see, hear, or speak in the Spirit, often seek to maintain their dominion of power in the ignorance. The movements of the Spirit and Powers tend to upset the balance of power in the world, and invoke a violent resistance or reaction from the rulers of the world. Those who are messengers of the Spirit and Powers, and those in the mystical journey, must be spiritual warriors, having the integrity, strength, and courage of a warrior, willing to sojourn their path in life regardless of whatever persecution or challenge they might face. Here we may recall Adonai Yeshua's blessing of those who are persecuted for his namesake and righteousness' sake, and his promise of great rewards in heaven. So it is with the Mother and those who are faithful to her, who love and serve her, who actively labor in the harvest of souls for the realization of the Heaven Earth Place, the "Divine sovereignty" or New Jerusalem on earth.

The Mother is, indeed, very gentle and immeasurably sweet, and yet, to meet her and to enter into her embrace, as said previously, there are challenges we must face, the Four Enemies taught in Toltec tradition: fear, clarity, power, and old age, or death. Juan Diego is being called to face death, which suggests that he has already faced the first three enemies and has come to the challenge of the final enemy. Aside from the suggestion of the Four Enemies of the spiritual warrior, and his entrance into the challenge of the final enemy, it is also true that once we are called by the Mother and meet her, which is meeting our destiny, we will be given sacred tasks by the Mother and by the Powers. We will be asked to fulfill our soul's purpose here, and to fulfill our destiny, our dreams. Going to the Mother, we will face many challenges, and when we meet her, there will be more challenges to face. Much like the process of our birth into this world, our process of rebirth from above in the Mother Spirit tends to be somewhat tumultuous, facing the resistance and opposition of our own karmic continuum and the world. There are labor pains in the process of giving birth and being reborn.

In this regard we might recall the vision of St. John of the Woman of Light whom he beholds crying out in the pangs of giving birth. Of course, we are not left alone in our labor and challenges. The Mother is present with us, and she blesses and empowers us, and to the extent that we surrender to her, her Presence and Power move with, in, and through us, and her Presence and Power accomplish everything. We see this with Juan Diego, willing to go to the bishop three times; the power of the Mother protects him and brings about his success. Indeed, in the story of the Mother's revelation, perhaps the greatest miracle or wonder of all is that the bishop does not harm Juan Diego, but eventually is actually brought to faith and convinced that Juan Diego's vision of the Mother is true. He agrees to build her Holy Temple on Tepeyacac!

What Juan Diego does in service to the Mother is truly amazing, as is what the Living Presence and Power accomplishes through Juan Diego, extending her Holy Light to the people. The Mother asks her precious child to go to the bishop and to tell him all that he has seen, heard, and experienced with her, and to share his knowledge and understanding, and the wisdom given to him. He is asked to be a messenger and voice of the Divine Mother, to inspire faith in her and bring about her reception by the people. This reflects another essential practice of the Mystical Path of Guadalupe: the telling of her story, the sharing of what we have seen, heard and experienced with her, the sharing of our knowledge and understanding of the Mother, and the wisdom we have been given, being an active messenger and voice of the Divine and Sacred Feminine in the world.

As we know and understand, there is a great need for the restoration of the Divine and Sacred Feminine among our people and in our world, and for a restoration of a spirituality of direct experience, a spirituality that is in the Spirit, rather than bound up in creeds and doctrines. Knowing that need and the desire of the Mother to fulfill it, when the Mother calls us to herself, we are also called to be her messengers, her voices, conscious agents of the restoration of the Mother and the reception of the Holy Bride. We must learn to speak of the Holy Mother and Bride, and to be voices calling others to faith in her, to the knowledge and experience of She-Who-Is-Our-Mother. Likewise, we must be advocates of a spirituality of direct experience, which is the Way of the Mother and Bride Sophia, reminding people of their innate Spirit-connection. We must be advocates of right relationships with all our relations, visible and invisible. What we receive from her we must share with our sisters and brothers, all our relations, serving as conscious co-creators with her, and as light-bearers, healers and peacemakers. In the Way of the Spiritual Sun and the Mother, we are all ordained to a sacred priesthood, and we are all called to a spiritual labor for the people.

Now, if we listen and hear what the Mother says to Juan Diego regarding his knowledge and understanding, and his wisdom—his *Habad*—we know that his experience runs far deeper than the tale of power that is told, and that there are dimensions of this experience that cannot be spoken or explained, at least not with words. Within the experience of the Mother, there is an energetic or Light Transmission, a transmission of her Living Presence and Power: a mind-to-mind, heart-to-heart and body-to-body transmission, a true initiation or empowerment. The true knowledge, understanding, and wisdom of the Supernal Mother—her Supernal *Habad*—is an experiential transmission, and it is communicated by the direct experience of the Mother, the *Shekinah* of the Supreme, the *Shekinah* of the Spiritual Sun. Receiving this Light Transmission, as much as telling the story of the Mother's revelation, and what we have seen, heard, and experienced with her, we are also called to facilitate something of this energetic transmission in the experience of others. We are called to teach and initiate, to serve as midwives in the process of the rebirth of souls in her, the Mother Spirit.

We not only speak with others about the Mother, the Spirit and Powers, but we also pray with them, meditate with them, and perform sacred ceremony with them. We create opportunities for the experience of Light Transmission in every way that we can, actively calling in the Spirit and Powers and actively developing spiritual community. In this spiritual labor, it is all about the direct spiritual and mystical experience of the Divine Mother, the Mother Spirit, and direct knowledge and understanding of her: True Gnosis, *Supernal Habad*.

You might say that in the Mother and Bride ours is an "energetic preaching," something more experiential than conceptual. It involves the belly, heart, and brow, sensing, feeling and intuiting, and direct seeing and hearing in the Spirit. It is as deeply rooted in the body as it is in the soul. Here we must say that in the Holy Mother and Bride, the body is included with the soul. We are not seeking to deny life or withhold ourselves from life, or to deny the body in seeking the "salvation" of our soul. Rather, we are seeking the reintegration of our energy being or soul with our body, to actualize and realize our energy being or soul, so we may embody the Divine Presence and Power. We are aspiring towards the dynamic balance of heaven and earth in our lives, the manifestation of the Heaven Earth Place here in this life, in this world, the Place of Flowering. In the Mother we "flower," we come to fruition, fulfilling earthly and heavenly desires, all our dreams. This is reflected in her promise of rewards to Juan Diego for his service to her, and her promise to us in our service to her. She promises not only heavenly rewards, but earthly rewards as well, the fulfillment of all our true heart's desires in heaven and on earth.

This is a central message of the Holy Mother, one reflected in her call for a Holy Temple to be built for her on the sacred mountain, a hill sacred to the Earth Mother. It is a call for the balance of heaven and earth in our spirituality, and the understanding of the role of our material and earthly being in the realization of our spiritual and heavenly being. Indeed, this exactly is the balance that the inclusion of the Divine and Sacred Feminine in our spirituality brings; the earth, our bodies, and even our sexuality are included, the whole of ourselves and our lives, leaving nothing out.

Now, as we consider the sacred task given to Juan Diego and the desire of the Mother that a temple be built on the sacred mountain in honor of her, we may gain insight into the spiritual labor to which we are called. The creation of a temple is the anchoring of Divine Power in the earth, and it becomes a vehicle for the transmission of spiritual power and blessings for the people. In the process of carrying her vision, her message, Juan Diego himself anchors and holds her Presence and Power for the people, and he actively labors to channel an even greater influx of her Presence and Power by participating in the creation of her temple, serving as an advocate of her intention. This is what we are also called to do: to anchor, hold, and channel the Living Presence and Power of the Divine Mother, bringing in the Spirit and Powers for the people, and channeling that Holy Light of the Spiritual Sun into this Good Earth: to embody the *Shekinah* of the Messiah, the Mother and Bride.

The embodiment of this Light-Presence and Light-Power is the very essence of the Mystical Path of Guadalupe, and each day we seek to bring in a greater influx of the Spiritual Sun, the Spirit and Powers for the people and this Good Earth. We pray, meditate, and perform sacred ceremony daily not only for ourselves alone, but for all our relations, all beings. If we who know the Mother and the Spiritual Sun do not do this, then who will?

The Mother's Force, the Light of the Spiritual Sun, enters the world through anyone opening to it. Divine Grace moves whenever we co-create the necessary conditions for her Action, her Movement. So we seek to open ourselves and create the conditions for Divine Grace to move in the world each day, actively worshiping the Divine Mother and offering ourselves as vehicles of her Light-Presence and Light-Power. Truly, it is as simple as loving the Mother and holding the conscious intention of opening our mind, heart, and life to the Mother's Force, taking the time to pray to her and meditate upon her. We commune with and in her, walking with her throughout the day. We take her Presence and Power into everything we do, sacred and mundane. In doing this, the Spiritual Sun shines from within us and we walk in beauty and holiness.

In this way, wearing the Body of Vision—living with and in the vision of the Divine Mother—we also bring a vision to the people, the vision of ourselves in her, the vision of all in her.

The Vision of the Holy Mother

When he arrived at the crest of the Holy Hill he found a celestial noble woman standing there, and he knew that she did not walk with her feet on the ground, and as he gazed upon her she called him to draw near, She-Who-Is-The-Mother-Of-All. When he drew near he was astonished by her radiance and glory, the radiance and glory of the Queen of Heaven, the Presence and Power of the Most High. Her clothes shone like the sun, and as that immeasurable brilliance shone on the rocks surrounding her, they sparkled like precious jewels and everything had voice. The entire ground on top of the Holy Hill became like a great rainbow of celestial glory in this Heaven Earth Place, and the trees, the Nopal cactus and all of the medicinal herbs that grew there were like green obsidian, their leaves like the finest turquoise, their stalks and thorns like gold, and in the air was something like gold dust, luminous sparkling particles of light-breath. Seeing this, Juan Diego was filled with holy awe and wonder, and he threw himself down at the feet of the Holy Mother, worshiping in the Presence and Power of the Supreme.

Repeating this account of the transfiguration of Our Lady speaks directly to the experience of Light Transmission when our sight opens to the energy dimension, the visionary dimension. Everything in the environment becomes transfigured in appearance, self-luminous, filled with the life and light of the *Shekinah*, the Divine Presence and Power. As in the disciples' experience with the Transfigured Yeshua, *whose clothes became dazzling white, such as no one on earth could bleach them* (St. Mark 9:2), and in

Saul's experience on the road to Damascus when, *Suddenly a light from heaven flashed around him* (Acts 9:3), so is the full-body Light Transmission of the Holy Mother with Juan Diego. In truth, nothing has changed, but we are seeing things as they are, their true glory and power as they are in the *Holy Shekinah*, the Mother and the Bride. Our consciousness has ascended, expanded, and the vibration of our awareness has been uplifted, so we perceive with renewed senses of our soul and spirit.

This divine vision of the Mother connects to two revelations in the New Testament. First, it connects to the Transfiguration, when Adonai Yeshua took close disciples up on a sacred mountain and revealed the true glory and power of the Spiritual Sun that was in him, becoming radiant with the Supernal Light of God. Juan Diego's vision also connects to the vision of the Woman of Light clothed with the sun in chapter 12 of St. John's Revelation. Here with Juan Diego however, the emanation of holiness was not up in the heavens and then coming down upon the earth, but she is on the earth, on the top of the holy hill, awaiting her meeting with Juan Diego. In the vision of St. John, the Woman of Light does not speak to him, but the Holy Mother speaks most intimately to Juan Diego. While the Woman of Light takes flight, on eagle's wings, from the Serpent, the Great Dragon, here her emanation as Guadalupe stands victorious. This is a most significant part of her message: the ultimate healing and spiritual victory of peace and joy she births forth into time.

Now, as we know in our own experience of the Gnostic and Light Transmission, whenever a holy being appears radiant with the Supernal Light and the environment shines with the glory of the Supernal Light, our bodies also shine with glory and we become aware of our energetic being, our body of light. Everything we might say of the experience on an external level is also an internal experience. If Juan Diego speaks of the glory of everything on top of the Holy Hill, then he also is experiencing the glorification of his body, and if he speaks of the stones having a voice, sound-vibration, then he is experiencing a powerful energetic vibration in his body. As we know in experiences of

Light Transmission, it may feel as though his body is expanding and as though he is going to disappear in divine rapture. Needless to say, he knows that Our Lady is a holy being that "she does not walk with her feet on the ground," and in this moment he knows that he, too, is a holy being, and knows the beauty and holiness of the Divine Presence and Power in all things. This is what we know and understand in moments of Light Transmission and the reception of the Holy Spirit.

In some oral traditions among Aztec elders, it is said that the Mother assumes the appearance of an Aztec princess. Assuming a form to which the person or being receiving the revelation can relate, this is how it is in the revelation of the Cosmic Christ and the *Shekinah*, the Divine Presence and Power, appearing like those to whom it is revealing itself. This image is significant in that an Aztec princess would never stand up to receive a person into her presence, but she would remain seated, unless that person was of equal or higher standing, in which case she would stand. Truly, the Mother is intending to reflect the holiness of being in Juan Diego and in all of us, and her reception of him reflects that, in truth, he is no ordinary "peasant," but a noble person, spiritual warrior and shaman, a holy man.

Of course, Juan Diego also knows that this Noble Celestial Woman is no ordinary woman. She is not a holy woman of this world, born of flesh and blood, but she is pure emanation, having no birth and no death, and she is the Woman of Womanhood, Mother God. Although appearing in the form of Our Lady of Guadalupe, she is the Supreme Mother, having countless aspects and emanations; Juan Diego bows down in her presence and worships the *Holy Shekinah* of the Supreme.

This reflects the very essence of the Mystical Path of Guadalupe, the Mystical Path of the Mother and Bride, and what may be called our "Tantra Yoga of Grace." When we receive the Light from above, when we meet the Holy Mother and Bride, the Way is simple: an active and dynamic surrender to the Holy Mother in communion with her, submission to the dance of the *Holy Shekinah*, the Divine Presence and Power. This surrender, of course, is not one of self-denial and the repression of desire, but rather it is embodying who and what we are in the Mother. Worshipping the Mother is all that we do, communing with her in the desires of our true and natural being, our heart's desire, rather than the desires of our ego. In this way we honor our Divine Mother and fulfill her wishes, our joy being her joy as a child of the Mother.

Now, when we hear the description of her glory reflected in the environment, all of the terms used are things of value and things sacred to the Aztec and Toltec peoples, things believed to carry great medicine or power: green obsidian, turquoise, gold, and precious jewels. This may very well be an exact description of how the plants and stones appeared in the vision, but it may also relate to another kind of perception, the perception of everything having equal value and power in the Mother, an awareness of the sacredness and spiritual power that is in all things.

Stones and the ground itself are, perhaps, our most ancient relations, the first peoples or beings to be formed on earth. From them—the mineral realm—the vegetable or plant realm emerged, developed, and evolved. There is great spiritual power in stone people and plant people. They all have spirits and powers, and they all are expressions of consciousness-force, energy-intelligence. Through the Light of the Mother, the Spiritual Sun and Holy Spirit, we know and understand how to call upon the spirits and powers of the stones, plants, and animals, as well as upon the elemental powers, celestial powers and the angels of Our Heavenly Father.

The ground beneath Juan Diego and the Mother itself appears like rainbow light. This points to the truth of Our Lady as a pure emanation of the Light of the Infinite—*Or Ain Sof*—but also points to the truth of all as energy, energy that we can draw upon in our action as co-creators. The light of the ground itself reveals the truth of everything as a play and exchange of energy. In the awareness of all relationships as an exchange of energy, we know that when we wish to draw upon the energy or power of a relation, we must form a true relationship, becoming acquainted with that spirit and power. We will ask and not demand, giving something back to the spirit for what we've received. We must be beneficial to our relations as they are beneficial to us. As people benefit each other socially, so also do spiritual practitioners seek to develop a reciprocal relationship with beings-forces.

In the time of Juan Diego following the aftermath of the conquistadors, the failure to honor the inseparability of all visible and invisible beings leads to great evil and ignorance escalating in our own times with even more extreme disbalance. The Spanish and other Europeans came to this people and land as rapists and thieves, as greedy takers, lustful consumers, intoxicated by impure, egoistic desire. Without regard for the people, the land, or the environment, without any concern for their relations, they stole and devoured and gave nothing in return. They had no interest in the welfare and well-being of their relations and environment. This, of course, is a great sickness in the world, one that is destroying us, our relations, and environment. This lesson of the formation of completely reciprocal relationships and the sacred interconnectedness of all life, from the ground and stones, to plants, animals, humans, and invisible beings, is essential to our survival and the healing of this terrible sickness. Reciprocity is a key lesson in our times, one we must learn if we are to go on to fulfill our true destiny as caretakers and co-creators.

Stones and plants are mentioned in the vision, and animals are mentioned also by way of the birds singing. The whole evolution of life leading to the generation of the human being is indicated by this, and the remembrance that all species are our relations. All life is in us and we are in it, our very existence from a physical to a spiritual level is inter-being, a profound interdependence and interconnection with all beings, in creation and cosmos. This is an important aspect of the knowledge or gnosis of the Mother, she who is this great matrix of life and light. In this holy awareness of the Sacred Unity and the dynamic exchange of energy, the Divine Mother empowers us to call upon the spirits and powers, to gather and acquire power so that we might act as conscious co-creators and fulfill our destiny.

A Practice: A Walk of Power

This description of the radiant glory of the Mother and Bride, the Woman and the Maiden, points to a practice in the Sophian tradition: a Walk of Power. When a seer and wonderworker, a shaman, goes on a walk of power it becomes a moving ceremony. Rather than doing ceremony in a stationary place of power or in a Sacred Circle, walking a line of power in the land, seers and wonderworkers invoke the Holy One and Powers, calling upon spirits as they are walking, gathering and acquiring powers, and engaging in spiritual work for the people. If we go out and walk in a sacred manner, walking in the Presence of Awareness, we may do something similar.

Go out into the great outdoors and take a walk. When you are walking it is good to take a bag with some offerings in it, and it is good to take a sacred walking stick or staff. If you are collecting power or sacred objects, it might be good to have a sacred bag to put them in as well. As you go, call upon the Divine Mother and the Powers, and walk in the company of the *Holy Shekinah*, the Mother and Powers. As you walk, be aware that you walk with and in the Holy Mother, in the company of the Bride, that all is formed of energy-intelligence, the emanation of the Presence and Power of the Great Spirit.

As you walk beneath and in Father Sky, and as you walk on and in Earth Mother—the Holy One—seek to look and see, and listen and hear the spirits and powers around you. Become acquainted with them and commune with them, and in your communion with them, commune with the Holy Mother and Bride. In this way, seek to know and understand the Great Mother, and enter into her embrace. Walk with God as Enoch the Initiate walked, *then he was no more, because God took him* (Genesis 5:24), and let the Holy Spirit, the Mother Spirit, take you up. If you walk with eyes of holy awe and wonder, open and sensitive to the spirits and powers, they will speak to you and they will share their power with you. Whenever you have need of power and receive power from the spirits, remember to give some offering in return, such as sage or tobacco, and only take power when a spirit wishes to give it to you. Walk in a sacred manner, walk in beauty and holiness. This is the practice of a "Walk of Power."

Touching the Mother & Seeing the Bishop

Juan Diego had risen up in her presence as they spoke together, but when she had said this he threw himself again at her feet, and he respectfully requested to be excused to go and carry out the sacred task she had given to him. When she granted him leave, he went immediately down the Holy Hill upon his sacred task, going by way of the causeway to Mexico City, to the place of the bishop's palace.

Juan Diego went straight to the bishop's palace, Right Reverend Juan De Zumárraga. He asked the bishop's servants to tell the bishop that he wanted to see him. After waiting a long time he was finally given an audience. He went in, bowed down, giving proper salutations to the bishop, and then he spoke the message of the Virgin to the bishop, recounting the entire experience to him and speaking to the bishop all that the Holy Maiden had sent him to speak.

When the bishop heard Juan Diego's story, however, he did not believe him and was not convinced. He sent Juan Diego away, telling him to return later so that they could continue their conversation. The bishop told him that in the meantime he would consider the matter thoroughly and have some word on it when he came again.

Juan Diego left the palace of the bishop deeply disturbed and in great grief, feeling that he had failed and was unsuccessful in his sacred mission. He went his way greatly troubled, going straight back to Tepeyacac, the Holy Hill of the Mother.

At the outset of his meeting with the Mother, Juan Diego bows down before her, and at the fruition of this first meeting he bows down again, requesting her leave and blessing to go and attend to the sacred mission she has given him. There is something to be said of this gesture of submission: it is a gesture of devotion and worship of the Celestial Maiden and Earth Mother. Placing the brow upon the earth or placing one's head between one's knees is a "prophetic position," one invoking an influx of *Ruach Ha-Kodesh*, the Holy Spirit. In our worship of the Divine, bowing down is a gesture of self-offering, a gesture of an active and dynamic surrender to the *Shekinah* of the Supreme, and it is an invocation of an influx of the Divine Spirit. Bowing down, the body is drawn near to Earth Mother, our energy is grounded, and as we bring the body into this position of submission, we still the vital and silence the mind, and commune in the Divine Presence and Power, listening and hearing the voice of the Spirit and Powers.

We know that Our Lady is the Queen of Heaven and Earth Mother, transcendent and immanent. She is the height and depth, and all directions of the Sacred Circle; all the powers arising from her and in her return to her, the All-In-All. There are seven directions of the Sacred Circle. Four are the directions of Earth Mother: four winds which are also four elemental powers. Three are the Gates of Heaven: the directions above, below, and the middle. The middle, the seventh direction within and behind our heart, is the depth of our being.

These directions are points in space, but are also dimensions of experience. We pass through the Gate of Heaven above by way of the generation of a body of light and the projection of our center of consciousness into the body of light, then passing in ascent through conscious intention, "rising through the planes." Likewise, we may also go within and behind our heart, and go deeper within, and as we go within we will experience a shift in the gradation of our being-consciousness, passing through levels of our being that exist in various inner dimensions, akin to our soul's journey into other worlds in dreamtime. Then there is also the Gate of Heaven in the depth, the Gate of Heaven in the secret center of Earth Mother. Traveling down in the Spirit through the seven earths, we come to a Gate of Heaven and passing through it in the Spirit, we experience an ascent. This heaven in the depth is a common path of the shaman into the heavens.

When an action is to be empowered in the material dimension or physical world, most often the path of descent as a gate into the heavens is ideal. For descending and ascending, running and returning in this way, brings the spirits of the seven heavens and seven earths into alignment and harmony with the movement of the Spirit. In this way, the world of angels and the world of spirits moves with us in the Divine Presence and

Power of the Mother. This is the path Juan Diego sojourns in the Mother, seeking the empowerment to accomplish his sacred mission, a path most common to devotees of the Earth Mother, the Mother God.

Her granting him leave to go on his sacred mission is the blessing she gives to those who descend and ascend in her Divine Body, the Living Earth, the Spiritual Earth. This is reflected when she speaks of his knowledge and understanding, and the wisdom given to him, the inner and secret dimensions of his experience of the Divine Mother. Bowing down, with our brow upon the Earth Mother, shifting consciousness into the energy body and Spirit, we descend in the spirit-vision through the seven earths to the Gate of Heaven in the center of the earth; passing through that Holy Gate in Tibel, we ascend through the seven heavens. This is a spirit-journey that a seer and wonderworker, a shaman, can guide us upon, and it is a journey of healing and vision quest.

This is also a spirit-journey the Divine Mother herself can send and guide us upon when we draw close to her and cleave to her. It may transpire through a movement of Divine Grace without the direct help of a shaman, if we know how to create the necessary conditions. Here we may speak of the wisdom of the Virgin Mother, the wisdom of Pure Emanation. When we live in complete surrender to the Holy Mother on all levels of our being and consciousness—spiritual, mental, vital, and physical—and we live in harmony with our true and natural being, the Spiritual Sun, the Messiah, all cosmic and spiritual forces, all spirits, will move and act in harmony with us. All will be subject to the Virgin Mother and the Spiritual Sun in us.

As we know, in these dark times, just as humankind is polluting and destroying the material environment of the earth and destroying the good creatures of the earth, so is humankind polluting and destroying the astral environments of the earth, the environments of dreamtime, the world of spirits and angels, and so the spirits are becoming angry and fierce in the astral earth and astral realms. Likewise, on account of the negativity we are taking into the dreamtime or astral, we are generating unclean and evil spirits in it, and we are invoking admixed and dark forces into the astral. The spirit world and world of angels is being cast into a state of extreme imbalance in the very same way as the material or physical world.

In the midst of this great darkness, this great ignorance, save through the grace of the Holy Mother and Spiritual Sun, there would be little or no working with the world of spirits and angels; for the most part we would meet only with hostility, a fierce or wrathful emanation. But through the grace of the Mother and Sun, we are empowered to pacify and enrich the spirits and angels, and when necessary, to subjugate or destroy unclean and evil spirits. Her Divine Presence and Power accomplishes this, as does the wisdom of emptiness.

This speaks to our need for the revelation of the Divine Mother in these times, our need on an energetic level for the influx of her Supernal Grace, her Supernal Light, for it is this that empowers our spiritual works in a dark and hostile environment, pacifying and enriching, subjugating and destroying the *klippot*, barriers. As we shall see, four aspects of the Mother correspond with these actions: Eagle Woman, Serpent Woman, War Woman, and Infernal Woman, respectively. Then there is her aspect as Spider Woman, healing and weaving all of these together into one Divine action.

This Divine Grace of the Mother is perfectly reflected in the story of her revelation to Juan Diego and his mission of bringing her vision to the bishop. Although he is not successful at first, neither is he harmed by the bishop, and although he is not successful in his second attempt, and the bishop is contemplating harming him, still he remains unharmed. Finally, on his third attempt, reflecting the three days of the Savior in the abodes of Hades and Hell before the resurrection, he is given a sign to take to the bishop that pacifies, enriches, subjugates, and destroys the ensnaring forces of ignorance. In a completely dark and hostile environment, through the grace of the Mother and Sun, he is ultimately successful in his mission, astonishingly so!

Now, Juan Diego sets out upon his mission in confidence,

having faith in the Divine Mother, but when he is not instantly successful his confidence and faith wane and he allows himself to fall into doubt and despair. He does not doubt the Mother, but he doubts himself and feels that he has failed her. Yet, doubting himself is doubting her, for she has sent him, empowered him, and is with him. This is a very important lesson to us all: When the enemy of fear or insecurity enters, causing us to doubt ourselves, or to view an initial apparent failure as a defeat, we restrict and diminish the Presence and Power of the Mother and Spiritual Sun with us, and in effect it is a compromise of our faith in the Holy One.

Regardless of appearances, regardless of the circumstances, situations or events that might arise, or whatever challenges we might face as we go about our sacred tasks and seek to fulfill our destiny and dreams, we must keep the faith and trust in the Mother Spirit, Divine Grace. Along with our spiritual humility, or surrender to the Divine Mother, we must abide in spiritual self-worth or divine pride, aware of our innate unity with the Spiritual Sun of God, a child of the Virgin Mother, and an emanation of her Presence and Power.

This is especially true in the midst of these dark times, and the hostile environment of the material and astral in which we are called to serve as light-bearers, healers, and peacemakers. We can only succeed in our spiritual labors if we abide in our faith and trust in the Mother Spirit, not allowing ourselves to fall into doubt and despair. We must walk in beauty and holiness, walking in the Mother, and wearing the Body of Vision as a sign of spiritual hope for the people in good times and bad times. A vision of hope is what the Mother brings us, and is what we are to bring to the people, all our relations, visible and invisible.

If, at times, we do find ourselves falling into doubt and despair, caught up in the ignorance and the "snare of the fowler," then like Juan Diego, let us return to the Mother, and let us ground and center ourselves in her, reorienting ourselves to the Spiritual Sun, holding and anchoring the influx of her Supernal Grace. Always, let us return to the Mother and cleave to the Mother, taking sanctuary in the Light-Presence and Light-Power that is in us. In a manner of speaking, let us go sit in the lap of the Virgin Mother as her Holy Child, the Sun of God, and remember ourselves among the children of the stars, remembering our dwelling in the Queen of Heaven and our place in Earth Mother. Running out upon her errand, Juan Diego returns to her.

As for the faithless bishop, what shall we say? He represents the channel or vehicle of an archonic force, a ruler, the servant of the demiurge, the false god, the half-maker, the servant of the ignorance, the darkness that rules the world. He is a "man of god" who does not know and experience the True God, the True Light, a child of the mother who is sorely lost and bound up in sorrow and suffering. It must be noted, however, that the Divine Mother intends the subjugation of the archonic forces, and that she intends to bring the bishop to faith, to uplift and illuminate him, just as she intends to uplift and illuminate Juan Diego. She wants to fulfill the true heart's desires of the bishop as well, and wants to see him fulfill his true destiny, his true dreams. The Holy Mother seeks the fulfillment of all her children, the enlightenment and liberation of all.

In this there is also an important lesson for us all. It is not ours to blame and judge anyone, not now, not ever. It is crucial that we do not carry anger or resentment, or allow ourselves to fall into hatred. All too often, seeing the great evil that religion has perpetuated, and continues to perpetuate in the name of "God," we blame and judge others, and fall into anger, resentment, and hatred. We carry this with us in our spiritual journey, and we let it poison our soul and corrupt our spirituality. We use it as an excuse to hold on to negativity, shades, and shadows in us, and do not recognize that, in effect, we are enacting the same ignorance, the same evil. That, or it becomes our excuse for rejecting spirituality, and we become among those impoverished souls who proclaim, "God is dead!" The truth is that this is the very same ignorance, the very same darkness, and it is a terrible plight, a great trap of souls in the potentially endless cycles of negativity and violence.

The Mother calls us to see this violent inclination for what it is, and to recognize it in ourselves and put an end to it in ourselves. She calls us to be true peacemakers, forgiving and loving people, free from blaming and judging others. Look and see! The Mother sends Juan Diego to the sworn enemy of his people, seeking to make peace, seeking to uplift and illuminate him, to heal him of faithlessness, to free him from sorrow and suffering. She speaks to Aztec and Toltec peoples, and to European Christian peoples, and all peoples, of all lands and traditions, saying, "Seek peace. Love one another and forgive one another. Let there be a weave of energy and wisdom between you. Labor together for the good of all, and seek to fulfill your destiny, your dreams, together as one people, one race, one humanity."

Appearing as an "Aztec Virgin" and proclaiming herself as the Virgin Mary, the Mother of Christ, she is saying that we all have one Holy Mother. One and the same True God speaks to us all when we listen. We are all children of Light, and she is proclaiming a universal salvation for all of her children, a universal enlightenment and liberation. She reminds us of the true Good News, the true Holy Gospel, the Spiritual Sun, Divine Illumination, born of Primordial Wisdom.

Indeed, religions err. Socio-politics err. Unenlightened societies and cultures err. We all err. Forgetting that we are asleep and dreaming, we all become bound up in the ignorance and perpetuate the ignorance. In this regard no one here is exactly innocent or without error. No one is so different. In the process of our coming into being, the development and evolution of our soul, how else is it supposed to be? Can we grow and mature without a process of trial and error, and the lessons we learn in this way? We must know and understand that the world is sacred as it is, even in the midst of the present ignorance and error. But more so, we must know and understand that we are the world and the world is us, and that if we want to see a change in our world, then, as Gandhi said, we must be the change we wish to see in the world. It is not us versus them, but it is we the people, all together. This is the central message of the Divine Mother to us. We are all in this play of creative evolution together, and we must all labor together to bring this creative evolution to fruition in the Divine or

Enlightenment. She calls us to assume full responsibility for our energy, for our lives, and ourselves, calling us to look after the welfare and well-being of one another, all our relations. This is what it means to be a human being.

A Practice: Touching Earth Mother

Perhaps you may recall the story of Moses at the burning bush, when the *Shekinah* of the Supreme, the Holy Mother, appeared to him; there in that holy place the Creator said to him, *Take off the sandals from your feet, for the ground upon which you are walking is holy* (Exodus 3:5).

Indeed, Earth Mother is holy, and it is good to take off your shoes and walk upon her, touching her and drawing strength from her through your feet. Sometimes, when you want to pray and you want to draw upon the power of Earth Mother and channel the power of Sky Father and the Sun into her, it is good to take off your shoes and touch her directly with your bare feet. It is a humble act, but also an action of spiritual self-worth, knowing your very body as her body, and knowing yourself as her Holy Child.

Now there is also a way of sacred ceremony going into living waters and then putting sacred earth on your body, drawing upon the power of Earth Mother as you pray and worship, singing and dancing in her, and calling out to the Spirit and Powers as an emanation of her. When you are done, returning to the living waters, as to the Womb of Earth Mother, she will rebirth you in the innate purity of your true and natural self, heavenly and earthly. Praying and worshiping in this way can be very powerful and healing.

So, too, like Juan Diego and many shamans, you can bow down at the feet of your Holy Mother and put your brow upon her. Call upon the Spirit and Powers, smudge yourself and make appropriate offerings. Bow down, placing your forehead on Earth Mother, receiving the Light from above and uplifting the Fire Snake to your brow. Sojourn into the depths of the Earth Mother in the spirit-vision. Running and returning in this way, she will heal you and make you whole in her, and the spirits will be friendly to you as a luminous child of the Earth Mother.

If you bow down in this way, when you rise up, with music and chant, and even with dance and worship, give praise and thanks to God and the Powers. Whatever sacred tasks you have been asked to do by the Mother and Powers, go and do them, and remember to walk in beauty and holiness, loving all of your relations as you love yourself and the Mother. Wear the Body of Vision. This is the holy seal. In these ways and many more, you can touch Earth Mother. It is always good to touch her and love her, knowing who your Holy Mother is and going to her.

Returning to the Mother

There he found the Glorious Celestial Maiden, the Heavenly Holy Woman, waiting for him, and he threw himself at her feet and said, "Patroness, special and holy person, noblewoman, my daughter, my mother, my grandmother, I went to the place you sent me to carry out your request. In spite of the great challenge of getting in to see the bishop, I was able to gain entrance and I gave him your message, just as you asked me to do, and at first he seemed receptive, listening to all that I said; but when he spoke, it seemed that he did not believe and was not convinced. It was clear that he thought I was making the entire thing up and that it did not come from you. I plead with you, Holy Mother, ask one of the noble born people, someone of position and standing who will be respected to go and deliver your message. I am just an ordinary person, a peasant. The bishop's palace is not my place, my daughter, my youngest child, special and holy person, Divine Mother. Please forgive me if I am burdening you or displeasing you in any way, Celestial Maiden."

The Holy Forever Whole and Perfect Maiden responded to him, saying, "Listen, my youngest child. The people I trust to carry my message and my presence, and to execute this intention, are many, but they are not the most powerful people. It is very important that you are the one to initiate this movement. My will and desire, and my presence, are to act through your hand, my word being placed into your mouth and your heart. I strongly appeal to you, my youngest child, and I order you: Go again to the bishop tomorrow. Recount my message to him once again and teach him for me, and help him understand my intention and my desire so that he will authorize the building of the Holy Temple I am asking for. Proclaim to him again that it truly is me, the Forever Whole and Perfect Maiden, Saint Mary, the Mother of Teotl-Dios, who sends you."

Juan Diego said to the Holy Mother, "Patroness, lovely lady, my daughter, my mother, my grandmother, may I not trouble you in any way. I will take your message to the place you have sent me with all my heart. No matter what happens, I will not leave it behind or abandon you. Even though the path is painful and difficult for me, I will manifest your desire. But they may not listen to me, or if they do, they may not believe. Regardless, I will return to you with the bishop's reply tomorrow when the Sun passes into the west, going down into the Underworld. So my youngest child, my daughter, my mother, my grandmother, special and holy person, noblewoman, I go as you wish. May you be well."

Then, Juan Diego departed and went home.

The Celestial Maiden is waiting upon the Holy Hill for Juan Diego to return, holding the portal of power open, a gate between heaven and earth, holding the sacred space of the Heaven Earth Place. So it is that the Holy Mother is waiting for us, always waiting for us to seek her out and return to her, waiting to speak with us and to embrace us. We need only open to her and become sensitive to her Divine Presence and Power, going to her. Indeed, the Holy Mother is ever-present; all arises from her and in her, and all returns to her. All is in her and she is in all. She is the Holy Light of our energetic being and the Holy Light at the center of every particle of matter composing our bodies, and she is the spaciousness underlying all, as near as our breath and the beat of our heart.

When it says that she is waiting upon the Holy Hill, it isn't that we must necessarily go to a Sacred Mountain to know and experience her, but rather we need only uplift our energy and vibration, shifting into a higher or more expansive state of consciousness. We need only generate the Presence of Awareness and awaken the Fiery Intelligence that is in us. Then we will know and experience the Divine Mother right where we are, in the power of the moment, here and now. She is right here with us, waiting for our ascent in consciousness so that we might know and experience her.

The same may be said of our energetic being and the energy dimension, and of the world of spirits and angels. The light realm is within and all around us. Here, in this moment, heaven and earth meet. Whenever the Presence of Awareness dawns and the Fiery Intelligence in us sparks, in that moment, in that space, we know and experience the Heaven Earth Place. The Gospel of St. Thomas teaches this in saying 113: *The Divine sovereignty is spread out upon the earth before our very eyes and people don't see it.* Again and again it must be said that we do not have to wait until we die to experience the Divine sovereignty, the light realm; it is right here, occupying the same space at the same time as the physical or material dimension. So it is with the Second Coming of Christ and reception of the Holy Bride. We do not need to wait until some future time to meet the Spiritual Sun in the air, the sky, but in this very instant we can greet the Spiritual Sun and let that Holy Light shine from within us. The Mother, the Sun, the Bride, the energy dimension or light realm are the eternal now, present here and now, always.

Here we may speak an open secret: Your future self, your enlightened self, is your present self in the eternal realm. Becoming aware of the eternal realm touching into this moment, your future self, your Christ self, is your present self, embodied in this very instant. This, exactly, is our experience of our energetic being in the energetic dimension anytime our consciousness opens to that dimension, the Light Realm and Light Continuum, Solar Being. So it is that the Celestial Maiden's robes shine with Solar Light, Supernal Light, and the Woman of Light's body is formed of the Light of the Spiritual Sun. She is the Mother of Solar Being, Stellar Being; hers are the Children of the Stars. The robe of the Celestial Maiden is the starry night sky. Her children, awakened, enlightened, are the holy stars or suns in her robe, for she asks Juan Diego, "Are you not in the fold of my robe?" We are in the fold of her robe when we let the Holy and Supernal Light shine from within us; as Yeshua Messiah has said, *You are the light of the world* (St. Matthew 5:14).

Indeed! Your energetic being, your light being, is a holy star in her robe. When you know and experience her, you will know and experience your Solar Being and future self which, in truth, is your present self, your true and natural self as you are in the Queen of Heaven, the Holy Mother. Returning to the Mother is returning to your true, natural self and returning to your true and natural self is returning to the Mother. Going to the Mother, going to your true and natural self, is one and the same, for that Holy Child, that Solar Being, is the emanation of her, the Celestial Maiden, the Forever Whole and Perfect Maiden. This is the truth of the Spiritual Sun, the Risen Christ: the Self-Made-Perfect, self-generating, self-begetting, bornless being.

Now, having gone down the Holy Hill into Mexico City, and into the hostile environment of the bishop's palace, the demon of unbelief or doubt in the bishop has caused Juan Diego to doubt himself. So naturally his vibration has lowered and he has lost energy. In need of regeneration and reintegration, he goes to the Holy Mother, actively seeking to uplift his vibration and restore his energy. This, of course, is a teaching that we must pay attention to our energy and guard our energy, and seek to maintain a higher vibration. We must nurture and nourish the Holy Child in us until it comes to full maturation. In the midst of this labor to give birth to our Solar Being, we must be careful not to let in the poison of negativity, or of archonic or demonic influences, the dark and hostile spirits. There is a need for constant purification and consecration, and for a continuum of spiritual practice.

When Juan Diego experiences a loss of energy, of lowered vibration, his spiritual self-worth is lowered; his confidence as a spiritual warrior wanes. He does not feel that he is good enough or worthy to carry the message and vision of the Mother. As he loses confidence, he shifts to the surface consciousness, self-identification with name, form, and personal history, and he falls into the delusion of the world of the demiurge and its hierarchal society, the unenlightened society and culture. He believes that a "noble born" person of some social standing and power should be sent, rather than a peasant or common person like himself who has "no place in the bishop's palace."

Although this happens, nevertheless he returns to the Holy

Mother and he is completely open and honest with her, opening himself to her Light and Truth. We are all familiar with this experience of the loss of spiritual self-worth, the loss of confidence, and in the story of Juan Diego and his return to the Mother we know what to do when we see this happening. We go to the Mother, and we pray with openness and honesty, opening ourselves to her Truth and Light. We cleave to her and let her heal and uplift us, reintegrating ourselves with her Divine Presence and Power. In everything we rely upon the Celestial Maiden; we rely upon Divine Grace.

The response of the Divine Mother to Juan Diego proves very interesting. When she speaks to him of how many of her messengers are not socially or politically elite, some might assume she's speaking only of the European invaders, the Spanish, and yet, as we well know, unenlightened society in all of its forms is hierarchic. The Aztec society and culture was also hierarchic, extremely so. The Mother is speaking of all unenlightened society, all society fashioned according to the dominion of the demiurge and archons, the ignorance and forces of ignorance. Essentially she says that those at the top of unenlightened, hierarchic society and culture, those who fashion it and dominate it and who have a vested interest in preserving the status quo, are not the individuals she would call upon to bring her message and vision. Indeed, she cannot, for such individuals are not open to the Divine Mother and have not the interest of the Divine or of others in mind, but they are intoxicated with selfish ambition and their own self-interests. Much of the time their self-interests even oppose the intention of the Divine they might claim to represent.

The message and vision of the Celestial Maiden is one of spiritual revolution, as was the message of her Holy Child, Yeshua Messiah. Those in power do not want to see a spiritual revolution take place. They do not want equality and freedom, or the illumination and empowerment of all people, for this would circumvent their dominion and power, their authority over people. Indeed, as we see with the dawn of orthodoxy and fundamentalism in the Christian stream, when people in the top of the unenlightened society's hierarchy take hold of a stream of Light Transmission and wisdom they distort and pervert it to serve their dominion. They divest the stream of its soul and spirit, and steal the spiritual power from the people, taking it for their own selfish ambitions. This had happened to the Aztec stream as well as the Christian stream. Such is always the way of large socio-political religious institutions in this world; always the influence of the demiurge and archons, the ignorance, enters into play over time and poisons the stream. Such is the same danger of the ego in spirituality, whether on a collective level or an individual level.

Essentially, the Mother appears in order to restore the Truth and Light to the stream, to restore the Holy Spirit to the people, to heal and illuminate the people. She sends a peasant, a common person, with no standing in the religious establishment, to the "spiritual authority," the bishop, bearing her message and vision, and her living presence and power. In so doing she reveals the truth of an enlightened society of equality and freedom, mutual illumination and empowerment, a society that is not hierarchic, but that holds the interests of all people in mind, and that seeks to facilitate the welfare, health and happiness of all, the true development and evolution of humanity.

In the Mother, in the True God, all are equal; all are Holy Stars, Suns of God. All are beautiful and holy. All have their place in the expanse of the Infinite and Eternal. This is the true message of the Messiah—Adonai Yeshua—and of the Holy Mother and Bride, the Forever Whole and Perfect Maiden. In an enlightened society founded upon God the True Light, the ancient shamans of Israel prophesied equality. The prophet Joel heralds, *I will pour out my Spirit on all flesh; and your sons and daughters shall prophesy, your old men shall dream dreams, and your young men shall see visions. Even on male and female slaves, in those days, I will pour out my Spirit* (2:28-29). This, and other proclamations by the ancient prophets, the shamans of Israel, point to a very different formation of human society, one that is truly human and illumined by the Spirit of Truth, the Spirit of Holiness. This is the revolutionary noble ideal the Mother brings. In speaking to common people, she fulfills something of ancient prophecies: those of Israeli prophets, Aztec prophets, and prophecies from other wisdom traditions.

Now the Mother says that her messengers are many, but that they are not the people at the top of the hierarchy of the dominant culture, rather, they are common people, and they are the poor, the outcast, and the oppressed. They are people who seek in the Spirit, who are called by the Mother, exalted by her, empowered and sent by her, bearing her living presence and power. Truly, they are anyone who seeks her out and cleaves to her, and who opens to her Truth and Light. Those at the top of the unenlightened society tend to be unwilling to surrender to her and to open themselves to her Truth and Light; they are bound up in extreme self-grasping, greed, and lust, sound asleep and unaware that they are dreaming.

When she speaks of her call to common people, she is saying that she is calling all of us, whoever will listen and hear the voice of their Mother, whoever is willing to open to her Truth and Light, the Spirit of the True God, the True Good. Likewise, she is telling us that what the unenlightened society and dominant culture lauds as "success" and tells us is our "destiny" may not be what we really want.

In this we must understand something differently. The message of the Mother is one of spiritual revolution. When we first enter into her presence and embrace her, there will, indeed, be peace and joy, but her presence and power will also turn our world upside down, and we will pass through a mystical death and rebirth. Arising as her messengers, there will be challenges, and we will meet resistance to her truth and light, both inwardly and outwardly. As much as being willing to receive her peace and joy, we must also be willing to labor in the pains of giving birth to a Solar Being and Solar Age in the midst of the present darkness.

Essentially, if we seek to bring a greater good into this world, we must experience the struggle and challenge of giving birth to it with the Mother, and first and foremost it must be born within our own lives and within our own selves. If we are willing to perform this labor as midwives of the Holy Mother, however, we will be richly rewarded with true enjoyment in this life and in the afterlife, rewarded with the fulfillment of both earthly and heavenly desires of the heart. Indeed, we will be living according to our true and natural self, that divine self, which is in the Spiritual Sun, the Messiah.

A Practice: Remembering Your Solar Being

If you wish to remember your energetic being, envision yourself in a great sphere of Solar Light, something like a luminous egg shape. Within that sphere envision your body as composed of Solar Light. Within and behind your heart, envision the image of the Spiritual Sun.

Then, envision the Holy Mother above your head, and open your mind and heart to her, and take up the sacred chant of *Eheieh* (I Am or I Shall Be): *Ah-Ha-Ya*. As you chant, envision an influx of Brilliant White Light from the Mother above, like the strike of a Thunder Being coming from the Mother above, and with the influx envision your Solar Being grow and increase in brilliance and glory, with Rainbow Glory streaming out into all directions of endless space.

When this transpires, intone *Ah*, and envision that with the strike of the Thunder Being you dissolve into that Holy Light of White Brilliance and flow in ascent merging with the Holy Mother above.

As the Holy Mother, chant the Blessed Name of Yeshua: *Ya-Ha-Sha-Va-Ha*. See a ray go forth from the Mother's heart womb, magically generating your reappearance in your Solar Being, the image of the Risen Messiah.

Walk as this Light-Presence and Light-Power in the world; walk in this beauty and holiness, and in the Holy Name of *Adonai*, bless all your relations. This is the practice of remembering your Solar Being, your being as you are in the Risen Messiah, the Spiritual Sun of God. Amen.

Places of Power & Walking Between Worlds

Then, the following day just before dawn, Juan Diego went to a place of the ancient way to attend to his spiritual essence, and he went to be counted at the mass and to go and visit the bishop. The mass was complete midmorning and when it was finished he went straight to the bishop's palace, seeking an audience.

He went into the bishop on his knees and weeping as he shared once again the message of the Queen of Space, the Sky-Dancing Maiden. He still did not know if the bishop would believe, or if he would understand that the Holy Virgin wanted her Temple built on the Holy Hill, the Heaven Earth Place. He told the bishop everything he saw and heard and experienced, all that he knew and understood, and told him that he truly believed and knew that the Celestial Maiden was the Holy Virgin, the Most Precious Holy Mother of the Spiritual Sun, Our Redeemer and Illuminator, the Christ, the Anointed of God. However, the bishop still did not believe and was not convinced. Nothing Juan Diego had said persuaded him in the least, but the bishop suspected that he was a heretic or had gone mad.

The bishop said that he could not build a temple on Juan Diego's word alone, but that he would need some sign, and Juan Diego inquired what sort of sign the bishop desired, and told the bishop that he would ask the Noble Celestial Maiden to produce it. Then, feeling some sense of sincerity in him, the bishop sent him away. Nevertheless, suspecting Juan Diego of heresy, the bishop sent trusted servants, officers of the Inquisition, to follow him and report where he went and who he met with. These servants were priests of a very dark evil.

As these men followed him down the causeway he crossed over the wooden bridge and they lost sight of him; they looked everywhere for him but could not find him. It was as though Juan Diego had vanished into thin air right before their eyes, and, unable to understand what had happened, they returned to the bishop and gave an evil report, saying that Juan Diego was a deceiver and was surely lying, intending to punish him so he could never enact a deception again.

Once again we are told that Juan Diego goes out in the morning to attend to his spiritual essence. Here it is said that he goes to a "place of the ancient ways," a sacred and holy place, a place of power in the land.

There are places of power in the land where lines of power, currents of earth energy, intersect, and in those places vortexes of power or energy form; they are like portals or gates between worlds, places where spirits and angels gather, and through which powerful influxes of spiritual forces come into this world. They are centers of power very much like the interior stars or "chakras" in our energy body, these being the "interior stars" of the earth, which is also a living entity and also has an energetic body or body of light. Along with these great places of power or vortexes of earth energy, there are also lesser places of power where spirits are also attracted and gather, and there are places of power generated by human beings through their reverence, devotion, and spiritual work in those places, to which spirits are attracted and gather.

These are places that people go for worship and spiritual work in the great outdoors, and they are often places where shrines, sanctuaries, and temples are built. Tepeyacac, the holy hill where the Celestial Maiden appears to Juan Diego, is one of the great places of power in the land of Mexico, the world navel in their Aztec cosmology, where a Holy Temple dedicated to the Earth Mother previously stood. Given the importance of the sacred mission given to Juan Diego, as a seer and wonderworker, as a shaman, he would likely go to another great place of power equal in strength to the holy hill. This other hill would offer some balance to the energy of the holy hill, a polarity of energy in resonance with the holy hill, and very likely one that carried energy of the Divine Masculine, balancing the strong Divine and Sacred Feminine energy he is carrying in his sacred mission.

Many sacred and holy places of indigenous people are hidden away, often in remote and difficult places to get to. This preserves their sacredness and energy, and it means that a person has to have a reason, a conscious intention, to go to them, that they must intend to go to them. It also means that they likely had to be shown where they were and had to be initiated into them. These are not places people would go too often, so the sacredness and energy would not be drained away or depleted from them. These are places that would be tended and fiercely defended by indigenous people, places especially powerful for spiritual work. Very often when there was spiritual work to do, a place would be chosen that naturally resonated with the spiritual task, a place that would attract spirits which had the knowledge and power a shaman might need to accomplish sacred work.

Learning to find places of power, to find and walk lines of power, is usually an art that we are shown. If we become aware of our energy body, our energetic being, and we become open and sensitive, through the energy body we can recognize and know places of power and lines of power. Likewise, at times, we can see a place of power because the land shows us, and the stone people and plant people and animal people show us. Its uniqueness and beauty reveal it. Indeed, it is very common that little children can find these places and paths in the land, for being in touch with their energy being, their soul, and their natural self, they know and understand such things. So when we are in touch with our true and natural being, we can know and discern such things too.

Although any positive place that attracts us and feels good to us can be a good place to pray, meditate, and perform sacred ceremony, from time to time we may need to go to a place of power for our spiritual work. Likewise, at times we need the blessing and empowerment that places of power give to those who go to them in a sacred manner. Here we may say, to know and love the Earth Mother is to know lines of power and places of power. The knowledge of sacred spaces is knowledge of the Divine Mother. Understanding this, it is no wonder that patriarchal religions which deny and reject the Divine and Sacred Feminine, do not know how to recognize true holy and sacred spaces, and do not know how to erect proper shrines, sanctuaries, or temples in such places. Whenever patriarchal religions come to erect places of worship in places of power, they are following the wisdom of indigenous or native peoples, erecting their places of worship to their male god where the worship of indigenous peoples used to be offered. Even in Europe, innumerable churches were built directly upon places of power long-revered by pre-Christian Europeans. This part of the story tells us that it is good to learn how to recognize and use lines of power and places of power. Here we may say that true walks of power, as we have previously discussed, follow along lines of power in Earth Mother.

Now here we may also share an open secret: in Sacred Circle there are two principle paths, that of the sun and that of the moon, that of day and that of night. Among indigenous Americans, the path of sun and moon are called the Red Road and Blue Road, respectively. The Path of the Sun corresponds to the east-west direction in Sacred Circle, and to the clockwise walking of the Circle. This is the path of life in this world. The Path of the Moon corresponds to the south-north direction in Sacred Circle, and to the counterclockwise walking of the Circle. This is the path of life in the spirit world.

Corresponding with these two paths, lines of power and places of power change by day and night, and there are lines of power and places of power that only appear by day or by night. Likewise, there are those that are peaceful by day, but wrathful by night, and those that are wrathful by day, but peaceful at night. The matrix of the Earth Mother changes by day and night, just as does the appearance of Sky Father.

At night, when the elemental forces are at rest, when the sky is reasonably clear, the places of power are "earth gates," and they become linked to "star gates" in the heavens, paths open to the "star people," and to many realms and worlds of other dimensions. It is a time of great cosmic and spiritual influx.

In the Holy Kabbalah, as taught in the Zohar, night's cycle of power is hinted at in three distinct ways. Rabbis teach of evening prayer, which corresponds with the patriarch Jacob, who wrestled with an angel of *Yahweh* by night. Another example of night's power is when Zohar speaks of the blessing of those who arise at midnight to pray and study the Torah. Such prayer and Torah study, of course, imply something more than it might religiously appear on the surface, for the Torah as understood in Kabbalah is the "foundation of creation." It is the primordial Torah that is being spoken of, the Torah as known in the energy dimension or spiritual world of the Holy Spirit. At the midnight hour, it is said that *Yahweh Elohim* enters into the Garden to disport Him-Herself with the righteous, the *tzaddikim* who are "there" eagerly waiting in study and contemplation of Torah. The third example of the power of night regards the lunar calendar that Judaism, like many indigenous traditions, followed and continues to follow even in modern times. The power of night may be understood as the play of earth gates and star gates, through which nocturnal influx of cosmic and spiritual forces, angels and spirits, are allowed in or shut out by the Path of the Moon.

If Juan Diego goes to attend to his spiritual essence before dawn, then he is going out at night, walking the Path of the Moon, then he greets the Spiritual Sun emerging from the womb of predawn as he shifts to walk the Path of the Sun. This is a walking of the Sacred Circle to bring in great spirit-powers, a way of walking the Sacred Circle when one is seeking a greater shift or manifestation in the material dimension and world. When we remember that it is the middle of winter, then we will know that to go out at such a time was not easy. One would face the bitter cold of winter, and the ferocity of the elemental forces of winter. In the face of such physical suffering, it would take the force of will and the discipline of a spiritual warrior to maintain a continuum of prayer and sacred ceremony for the people.

This, of course, was quite natural in times past among indigenous peoples. Unlike our modern societies and cultures, especially in the West, they were not so focused upon creature comforts and conveniences, and were not so afraid of hard work and hardships. Thus, following in the way of the natural order, walking in the harmony of the natural flow of things, and catching hold of currents of spiritual power that might require some discomfort and inconvenience, or require some hard work and hardship, wasn't something that discouraged indigenous people or put them off. They were better able to move with the Spirit and Powers, and to develop powerful relationships with the spirits.

This is an important message in our times, even in the midst of the prevalent trends of modern spirituality and the new age movement. Many people seek great spiritual knowledge and power and are prone to lay claim to all manner of spiritual attainments, but are unwilling to endure true spiritual training and discipline, the hard work and sacrifices such attainments require. We must be willing to do whatever it takes to acquire spiritual knowledge and power, divine illumination, and to be empowered to labor in the Spirit for the people, to be empowered to be of true benefit to our relations.

Although much of Christianity might speak of a collective and vicarious salvation through the suffering of the Christ, in truth the Holy Gospel calls us as participants in self-offering for the people, as when Yeshua said in verse 55 of St. Thomas, *Take up the cross and follow in my way*, teaching an active spiritual labor to bring the light of the Spiritual Sun into this world. While this indeed includes the bliss of communion and union with the Divine, this also includes a call for our own sacrifice, our own suffering for and with the people, a true offering of our lives and ourselves for the sake of a harvest of souls and the advent of the Second Coming.

By this we do not mean a vain and meaningless self-martyrdom, or the perverse self-flagellating and self-destructive behaviors ascribed to many "saints" of the Roman Church. What we mean is a willingness to submit to true self-discipline, the hard work and hardships that are often required for true spiritual breakthroughs that bring in greater spiritual power for the people. Spiritual works for the people such as prayer and fasting to seek a vision, or prolonged vigils of prayer and meditation, holding sacred space and energy, going out on treks of power into the wilderness to do spiritual works, maintaining a significant continuum of daily spiritual practice, and calling upon the Spirit and calling in the Divine Powers, are actual spiritual works and a true offering of oneself for the people.

The spiritual life is also a progressive change in our lifestyle and the way we are living. We can simplify our needs and demands on the environment and our relations, reduce our consumerism and need for idle entertainments, let go of our fixation on excessive creature comforts and conveniences, and instead, pay more attention to our energy, our spiritual life and practice. We can seek to live more in harmony with the natural order, working to live in a deeper communion with the angels of our Heavenly Father and Earthly Mother. We can choose a more peaceful and loving way, with an aim of active compassion and charity, "walking lightly upon the earth."

When the story hints at Juan Diego's devotion and sacrifices, it encourages us to consider how we might actively engage in a more zealous spiritual life and practice. We can consider what works we might take up and what sacrifices we might make to manifest a greater good in this world, to have a more positive and uplifting influence and effect on our relations, environment, and world. We are encouraged to become true spiritual warriors and a holy people, a true sacred priesthood.

Now, Juan Diego first goes into the great outdoors, to a place of power, to attend to his spiritual essence, and then he goes to a church to attend morning Mass. As we know all too well, most often, there is little, if anything, of the Light Transmission or power of the Holy Spirit in the mass of the Roman Church, save for that Holy Light and Spirit that is brought in by the truly faithful. Thus, just as the Holy Mother is seeking to restore the Spirit and Light to two streams, and to call for the weaving of streams, so Juan Diego goes out, invokes and receives the Spirit and Powers, and he brings the Holy Light and Spirit into the church and its celebration of the Mass on Sunday morning. He brings the Divine Presence and Power with him, and in so doing he weaves the two streams through his own actions.

This, too, is an important teaching for us. If we are seeking the Divine Light and Holy Spirit, then we must invoke and receive that Light and Spirit ourselves, and bring it with us. We must walk as conscious co-creators and conscious agents of the good that we are seeking, and not just rely upon those outwardly ordained as priests or recognized spiritual leaders to facilitate our spiritual and mystical experiences. We must take responsibility for our own spirituality.

As we have noted previously, a society based upon the Divine Mother and enlightenment, a spirituality rooted in the Divine and Sacred Feminine, is not hierarchal. Although, indeed, there may be very gifted individuals that we recognize as spiritual leaders, as teachers and guides, and as seers and wonderworkers, shamans, we do not rely upon them exclusively for our spirituality, or for our spiritual life and spiritual experience. Rather we all carry spiritual knowledge and power. We all have direct access to the Spirit and Powers, and we all have a responsibility for our own spirituality. We all have a priestly role to play, even if we are not called to the outward role of the spiritual leader in community. Consider everyone present in a sacred event, in worship and spiritual work. Isn't everyone responsible for what happens? All who are present are co-creators with the Spirit and Powers of what transpires. As we go to sacred events of any kind, we must walk in a sacred manner and pay attention to our energy, and bring the Spirit and Light with us to the gathering.

When Juan Diego has attended to his spiritual essence, and has attended Mass, having called upon the Spirit and Divine Powers in full, he goes to attend to his sacred task, going to see the bishop again. He goes in all humility, as we see from his bowing down and weeping, but he also goes in spiritual self-worth, carrying something of the Divine Presence and Power with him. We wish to begin every day in the same way as Juan Diego. Calling upon the Spirit and calling in the Powers, we want to walk with humility, openness, and sensitivity, and walk with spiritual self-worth or divine pride. Whether an apparently sacred or mundane task, it is just the same; we wish to walk in the beauty and holiness of the Spiritual Sun, wearing the Body of Vision.

Although the bishop does not believe Juan Diego, he does sense some sincerity, perhaps even some holiness, with Juan Diego. Although he suspects heresy or madness, because of the sincerity, or holiness, he does not cause him immediate harm, but rather he asks for some proof, some sign, some wonder. Confident in the Holy Mother, Juan Diego agrees to bring him his sign. Sincerity and integrity come from our true and natural being, and they come from standing in our truth and standing in our power, aware of our energetic being. When we abide with and in the Holy Mother in this way, abiding as her Holy Child, her presence with us can act to pacify and enrich, and to subjugate and destroy, admixed and dark spirits.

Abiding in the Mother, even in the face of the enemy, we need not fear, and we may say, where there is no fear, typically a predator has no reason to attack; peace within invokes a peaceful response without. The faith and confidence in the Mother that Juan Diego expresses, specifically his faith and confidence in the power of the Mother to work wonders, is the faith and confidence we wish to cultivate and walk with. As is well known in the wonderworking art, when one enters into the play of wonderworking, one must act as though the wonder has already transpired, with no doubt that the wonder is coming to pass, and so it shall come to pass just as it is spoken.

Now, the bishop sending spies to follow Juan Diego, priests of the office of the Inquisition, and his vanishing from their sight as he crosses a bridge, is very significant. Essentially, crossing a bridge indicates a passage into the spirit world and the ability of a shaman to cross into the spirit world, their ability to walk between worlds. Naturally, this is a place into which most Catholic priests and ordinary people cannot see, let alone go, and, in fact, it would likely be a world hostile and frightening to them. It is no wonder that the priests become frightened of Juan Diego and return with an evil report of him to the bishop. To the extent that the bishop represents a channel of an archon, these priests represent "angels" of the archonic realm. As the Gospel of St. Philip teaches us, when we put on the True Light, the Light of the Spiritual Sun, the demiurge and archons, and their servants, their "angels," cannot see us; we are invisible to them and cannot be bound by them. This, too, is implied by the vanishing of Juan Diego from the sight of the spies of the bishop. He cleaves to the True Light, and he leaves the servants of the false light behind.

One is reminded of the many times we are told that Adonai Yeshua vanishes from the sight of people, or "disappears in the crowds" at a critical moment. There are, of course, many deep and esoteric teachings in this. While many individuals might think that this part of the story is only a metaphor, it may also reflect actual experiences we may have with some very powerful and holy people; in sacred moments they may go in and out of phase with the material dimension and with other dimensions in which they may appear. In effect, to those who remain in phase with the dimension of appearance, they may be seen to disappear and reappear. There are many initiates who can bear witness to this phenomenal wonder in their experiences with some holy people in moments of power. In the world of the seer and wonderworker, the world of the shaman, this is not unusual or uncommon. Neither is shape-shifting uncommon in the world of the shaman. It is a wonder that is based upon the same principle of going in and out of phase, or the dissolution and reformation of the energetic body.

Essentially, as we have said, all reality is dream-like; all reality is a radiant display of the mind, consciousness, or soul. It is all in consciousness. The energy body and material body are, in truth, inseparable, and they are expressions of the same radiant energy of consciousness in two worlds, the spiritual and material. In essence, the "body," whether the energy body or material body, is a body of consciousness, and the body shares the very same essence and nature as consciousness: the emptiness, the spaciousness, which is radiant or energetic, and which is aware, intelligent. If and when consciousness can be dissolved into its essence and nature—the Clear Light—then the body of consciousness may also dissolve and be radically transformed in a new arising or emanation of consciousness. Likewise, if and when a more radical shift can be brought about in the energy and vibratory frequency of consciousness, then a corresponding shift and transformation of the body of consciousness can occur. In this way, the body of consciousness can go in and out of phase. It can shape-shift, shine with visible light, pass through seemingly solid objects, move with great speed, or have other very magical effects upon the dimension in which it appears, including the material dimension.

In terms of Juan Diego disappearing, this could indicate many things. He may have gone out of phase to become invisible, eluding his enemies; he may have also shape-shifted, with the same result. Those who might have been watching were not able to process what they had just seen. He might have gone out of phase in such a way that his body of consciousness actually passed into a completely different continuum of space-time, or shifted completely into another more subtle dimension. Perhaps he did not go out of phase at all, but spirits helped him elude those who were following him, distracting or blinding the bishop's spies. Of course, the bishop's spies could have simply lost sight of him in broad daylight, or knowing they were following him, he could have taken action to duck out of sight like an ordinary person might do if they were being followed. All of these are possibilities, and all of them can offer spiritual teachings. If nothing else, it is a call for us to open to greater possibilities, awesome and wonderful possibilities, walking with a sense of the magic and openness that is essential to the spiritual and mystical journey.

Now, all of this happens on Sunday, the Shabbat in Christian tradition, and according to oral teachings of the story, when Juan Diego disappears from the sight of the bishop's spies, he goes to a secret meeting with the Celestial Maiden, a meeting not recounted in the story, though it is hinted at in oral traditions of Guadalupe. What transpired between the Sky-Dancing Maiden and Juan Diego on Sunday is said to be in teachings held by elder women of the tradition, which only they can impart, or it is said these teachings must be revealed to a faithful person directly by Our Lady in a luminous dream or vision. As for the elder women who hold these teachings, it has often been said that they also appear in dream and vision to communicate them to those ready to receive this secret knowledge, and the spiritual power that it gives.

Part of this secret knowledge is said to be about the disappearance of Juan Diego and his journey in the Spirit on Sunday to the Queen of the Shabbat, the Celestial Maiden, who reveals teachings about her Celestial Palace among the "star people." Sacred chants and secret Divine Names of the Holy Mother, and many other mysteries and spiritual practices are held in this oral teaching. If nothing else, the stories of a secret meeting and secret teachings certainly pique our curiosity. In the journey, that is a good thing, for such curiosity invokes questions that we may take to the Mother, and when we know to ask the question, we might receive an answer, all in the Good Mother's time.

The Benefactor of the Ancient Ways

The next day, Monday, Juan Diego did not go to the bishop's palace with the sign he requested because his uncle, Juan Bernadino, had become extremely ill and was nearing death. Although Juan Diego had fetched a doctor for his uncle, it was too late, so in the wee hours of the morning, while it was still dark, his uncle asked him to go for a priest to hear his confession and prepare him for his responsibility to death. He was certain that his time had come and he would not arise from his deathbed.

In the ancient Aztec society, "uncle" was the brother of your mother, and the uncle was the benefactor to his nephews, passing knowledge, wisdom, and special blessings of a loving, energetic transmission on to them, something like what we see in the Torah in the passing of the patriarchal blessing between a father and his firstborn son. Uncle may also be taken as a spiritual benefactor, a teacher and guide in the ancient ways of the spiritual warrior and shaman, a holy person to whom a younger seeker might be an apprentice. Juan Bernadino represents the ancient tradition of the indigenous people, the Aztec and Toltec people, and his death at this time heralds the death of the ancient ways, or more truly, their healing and transformation as they pass into a new generation and new era. He is the spiritual benefactor of Juan Diego.

Indeed, the ancient ways were dying. They could no longer remain in the form they once were, but nevertheless the essential wisdom and Light Transmission could continue on, purified of the shades and shadows that had come to dominate Aztec spirituality in its decline, in the extreme darkness and violence of human sacrifice that had become so prevalent in the late period of the Aztec empire.

In much the same way there was, and is, a need for the death and rebirth of the European Christian stream, the drawing out of its essential wisdom and Light Transmission, and the restoration to a pure spirituality of direct spiritual and mystical experience, a return to its mystical and gnostic roots. The Office of the Inquisition, the "Holy Wars," the slavery of indigenous, "godless pagans," and all of the psychological atrocities committed by the Roman and Protestant churches infected by arbitrary creeds and doctrines encrusting the Christian stream, all represent the same shades and shadows, the same encrustation of ignorance, darkness, and evil as that which plagued the late Aztec and Toltec stream. The Mother comes to banish these shades and shadows, and to heal the two streams, restoring their essential wisdom, light, and Spirit. This is manifest as a weave of the two streams of two wisdom traditions.

The weave of the Aztec and Toltec tradition and the Christian tradition in Our Lady of Guadalupe is a very important message for our times. Essentially it tells us that a weaving of streams of Light Transmission or wisdom traditions is essential for the development of the new world-view or paradigm we need to survive and to usher in a true new age. What Christians might call the Age of the Holy Spirit or Second Coming of Christ, Aztecs and Toltecs might call the Sixth Sun. Aztec and Toltec prophecies seem to insist that the wisdom of many indigenous peoples of many other lands will be essential to integrating a new paradigm. This paradigm is more "shamanic," a spirituality of direct spiritual experience that is more inclusive of our whole being, of the earth and nature. It includes the Divine and Sacred Feminine in a more dynamic balance of heaven and earth, the spiritual and material worlds. Here, in North America, like the Aztec and Toltec peoples of Mexico, the various Native American peoples hold essential wisdom that is crucial to the new paradigm, and quite harmonious with the way of Adonai Yeshua and the healing, Holy Gospel.

These weaves, however, need to be founded upon direct spiritual and mystical experiences, upon true dreams and visions, true revelations of the Divine, and upon an actual enlightenment experience or self-realization. Their foundation must be experiential, based upon actual experience of the Truth and Light of the Divine. In this process the questions Juan Diego presents us with at the very outset of his experience are crucial, most especially, "Am I dreaming? Am I imagining all of this?" This is well evidenced in much of modern spirituality, the "new age movement," and popular occultism, which can often put forth many nice ideas devoid of any actual spiritual and mystical experience, or any actual realization or energetic current. Confusing fantasy and daydreams with true dream and vision, or falling into influences of deceptive, even dark and hostile forces, and presenting some very strange and harmful ideas, are distortions that are balanced and focused by the critical process of spiritual discernment, something very essential, as we are taught in the story.

Now, in a weave of streams of wisdom and Light Transmission, the streams that are woven together are transformed, rather like a man and woman who couple and conceive a child. The genetic and energetic influence of the parents is in the child and the child has a resemblance to them on a material and energetic level, and yet the child is a unique and individual person, a different entity from either of the parents. In the same way, when living wisdom traditions are woven together, those streams undergo a death and rebirth, and are transformed, and in effect an entirely new stream of wisdom and Light Transmission is born, one vibrant and alive, shaped for the time and place in which it comes into being.

Our own tradition is much like this, especially since the time of Tau Miriam, my teacher's teacher. Receiving the stream of our lineage from her teacher and then experiencing Supernal realization, she transformed the teachings and practices of the lineage into a vehicle of the Light Transmission or energetic current of that realization. In so doing, the tradition, the lineage, died and was reborn. It was revolutionized and transformed based upon her spiritual and mystical experience, her dreams and visions, and the influences of many streams were drawn into the lineage, all reflecting and expressing something of her enlightenment experience. Since that time this process of the death and rebirth of the lineage has continued with the lineage-holders that have come after her. Based upon their experience of Supernal realization they have continued to weave and regenerate the teachings and practices of the tradition, so that the tradition remains alive and vibrant as a unique vehicle of enlightenment for contemporary, Western people.

Such spiritual works of weaving streams of wisdom and Light Transmission are going on throughout the world today. While some might be a nice idea, or something conceptual, theoretical, or even fanciful, all do have something of this spiritual impulse—revolutionary and evolutionary—founded upon actual dreams, visions, and divine revelation, and an actual experience of enlightenment or self-realization. This very impulse and inspiration is the Holy Mother, a first and foremost expression of which comes in the form of Guadalupe as a tangible emanation of Daughter, Mother, and Grandmother Sophia. Indeed, while the impulse and inspiration of a new age bursts forth, as yet we remain in the dark age of the Mother's womb. The birth or dawn of the new age has not yet come, though surely, messengers and prophets of that time are among us, and many who co-labor as midwives with the Divine Mother to give birth to the true and full advent of the Spiritual Sun and Holy Spirit are among us.

On a symbolic level, perhaps even an actual level, we can say that Juan Bernadino represents all religion, all tradition, of the former age and ages, and the need for a death and rebirth of all wisdom traditions in a greater global weave of essential wisdom. The old time religions, and old time wisdom traditions, can no longer serve us effectively, for they are of a world of the past, a world gone by, and cannot keep pace with the acceleration of consciousness in a new world, nor facilitate the Second Coming that is destined and already here. Here we can say that the appearance of the Celestial Maiden heralds the coming of a new age, world, and order, one that is global. And if we know and understand the meaning of her robes, especially the outer robe of the starry night sky, we will know and understand that this will lead us to an awareness of a greater galactic and universal order, one that is cosmic and primordial, divine and eternal.

The noble ideal of a new age or new era of humanity on earth is by no means wrong or incorrect, neither is the suggestion that if we choose to, we can live in that age of the Holy Spirit or Second Coming here and now. Indeed, we can, and some among us do! But, there is a spiritual work, a labor to give birth to a new age in full, and a greater number of people must be willing to let go of old religions and traditions to embrace the weave and the new streams of wisdom and Light Transmission emerging from it. More individuals must seek a spirituality of direct experience and an actual self-realization. Are we willing to undergo this spiritual death and rebirth, to bear the pangs of giving birth to a new era? This is the question of the dying and death of Juan Bernadino, as well as the message being taken to the Catholic bishop, a message from an Aztec Goddess, who is also the Virgin Mary. She is the Holy Mother of us all, Our Mother God.

Now Monday is the Day of the Moon, and as we know, moon wise in the Sacred Circle is the path of the spirits. Likewise, as we know, it is the astral dimension and dreamtime, and all of the dimensions beyond the astral, the astral being the gate to the world of spirits and angels, and great cosmic forces and the Supernal. The pending death of Juan Bernadino on the day of the moon implies a great cathartic movement or shift in the matrix of spiritual forces within and behind the weaving of these streams, and the generation of a new stream of wisdom and Light Transmission. In this regard, energetically, it is much like the great tumult that follows in the heavens as described by the appearance of the Woman of Light in Revelation; the balance of spiritual forces is shifted by the influx of the Solar or Supernal Light. As Juan Diego attends to this movement with his uncle, he tends to a theurgic or magical movement in the play of spiritual forces, laboring to integrate the influx of the Mother's Force and to bring forth the new weave.

The need for confession reflects this process of integration. The "responsibility to death" is the need to let go of the past and all that is obsolete, all that is no longer useful, and to address all shades and shadows with rigorous openness and honesty, opening the way to the new Body of Vision. As Juan Diego attends to this, as we know, his uncle does not actually die, but he is healed and made whole, restored to health and given new life by the Mother. He is made a new man, a new stream of Light Transmission.

This tale of dying and death, of course, implies much more and holds many more teachings. As we know, aging and dying is the final enemy, and as we also know, our responsibility to death, our full reintegration with the Light Continuum, the Pleroma of Light, is perhaps the most critical time of our incarnation. If in our life time we have fulfilled our soul's destiny and we have lived in a conscious way, if we have developed consciousness beyond the body, the full awareness of our energetic being, and if we have cultivated awareness in all states of consciousness, waking consciousness, sleep and dream, and death and the afterlife—then when the hour of death comes we may be conscious in our dying, as in our living. When we die, we will not fall into unconscious oblivion, but rather we'll undergo a conscious transition, a completely conscious reintegration with the ground or source of our being, and we will no longer have need of physical rebirth. We will pass into another level of the soul's journey and evolution. While dying, if we do fall unconscious and we are not able to meet and fulfill our destiny, still, in truth, we will not "die," but we will continue to be reborn into the material dimension until our soul is actualized and realized, fully awakened and embodied with physical purpose.

Although Juan Bernadino is said to be healed and brought back from the threshold of death, we may also understand that all healing does not necessarily take place in the body, but that our ultimate healing takes place beyond the body, with reintegration of our soul or energetic being into the greater energetic continuum, the Light Continuum. Indeed, our healing or reintegration in the Divine Mother is not only in this world and in this body, but it is also beyond this world and this body, in transcendence, the great resurrection and ascension.

This, too, is a mystery spoken here, for when it is said that Juan Bernadino is called back from the threshold of death, healed and made whole, this speaks of another mystery of the Supernal influx, the Mother's Force. Not only does it bring about the great ascension, the great liberation, but the Mother's force transforms every level of our consciousness, every level of our being, potentially the very substance of matter itself and the material world. For this reason, the Mother's Force is the great transformation. In this regard, we must remember that the emanation of the Holy Mother becomes material: something that may be touched, smelled, tasted, heard, and seen. She is not just an energetic appearance in the visionary dimension with Juan Diego, but she appears in the material dimension. Likewise, when she gives a sign, producing her wonder for Juan Diego to take to the bishop, it is a distinctly material sign, a materialization of spiritual energy, which also implies a spiritualization of matter.

In the Mother, on one hand we labor for transcendence, the great ascension, yet, on the other hand, we labor for the refinement and spiritualization of matter and the material world, the great transformation. This is the great and holy mystery of our destiny in the Holy Mother, the *Shekinah* of the Supreme. In her we know a twofold movement of Creative Evolution, which in the end we understand as a movement of one single direction, the "Seventh Direction:" the Divine centered within us.

There is also another teaching here of Juan Diego tending to the needs of his uncle as the need to work out our karmic continuum. Family represents this need, and it is the thrust behind the Fifth Commandment in the Torah, the honoring of father and mother, which is the working out of our karma. Likewise, it is a teaching on duty, responsibility, honor, integrity, and justice, and true righteousness—qualities we all can see are severely challenged in this modern world, especially among our economic, political, and spiritual leaders. Although, perhaps, these words imply a burden to our egos, they are the truth of the good in our soul, our energetic being, and they are the healing of the soul, true *tikkune*.

Juan Diego is truly a righteous man, a righteous person, a *Holy Tzaddik*. According to the Holy Kabbalah, the *tzaddikim*, righteous ones, are the foundation and sustenance of the world. So we see in the story of Juan Diego and his encounter with the Mother our own aspiration to live as the *Holy Tzaddik*, a spiritual warrior and holy person. If Juan Bernadino taught Juan Diego, then he taught him very well. In that he is healed by the Mother and restored to the fullness of life, it would appear that he also is among the *tzaddikim*.

The Mother Comes Down in Divine Mercy

In the darkness of Tuesday morning, Juan Diego set out to bring a priest from his spiritual home to see his uncle through the crossing over. When Juan was passing by the west slope of the Holy Hill on his way, he thought to himself, "If I continue along the same path the Celestial Maiden, the High Holy Woman, will surely see me and command me to go to the bishop with her sign, but if she does that, I will have to go and my uncle will die without the guidance of a priest of the Way. It is my duty and responsibility to honor my uncle, so I will go around the backside of the Sacred Mount, going around by a different path. I cannot leave my uncle waiting. There is no time for that." By going around the Sacred Mountain he thought She-Who-Sees-Everywhere would not see him.

So Juan Diego went around the eastern slope so as not to be seen and detained by the Sky-Dancing Maiden, the Queen of Infinite Space. Seeing him, she came down the Holy Hill to meet him from where she was watching.

She said, "My youngest child, my messenger, where are you going?"

This time he was disturbed, ashamed, startled, frightened!

The world of spirits and angels, and the world of the Divine, truly is a strange and mysterious realm. Very magical and powerful, awe-inspiring and delightful, it can also be dangerous and frightening, extremely unpredictable, for the intentions and interests of the spirits and angels, the Powers and the Divine, can be very different from that of human beings. Their intentions and interests sometimes are incomprehensible to us, and can often pose a sharp contrast and come into conflict with our own intentions and interests. Not only that, but at times we find the intentions of the spirits and angels in apparent conflict with one another, so that in carrying out sacred tasks aligned with one group of spirits or angels, at times, we can find another group of spirits or angels that might be opposed to it. This plethora of intentions and works can reach up into the realm of archangels and great cosmic forces, and even between emanations of the Divine or enlightened being we can encounter very different works, very different ways.

In terms of the radical differences that we might find one can consider the opposing views of Christ and Buddha on the resurrection of the dead. Christ raised a child from death, like the prophets Elijah and Elisha before him, having compassion on a grieving parent and the suffering child. When approached by a grieving mother, however, the Buddha, also lead by compassion, refused to raise her child back to life, and instead taught the woman about impermanence and the Four Noble Truths, setting her on the path in a very different way. These two holy ones embody the same Light-Presence and Light-Power, the same basic enlightenment, and yet their response to the same circumstances was quite opposite from one another. Though embodying one and the same Living Presence and Power, their way is very different.

If this is true in the world of the Divine, between emanations of the Divine or enlightenment, then it is even truer in the world of archangels and great cosmic forces, and in the world of angels and spirits. The spiritual world can be much like this world with all of the different views, ideologies, and interests that are served among the masses of humankind and nations. Juan Diego is very experienced with the world of spirits and angels, and the play of great powers, and as a spiritual warrior and shaman, he knows and understands this, and accepts this. He knows that the spiritual world is very sacred and holy, and that it is very mysterious, magical, powerful, awe-inspiring, and delightful, and yet sometimes very dangerous, very unpredictable. He knows that, potentially, his sacred task and duty to his uncle, his spiritual benefactor, might oppose and come into conflict with the sacred mission given to him by the Celestial Maiden.

This is very significant on many levels. First and foremost, before actual contact and experience with the spirits and angels, Juan Diego's challenge teaches us that the spiritual world may not exactly be like what we imagine or conceive it to be. It also suggests that contact with the admixed world of spirits may often be presented fancifully by some forms of modern alternative spirituality, like a daydream rather than the actual experience of the spirit world and angelic world. Contrary to what psychism might say, the spirit world can be very different from how we might imagine it or want it to be. A second layer in Juan Diego's challenge teaches us about the courage and integrity of a spiritual warrior. Although he fears that his two sacred duties might be in conflict with one another, nevertheless, by choosing to honor his duty to his uncle, he is willing to take both the responsibility and the consequences for his choice upon himself in service to his uncle, attending to his uncle's needs as he meets with death. A third layer in Juan Diego's challenge also teaches us how very important the time of dying and death is, how sacred and holy attending to the dying and the dead is, a very sacred duty that must take precedence over any other sacred or mundane responsibility.

Now, fearing he will encounter the High Holy Woman if he goes by the same path to the west of the holy hill, he goes by the eastern path around the holy hill, seeking to bypass the place of power where he encountered her voice and presence. Attempting to go unseen by her, perhaps even using his knowledge and power as a warrior and shaman to go out of phase and be invisible as he passes by the Holy Hill, is to no avail. The Sky-Dancing Maiden is She-Who-Sees-Everywhere, Mother God, and there is no hiding from her. All is in her and she is in all, and her presence and power is everywhere in the material and spiritual world. His attempt to avoid the Holy Mother is a very human act, and it is both child-like and comical. Given that he does so out of love and respect for his spiritual benefactor, to attend to a most sacred duty, there is an innocence and good intention behind it. Listening and hearing the response of the Divine Mother, clearly she knows her children and understands them, and she knows their hearts and minds, their intentions.

Seeing Juan Diego passing by, she does not call to him from afar, but she goes down to him and meets him where he is, and she does not go in judgment or wrath, but she goes to him in love, in mercy and compassion. Her appearance startles and disturbs him, and he is afraid when he encounters her this time, but as we see, whatever judgment there might be, it is in his own heart and mind, in his own worries about a conflict between his sacred tasks, and between the intention of the Divine and the intention of the human being. This is a very significant teaching to us. There is no judgment in the Mother, there is no judgment in the Most High, the Supreme, but the judgment is in us, in our own internal conflicts, our own energy and karmic continuum. If and when there is an appearance of judgment, it is that we are not aligned and in harmony with the Light Continuum and the divine, and we are not aligned and in harmony with our true and natural being. We are in conflict with ourselves, and so we are in conflict with the Divine, the source of our being. The result is an appearance or experience of judgment, or what may seem to be a wrathful manifestation of the Divine presence and power.

This is a very powerful message to a Toltec or Aztec person of the time, for the shades and shadows of violence and human sacrifice that plagued the later period of their tradition presented a very different view of the Divine, one very severe and judgmental, potentially very dark and hostile. Likewise, it is a powerful message to many Christians who hold a similar view of the Divine as extremely vengeful, judgmental, and bloodthirsty, calling for genocide, "holy wars," and torturous persecutions of people. Mediated by religious traditions, the world of spirits and angels can indeed be dangerous and unpredictable, just as life is a dance of great beauty and great danger, completely unpredictable. But the reality of our experience on all levels is a radiant display of our own mind, consciousness, or soul, our own energy reflecting and expressing our karmic continuum. The experience of "judgment" is simply the consequence of our own actions in a play of cause and effect, the result of being in an imbalanced state or out of harmony with the natural and Divine Order.

Now, the High Holy Woman comes down and meets Juan Diego where he is, and there is no judgment in her, but she comes in mercy, as the embodiment of love and compassion, seeking the fulfillment of her intention and desire, and the desire of Juan Diego. As before, she inquires where he is going, about the direction he is walking, his orientation, the intention, and desire of his heart. He responds with complete openness and honesty, surrendering and reintegrating himself with her Divine presence and power, and when he does, Divine Grace, Supernal Mercy, pours out, and wondrous miracles, happen, fulfilling his heart's desire.

This is a most important message from the Mother. She comes in mercy and love, the Compassionate Mother, and she comes down, meeting us where we are, assuming a form with which we can interact and relate, revealing herself according to our desire and capacity to receive her. To the extent that we are willing to surrender, to become open and honest and reintegrate ourselves with her living presence and power, she will bring about the fulfillment of our heart's desires, our dreams, and she will empower us to meet and fulfill our destiny. She does not come in judgment, but in mercy and love, and yet, in her presence all shades and shadows, all that is unreal, is exposed. While she has a bright and peaceful face, she may also have a dark and fierce face. But when we encounter her dark and fierce face, all that distorts, hinders and obstructs the fulfillment of our inmost heart's desire and dreams is being exposed and dispelled, all by her compassionate, loving, and merciful embrace. Indeed, there is no judgment in her, but rather illumination and liberation, our fulfillment.

Here we may say, God the Father has been revealed, but was too lofty and transcendental for us to comprehend or cleave to, and likewise, the Spiritual Sun—the image and likeness of the Sky Father—has come. But loving the darkness and identified with the darkness, the light of the Spiritual Sun was a blazing glory and too intense and bright for most. The Spiritual Sun became to us as judgment, and that judgment was severe. God therefore has come down as the Compassionate Mother, tending to her little ones, nurturing and nourishing them to their fruition and maturation in her. She comes down to dwell with us and be with us, meeting us right where we are, embracing us just as we are, taking us into her heart womb, healing us, transforming us, and making us whole, uplifting us and restoring us to the Great Natural Perfection of our true being, the Primordial. The Mother comes down to us; such is the nature of the Holy Mother, God the Mother. And like the Spiritual Sun, she assumes any form that will touch us, one with which we can connect and relate, know and understand, one we can embrace with the fullness of our being. In her we receive the Supreme—Mother God and Father God—and we receive the Spiritual Sun, the Messiah, and the Light of the Spiritual Sun, the Holy Bride, the Holy Spirit, all as is good and beneficial for us, all in due season.

Now, there is also another mystery embedded in this point of the story, for going round to the east of the holy hill, Juan Diego has changed directions in Sacred Circle. From his first encounter, he was standing in the west and facing east when he sees the Mother; now he is standing in the east and facing west. As he experiences the Celestial Maiden, he is walking the directions, walking the Sacred Circle, for she is all the directions and the circle. As we remember at the outset, he stands in the west, the direction of the *Holy Shekinah*, and walks east, the direction of the Spiritual Sun; now it is reversed as the vision and movement approaches its fruition. This reversal occurs through Monday, the day of the moon, when he is walking the Sacred Circle moon wise, the movement in circle corresponding with the Divine and Sacred Feminine.

Here we may say something about the secret meeting on Sunday between the Celestial Maiden and Juan Diego, the day he disappeared from the Bishop's guards. On Sunday, when she tells Juan Diego to take a sign to the bishop, asking him to return to her on Monday, he is set standing in the south facing the north. According to one oral tradition, after the bishop receives the sign and agrees to build the Holy Temple, there is a second secret meeting between the Celestial Maiden and Juan Diego. Returning to her in fruition to report the success of his sacred mission with the bishop, he stands in the north facing the south. Beginning to end, Juan Diego goes full circle with the Sky-Dancing Maiden, the High Holy Woman.

In this we receive instructions for several ceremonies in Sacred Circle invoking the Divine Presence and Power of the Mother. In fact, as the story unfolds, we are given Divine Names and images for her in the directions to empower the sacred ceremonies invoking her. Although this is not the place to discuss them in detail, here we can give the correspondences of the Divine Names and images to the directions, forming the Sacred Circle of the Celestial Maiden.

A Practice: Directions of Guadalupe

The holy emanation of Our Lady of Guadalupe is in the sacred center of the circle, and above her, in the height, is Weaving Woman, Spider Woman, in her luminous web matrix of stars. Within and beyond her is Grandmother Deep Space. To the east is Eagle Woman and to the west is Serpent Woman; to the south is War Woman and to the north is Infernal Woman, the Woman of the Underworld, the In-Betweens. The depth, of course, is Earth Woman, Earth Mother. This is the Sacred Circle of the Celestial Maiden, Our Lady of Guadalupe, and the path of invocation. The Sacred Circle of the Holy Mother is walked moon wise, for her Sacred Circle is invoked following the Path of the Moon. The new and full moon are most sacred and holy. In her image the Mother stands on the moon just as the Woman of Light in Revelation.

There are many other emanations of the Celestial Maiden, the Holy Mother-Bride, but these are the emanations that form her Sacred Circle, and thus they are considered her principle ones. We will discuss these emanations, and others, in greater detail later, but by giving their correspondences to the directions of the Sacred Circle and pointing out Juan Diego's walk of the Sacred Circle, it is an empowerment for you to invoke the circle of the Divine Mother-Bride, and to walk her Sacred Circle to acquire knowledge of her principle emanations through direct spiritual and mystical experience. Here we may share one of the sacred ceremonies to help to acquire deeper knowledge and understanding of Our Lady of Guadalupe.

A Practice: Going to the Mother's Heart Womb

On, or near the full moon, go to a place of power and create a Sacred Circle. Go out with offerings of lights, sweet fragrances and flowers, bread and wine, a smudge pot and smudge, a sacred feather and staff, and go to pray to her and commune with her, She-Who-Is-Your-Mother. Create the Sacred Circle as you are inspired and as resonates with the place of power. As you do, love and adore the Divine Mother and know the light of the moon as her smiling upon you.

Place a sacred blanket or rug in the center with your sacred items and offerings on it. When you are ready, perform a smudging ceremony calling in the Spirit and Powers as the Holy Mother, and smudge yourself and the Sacred Circle, and everything in the Sacred Circle.

Then go stand in the west facing the east, facing the sacred center of the circle, and envision Guadalupe magically appearing in the sacred center as you invoke and call upon her. Go into her at the center and merge yourself with her presence and power, and make offerings to her as you pray and commune in her.

Then, standing in the sacred center and facing east, invoke Eagle Woman, and make offerings to her, praying to her and communing with her; then, go to the east and turn to face the west, and invoke Serpent Woman in the same way.

Then, return to the Sacred Center and go to the south, and facing the north invoke Infernal Woman in the same way; then passing through the Sacred Center again and going to the north, turn and face the south and invoke War Woman.

When you have done this, return again to the Sacred Center and invoke Spider Woman, and then Earth Woman in the same way, making offerings, praying and communing.

Then, with sacred feather and sacred staff in hand, go to the west and begin to walk or dance the Sacred Circle moon wise, counterclockwise, intoning sacred chants or heart songs of the Mother, invoking the fullness of the Holy Maiden, the Mother and the Grandmother, rejoicing in the living presence and power of the Holy Mother-Bride, Our Lady of Guadalupe.

When the Sacred Circle of our Lady is manifest in full glory and power, remember to look and see, and listen and hear, and to commune deeply in her Divine presence and power, coming to rest in her. Remember to pray for all your relations, extending the blessings of the Divine Mother to all beings, to all realms, worlds and universes, material and spiritual.

When all is said and done, celebrate an essential Wedding Feast of bread and wine, sealing the sacred ceremony. When you are finished, perhaps gaze at the moon, beholding the Holy Mother-Bride standing on it and smiling upon you.

If you behold the Celestial Maiden as you gaze and you know how, send your spirit into her heart womb, offering yourself to her and merging with her, walking full circle with her on the full moon. This is a fruition of the sacred ceremony in perfect delight and all beings are greatly blessed by it. *Hallelu Imma! Praise the Mother!*

If in this movement you are given sacred tasks by the Holy Mother and Powers be certain to do what you have been asked to do and to honor your Divine Mother as Juan Diego and those who have sojourned the Sacred Circle before you have done. This is the ceremony of Going to the Sacred Center, Mother's Heart Womb. It is very good. *Tov Meod.*

Emanations of the Noblewoman

He fell at her feet, knowing in her Eagle Woman, Snake Woman, War Woman, Infernal Woman, the Woman of All Womanhood, the Great Mother. He prayed to her, speaking with her, saying, "My daughter, my mother, my grandmother, great grandmother, noblewoman, may you be happy! Did you wake up well? Are you in sound health, patroness, Sweet Princess? I am going to make some trouble for you. One of your humble servants, my uncle, is very ill and he is going to die soon. With haste I must go to your home in Mexico City to fetch a priest for him to hear his confession and prepare him, for he is about to face that for which he was born, his responsibility to death. When I have done what I must do, I will return to you and take your message, special and holy person, my daughter, my mother, my grandmother. I will come first thing tomorrow."

The Forever Whole and Perfect Maiden replied, "Understand and know, my youngest child, nothing should frighten or concern you. Do not worry. Do not be afraid of the sickness, or any other illness or hardship. Am I not right here who is your Mother? Are you not under the shadow of my wings, under my protection? Am I not the foundation of your being, your sustenance, your happiness, peace and effortlessness? Are you not in the fold of my garment, I who am the Weaver-Of-All, the Weaver of the Web of Life? Do you need anything else? Do not allow anything to worry or disturb you anymore. Do not worry about your uncle's illness. He will not die; already he is healed and well, rejoicing in the dawn of a new day and the renewal of light and life, tending his spiritual essence.

As it turned out, it was discovered that Juan Bernadino arose completely healed at that moment.

Juan Diego's response to the Noble Woman's question proves very intriguing, for he speaks to her as though she is a human person or physical being, saying, "May you be happy," and asking, "Did you wake up well?" We naturally might inquire, "Does the Divine Mother ever sleep so that she wakes up well or not well?" This, of course, speaks to the mysterious nature of emanations and embodiments of the Divine, and to the mysterious nature of the great cosmic forces and the play of sentient existence that includes the whole spectrum of beings in creation, from beings of the physical worlds in *Asiyah*, to those of lofty spiritual worlds in *Yetzirah* and *Beriyah*. All of this is the Emanation Body of the Divine Mother, within and behind which are her Glory Body and Truth Body. The Emanation Body of the Mother appears in the dualistic play of creation, forming the matrix of creation; the experiences of all living beings—all creation—is her experience, while she is transcendent of creation.

Now, in terms of an actual Body of Emanation, whether a direct emanation within space-time, as in the case of the appearance of Our Lady of Guadalupe, or as a realized individual who embodies something of the Divine, as in the case of the Christ-bearer, these are appearances within the material dimension; the laws of the natural order within the material dimension to some extent, more or less apply to the Emanation Body. In a manner of speaking, Divine or enlightened being, appears as a human being, or any other sentient being, taking on the experience of sentient existence while appearing in the material or physical world. Indeed, the Divine or Enlightened Being becomes a person like us, although completely lucid, awake, in the full power and glory of Divine or enlightened being.

How Juan Diego speaks with the Celestial Maiden, the very physical sign she gives to him, and the fact that he can touch her, as well as see and hear her, speaks to an appearance in Emanation Body. As something more than an appearance in vision within the energy dimension in a Body of Glory, no doubt, there is a Glory Body and Truth Body dimension to the appearance of the Divine Mother, but she assumes a body of pure emanation, becoming, in effect, tangible, material, and physical. This is a great and holy mystery, and as we know it is a relatively rare event, for more often the Emanation Body appearance is that of a realized individual born into this world like anyone else, yet who embodies something of the Divine or enlightened being, unlike a direct emanation of the Divine not born into this world.

The appearance of the Noble and Holy Woman is a great wonder and is something much more than a vision! Such experiences of the pure emanation of Divine or enlightened being, though relatively rare, are not isolate to Juan Diego. There are other mystics who have had similar experiences with the Mother, as well as with other divine beings, in which an apparent material or physical form was generated. When this occurs, of course, it represents a radical influx of Divine power into the material dimension and world, a distinct shift in the balance and play of spiritual forces. This is why Divine or enlightened being chooses at times to appear in this way, to shift the matrix of spiritual forces in the world.

Now, here we are given five names of the Divine Mother, names that indicate her principle aspects or emanations: Eagle Woman, Snake Woman, War Woman, and Infernal Woman, as well as Spider Woman. As we have discussed, these correspond to the Powers of the Divine Mother in the directions of the Sacred Circle, and through an understanding of the directions, we may glean something of the presence and power of these emanations.

Eagle Woman stands in the east, the place of dawn and the powers of the light-bringers, the direction corresponding to the element of air, knowledge and healing power, and to the kerubic guardian with the face of the human one. Eagle Woman in the east is represented by both the Bald Eagle and Golden Eagle, uniting the *Shekinah* and the Messiah. As the bird that soars to the greatest heights, the eagle bears the power of passing between worlds, between heaven and earth, bearing full knowledge of Sky Father and Earth Mother, the Holy One. This reflects something of the power of Eagle Woman. As you may recall, the Woman of Light is given the wings of an eagle to fly into the wilderness and escape the power of the dragon or great serpent that pursues her (Revelation 12:13).

Serpent Woman stands in the west, the place of sunset and the emergence of night, the place of the great Thunder Beings, transition or crossing over, dying and death, the direction corresponding to the element of water, devotion or love, and to the strength of the Divine manifesting as luminous dreams and visions, as well as to the kerubic guardian with the face of the eagle. Serpent Woman is any form of serpent or snake, though here in our land most especially, it is the rattlesnake that represents her. This is the power of sound-vibration and radical transformation, and it is the serpent power, the Fiery Intelligence in us, that must be sublimated, uplifted, and redeemed, a power for great good or great evil, a power mastered by the Woman of Light and her Holy Child.

War Woman stands in the south, the place of noonday and the powers of ancient warriors, righteous warriors, the direction corresponding to the element of fire, the force of will or power manifest in all kinds of wonderworking, the path of the Milky Way that spirits travel, and corresponds to the kerubic guardian with the face of the lion. War Woman represents the Mother of Justice and Truth, the Divine Mother maintaining a balance in the play of great cosmic and spiritual forces, and she empowers spiritual warriors, angelic and human. You may recall, when the Woman of Light appears, a war breaks out in the heavens between the hosts of Michael and Satan, and the hosts of Archangel Michael are victorious, casting Satan and his minions out of the heavens.

Infernal Woman stands in the north, the place of midnight and the powers of the afterlife and star people, the direction corresponding to the element of earth, the light of God or Divine

Illumination, and to the powers of manifestation and powers of the underworld or otherworld, as well as to the kerubic guardian with the face of the ox. Infernal Woman is the Dark Face of the Divine Mother, her cathartic power. Specifically, she is the Divine Mother manifest as all creation, order and chaos, light and darkness, good and evil alike. In this we may understand a deep connection between the Whore of Babylon and the Woman of Light, the wisdom nature in ignorance or agnosis, and wisdom nature in enlightenment or gnosis—two expressions of Sophia, unenlightened and enlightened.

Spider Woman stands in the Height, the place of the heavens and the celestial spheres, the direction corresponding to the element of space, Union with God, and to the powers of transcendence. In the night, Sky Father becomes Heaven Mother, Queen of the Heavens, Queen of the Stars. The great matrix of stars and galaxies is the web of Spider Woman, Weaving Woman, and she holds the power of karma as a force of evolution, the power of fates and destinies. Although she is associated with the matrix of stars and galaxies, she is the weave of all, the formation of all. She is the energetic matrix underlying all creation, woven of the light of the suns, the Light of the Divine.

These emanations all point to Earth Woman, Earth Mother, the focal point of our experience as we walk the Sacred Circle of life. Earth Woman stands in the Depth, and she is this good earth understood as a living entity of divine intelligence, the good earth and nature as our Mother, as a Holy and Divine Being. We are in her womb, and when we die, when we have come to maturation in her womb, she gives birth to us in the infinite, in the eternal realm, the light realm. The earth and our very bodies are as her holy womb. In the Divine Mother we behold a complete and integral weave of the sacred and the mundane, and in the fullness of her Divine Gnosis we find no difference between the sacred and mundane, a non-dual Supernal realization.

Along with these emanations of the Celestial Maiden that are named—all intimately connected to the vision of the Woman of Light and to well-known Aztec Goddesses—we are told that the Divine Mother is the "Woman of All Womanhood." This indicates countless emanations of the Divine Mother that are not named such as Owl Woman, Deer Woman, Elk Woman, Bear Woman, Mountain Woman, River Woman, Ocean Woman, Dancing Woman, Weeping Woman, Tree Woman, Raven Woman, Hawk Woman, Lizard Woman, Stone Woman, Happy Woman, or White-Buffalo-Cow-Woman, and so on. This also indicates every woman as a potential emanation of the High Holy Woman, the Holy Mother-Bride, if and when the communion of the Divine Mother comes to fruition in Union, self-realization.

As has been previously mentioned, this is the wisdom of the use of the word Woman rather than "Goddess," for the word woman does not distinguish between the heavenly and earthly, or between divine and human womanhood; it is a weaving and a non-hierarchal term that flickers in its meaning, and that alludes to the perception of reality in a non-dual realization. In this respect we could very well speak of Eagle Man, Serpent Man, War Man, and Infernal Man as Divine and Sacred Masculine manifestations of the same powers, and speak of a play of Divine Consorts. The Divine Man and Divine Woman are innate to Christian Gnosticism in the persons of Yeshua and Mirya, the Groom and Bride, and the mystery of their Sacred Marriage. In the use of the word Woman for the Divine Mother there is a distinct message of the embodiment of the Divine in the awakened human being, whether in a woman or a man, hence the aim and fruition of the Gnostic experience in the direct knowledge of the Divine and unification with the Divine.

This is strongly reflected in what the Holy Mother says to Juan Diego, that she is "the foundation of his being, his sustenance, happiness, peace, and effortlessness," all indicating his innate unity with her, the innate unity of us all with her. In the Mystical Path of Guadalupe we seek unification, for this union is realized being, the culmination of the Mystical Path. Now here the Mother speaks the true nature of the Mystical Path in the Mother-Bride. She tells us not to fear or be concerned, "Don't worry about anything." This implies a calm abiding in the Divine Mother, and it implies something more: the cultivation of joy, the joy of life, the joy of being, the joy of the Divine, and delight in the dance of the *Holy Shekinah* on earth and in heaven. The *Holy Shekinah* comes to rest on those who abide in joy and who seek to truly enjoy life in communion with the Divine, weaving the sacred and mundane in an integral self-realization in the Mother.

Indeed! The Mother tells us to enjoy ourselves, to live life fully, free from fears and concerns, free from worries. In living fully she encourages us to be and become all that we can be, to be and become what we are in the "fold of her garment," a true human being and more, a Solar Being, a shining one, a holy star. This message of the spiritual and mystical path is very different from what we have been taught by old age religions and traditions bound up in patriarchy. On the mystical path, there is no denial of the body, earth, and nature, or of the sensual and sexual, or of life on any level. There is no foolishness of divorcing or dividing our spiritual and material being, or the sacred and the mundane. All is in the Divine Mother as we seek an integral realization, offering up the whole of our being and our lives to the Divine Mother, our love and enjoyment being her love and enjoyment, her delight.

We enact an active and dynamic surrender to the *Shekinah* of the Supreme–the Holy Mother-Bride. When we receive the Light from above—the Mother's Force and the Fiery Intelligence—the Bride's Force is awakened and uplifted in us, the whole of life and our being becomes Divine, Supernal. We live the Life Divine, all in the Pure Joy of the Mother. While we are not oblivious to the plight of souls in sorrow and suffering, or to what's happening moment to moment, even in the midst of sorrow there is this peace and joy of the Divine Mother, calm abiding that is passionate and radiant, all in the Mother, the Divine.

We bring delight to the Mother in our enjoyment. Just ask any noble mother what she feels in her child's enjoyment and fulfillment! Here we may note that Juan Diego does not ask the Mother to heal his uncle, but nevertheless she heals him, fulfilling the heart-wish, the deep desire of Juan Diego without him even having to ask it of her. So it is often times in the worship of the Divine Mother: there is a spontaneous flow of blessings and boons, and often even prayers we have not spoken are swiftly answered, our heart's desires being fulfilled by the Mother's Love, her Good Grace. We need give way to the passion of loving her and open our mind, heart, and life to her, seeking her most intimate embrace. When we do, she is, indeed, our happiness, peace, and effortlessness.

A Practice: Bringing Joy to the Mother

Any action, any activity, which we consecrate and offer up to the Divine Mother becomes a way of worship, devotion to her. If you want to make your Mother happy, then cultivate joy in all that you do, and in everything you do seek to enjoy yourself and seek to facilitate the enjoyment of others.

Choose some activity that brings you joy—something that you enjoy doing or experiencing—and when you go to take up that activity, consecrate it to the Divine Mother and offer your joy in the activity to her. Be completely present in the action and experience, aware of the Mother-Bride with you, and truly let go and enjoy yourself, and you will make your Divine Mother happy. Your enjoyment will be her delight. This is a good way to worship the Holy Mother-Bride; like children at play, enjoying themselves, we too may worship in this way every day, being a great joy to our Mother!

Any time you bring enjoyment to yourself it is good to seek to bring enjoyment to others as to the Divine Mother; the joy of others is a great joy to us, and in the enjoyment of others is the peak and perfection of our joy, the greatest joy of all. Later, when all is said and done, remember to reflect upon the enjoyment you experienced and the innate goodness of life in the Mother, and give thanks to the Mother and pray that all might experience true happiness, true enjoyment. This completes the movement of your worship.

Gathering the Flowers & Making the Bundle

Juan Diego believed in the Great and Holy Mother, and he was comforted by the Weaving Mother's words. So then, he prayed and pleaded with her to give him a sign to take to the bishop, a gesture that would bring the bishop to believe in her.

The Celestial Sky-Dancing Maiden, the Queen of Heaven, instructed Juan Diego, "My precious little child, go to the top of the Holy Hill where you saw me and where I spoke with you. You will behold different kinds of colorful flowers growing there. Go and gather them, and bring them down from the Holy Hill to me."

Juan Diego ascended the Sacred Mount and when he arrived at the top, in dawn's first light, he was in complete awe and wonder of the vast variety of Spanish-essence precious flowers that were there, all bursting forth in bloom with celestial dew upon them, all setting forth their sweet fragrance as the pure sweetness and beauty of the Holy Virgin, the emanation of her presence and power, and the sign of her prophecy set into his heart, now manifest before his eyes. He was very surprised and amazed, for it was in the depth of winter, the most cold and icy time of the year when nothing can grow, let alone bloom. It was a great and delightful wonder, one reflecting the grace of the Mother's blessing upon those who love her and draw close to her, entering into her loving embrace. The top of Tepeyacac was no place for such flowers, even in the springtime. It was totally overgrown with thorns and thistle, wild bushes, Nopal cactus and mesquite. At that time of year, even medicinal herbs that grew there would have been destroyed by frost and the bitter cold, but there, where she touched down, in the Heaven Earth Place of her Divine Grace, the flowers were in full bloom, full glory.

This humble wise man, the servant of the Holy Mother, harvested every flower, every blossom, and he put them in his cloak—the warmth of the Precious Maiden filling him—and he carried the bundle back down the Holy Hill to the Celestial Maiden who was waiting for him at its base. She took the bundle in her arms, opened it and held the flowers, smiling upon him, and then she put them back into his cloak, restoring the bundle and passing it back to him. She said, "My youngest child, my messenger, these flowers are my blessing upon you and the people this day, and they are the bishop's proof so that he might believe. Take them to him. Tell him for me that he ought to set my desire and will into action, and that you, as my messenger, can be trusted. Unfold your bundle only in front of the bishop. Show him what you bring. Tell him exactly what has transpired between us this morning, bearing witness of everything you have beheld and heard, and speak to him of the healing of your uncle, and speak of the wonders that are yet to come, and remember the time that is coming and the time to come that I spoke about with you, abiding in the confidence of my blessing and grace. Inspire the bishop so that the Holy Temple I have invoked comes into being and is built immediately."

Juan Diego's faith waxes hot and strong, and he is uplifted and encouraged by the words of the Celestial Maiden. Specifically we are told that he is "comforted," and the subtle implication is that something of the Comforter, the Holy Spirit, was transmitted to him, a spiritual empowerment.

According to the tradition, when the Risen Messiah empowered the disciples as apostles he communicated the Holy Spirit to them through mystic word, radiant holy breath, and the laying on of hands. Here, as the Divine Mother reveals herself in full to Juan Diego, she empowers him as her apostle. The actions of the Risen Messiah reveal the inner form of the Threefold Rite of Initiation in the tradition, an initiation into the Interior Church and the Mystical Path of the Christian stream. They are parallel to another spiritual empowerment communicated by the Holy Bride in the tradition called the Mantle of the Bride. When we are taken under the Mantle, there is also a play of sound-vibration, a mystic word, and blessing spoken, and there is radiant holy breath, anointing and laying on of hands under the Mantle, and we are received into the company of the Bride, receiving the *Shekinah* of Messiah.

We also know that when a divine and holy being speaks, or when a person of knowledge and power gives sacred discourse, there is an energetic transmission, a play of radiant holy breath and the Fire Snake within and behind their speaking. Their words may become a spiritual empowerment that invokes true knowledge and understanding, for their speech arises from the direct experience of the knowledge they are communicating in the moment, and may facilitate something of that spiritual or mystical experience. Such is the way of true sacred discourse and visitation with a holy being or holy person. In the midst of such a transmission, we merely need to be open and sensitive, and abide in faith, hope and love, and we will form the circuit and conditions through which we can receive the transmission of spiritual energy.

Now, such transmission can be received in dream and vision, or in the inner dimensions, but the full spectrum of a spiritual transmission and empowerment occurs when the divine energy or Light Power can move on all levels, including the physical or material. As we contemplate the Risen Savior coming in an Emanation Body that disciples may touch, and the Mantle of the Bride, a physical talisman of the *Shekinah* that goes over our body, so we see in Guadalupe generating a Body of Emanation that can also be touched. When a spiritual transmission and empowerment can be experienced on all levels, including the physical or material, then it becomes fully grounded, anchored, and it is integral, complete. The Divine Influx is brought down in full, the Light Transmission moving in this world, in this continuum of space-time. This naturally extends greater blessings and light in this world.

In this part of the story, of course, we are hearing of a spiritual empowerment in the Mystical Path of Guadalupe, one that has a deep resonance with the Mantle of the Holy Bride: The Passing of the Bundle. Flowers are collected in a sacred manner as an offering to the Celestial Maiden and as a prayer for the empowerment of faith and hope among the people. Gathering sacred flowers and making a bundle, using the colors of Our Lady to make the bundle, we pray for her full revelation to us and we carry the bundle to a man or woman of knowledge and power who knows how to enter into union with the Sky-Dancing Maiden, and we pass the sacred flower bundle to them. Taking the sacred flower bundle, they also pray and offer it up, but they pray in union; praying in union, they speak a blessing, a word of the Holy Mother, and they communicate the spiritual energy of the empowerment by passing the bundle back to us. Receiving it from their hands, we then must go out and create a Sacred Circle and call upon Our Lady of Guadalupe, and we offer the sacred flowers to her spirits and powers, and we pray for all our relations. The cloth that was used to form the bundle is made into prayer-ties afterwards, our prayers for the people and the land tied to the limbs of a sacred prayer tree, offered for the full reception of the Mother-Bride, the Age of the Holy Spirit, the Sun of Flowering. This completes the movement of the empowerment ceremony.

Usually, the sacred flower bundle is passed in a sacred ceremony that is created for this purpose, but at times a shaman of the Mystical Path of Guadalupe may call a person to a sacred visitation for this, or may agree to a sacred visitation if asked to enact this with a sojourner of the Way. Though simple, it is a beautiful and powerful ceremony and many luminous dreams and wonders have been invoked through it. Here, too, we see that the creation of sacred power bundles is a way of extending blessings in the Mystical Path of Guadalupe, and that the creation of power bundles extends to the creation of power bags, or medicine bags, and prayer-ties for people, various talismans that communicate blessings or spiritual power to help people. In the Mystical Path of Guadalupe, flower essences are a central part of such talismans, coupled with other power objects that might be included. Usually, after they're made, they are placed upon the Shrine of Our Lady to be charged when we consecrate them.

The making of the bundle and passing the sacred flower bundle also alludes to another sacred ceremony in the Way of the Mother-Bride, the sacred ceremony of baskets. In the most basic form of this sacred ceremony there are four baskets and they are laid out upon a sacred blanket, and an altar is built to the Divine Mother. The Spirit and Powers are called in as her holy emanations, and offerings are placed into the baskets; with the offerings, power is gathered into the baskets. Then, a person of knowledge and power may draw out blessings for the people from the baskets using a sacred feather and rattle, or other sacred tools. When the ceremony is complete, the contents of the baskets are taken out to a place of power and offered up with prayers for the people and the land. This sacred ceremony may include the passing of a bowl of water in which flower essences are placed, the fragrance of the flowers and flower essence water becoming an extension of the Mother's blessing upon all who are present in the sacred ceremony.

As revealed in the story, naturally, those who sojourn the Mystical Path of Guadalupe will often go up on sacred hills for special spiritual work in prayer, meditation, and sacred ceremony, going to where the sky and earth meet to take up their spiritual labor for the people and entertain their communion in the Holy Mother-Bride. Holy hills are sacred to her and there is great power on them, as is well known in indigenous wisdom traditions around the world.

Now, as we have said, the uncle of Juan Diego is healed without him even needing to ask the Mother, and already the Mother has told Juan Diego that he would take a sign to the unbelieving bishop so that he might believe, yet here Juan Diego must ask the Mother for the sign. This is an important lesson to us. Indeed, the Mother fulfills many desires without our needing to ask, but there are also things we need to pray about and ask her for, things for which we must pray and co-create the conditions necessary for the flow of her blessings and grace. Although many blessings and boons will come to us naturally and spontaneously in our worship of her, nevertheless we are to be active and conscious agents of her Divine Presence and Power.

Here, Juan Diego prays for a sign and is told to go up the holy hill and to gather flowers in a sacred manner and bring them back to the Celestial Maiden; he is told to make an offering to her of sacred flowers, and so he does. Bringing them to her, she takes them from him and blesses them, and gives them back to him to take to the bishop, along with the Divine Image of her that she has secretly imprinted upon his cloak containing the bundle. Juan Diego and the Holy Mother act together as co-creators of this wonderworking play, and throughout she gives him specific instructions and he follows them. This exactly reflects our labor of co-creation with the Divine Mother in her Mystical Path. We pray for the needs of the people, and we perform sacred ceremony calling upon the Mother and Powers for the people, and in our spiritual labor we do whatever the Mother and Powers ask us to do. In a similar way, whatever we see in dream or vision, we seek to bring into this world, anchoring and holding the Body of

Vision for the people.

It is a path of direct communion with the Divine Mother, and spiritual works for the people and the land, a labor to continually manifest the Heaven Earth Place, the Place of Flowering. Here we must emphasize that physicality and physical actions are essential to the Mystical Path of the Mother, for these actions ground her spiritual power in our physical or material being, our bodies, and the physical or material world. Actual movement and sacred ceremony is an integral part of her Mystical Path and her Divine Message. Her call to build a Holy Temple is the very sensory and physical sign she gives. Always we must remember, the Mother's Path isn't merely conceptual, but it is experiential; it isn't just in our head or heart, but in our bellies and bodies as well. The spiritual, mental, vital, and physical move together as a unified being in her. The whole of our being on all levels is included in her movements, her sacred dance of the circle, all of life.

Now, as much as any miracle told in the Holy Bible, this sign the Mother produces with Juan Diego in the midst of winter is a wonder of wonders. In a completely frozen, inhospitable environment, she makes flowers bloom on the holy hill. What's more, these aren't any indigenous flowers of Mexico, but Spanish essence flowers, roses from over an ocean away. This is a play of the presence and power of pure emanation, and it is a play with space-time, a very special magical power of the Divine Mother and those who carry something of her presence and power. As you might imagine, there are many layers of teaching within this sign, beginning with a promise of flowering, blooming, thriving, even in the midst of great tumult and darkness, a vision of hope for the people.

We have spoken often of the Mother's Path as a cultivation and refinement of desire, and as a path of joy, true enjoyment. In place of human sacrifice and Inquisition, whether Aztec or Christian, the Mother makes flowers the principle offering to her. Flowers, sweet fragrances, lights, artistic creations, sacred herbs, stones, and other natural things reflect her beauty and grace, and invoke peace and joy. The symbolism of flowers, however runs deeper, aside from the Aztec and Toltec association with maturation and fruition. It is the pollen path, the path of the sacred bees and butterflies, the goodness of the play of desire from which all life comes: cosmic orgasmic bliss.

There is a very deep and profound suggestion of the inclusion of the sensual and sexual in her worship. The suggestion of flower offerings is entirely opposite of any "original sin" of religion. All of life is sacred. The remembrance of the truth of the original blessing in which we are conceived affirms that sensual and sexual play may also be an offering to her. There is an affirmation of family and the raising of children as sacred to her and as an offering of worship to her. After all, she is the Divine Mother, not the cold and sterile male god devoid of the fertility and dynamism of the Divine and Sacred Feminine! This speaks of a special practice in motherhood: mothers seeking to embody something of the Divine Mother in their relationships and family, taking their labor as a mother for a vehicle of union with the Great Mother and as a holy offering to the Divine Mother. In a similar way it speaks of a noble view of womanhood by men who sojourn her Path, the view of women as the embodiment of the Mother-Bride, the manifestation of the Sacred Feminine.

Naturally, in this there is an equivalent view of the Divine and Sacred Masculine playing out through men. There is something of the play of the Sacred Marriage in the Mystical Path of Guadalupe, for in her is Father and Mother, Son and Daughter, God, the Supreme, and the All-In-All. As we shall see when we examine the little child angel or angelito associated with Guadalupe in images of her, children are very sacred to her, and there is a prophecy and teaching concerning the conception and raising of children who are older souls that might enter to help bring about the Sun of Flowering, the Age of the Holy Spirit. Again and again, the Mother's message is one of integration, transformation, and embodiment, the healing of the great division that has been made between our spiritual and material being in patriarchal culture and old age religion, restoring our wholeness through a pure spirituality of direct experience.

We may also say here that the sign of flowers and her Divine Image alludes to the opening of the interior stars, which have also been called "roses" in Christian mysticism, and to the awakening and uplifting of the Fire Snake, desire-energy, and the full generation of the body of light represented by her Image; hence, there is something akin to a "Kundalini Yoga" in the Mystical Path of Guadalupe, free of the sexual repression so common in most Eastern schools of the old age, or in religions of the West.

A Practice: A Sacred Flower Essence Bundle

It seems good to speak in more detail about creating the Sacred Flower Essence Bundle for the Ceremony of Passing the Bundle. Creating the bundle is a prayer ceremony itself, invoking the Mother Spirit and Powers, and praying for the people and the land, all the while offering up yourself, your energy and life to the Celestial Maiden. In dream and vision we have learned the way to create the sacred bundle, and we bring in the spiritual power of what we have been given in dream and vision when we make a bundle and enact the Ceremony of the Passing of the Bundle.

We may very well use a coarse material, like rough hemp, reflecting the sacred ayatl—cloak or cape—Juan Diego used, but in dream and vision, another way has been given for the sacred ceremony, a bundle made of cloth in the colors of Our Lady's robes: peach colored cloth enshrouding jade-green cloth, with three rainbow colored ribbons binding the bundle. If you contemplate this arrangement of colors, the color of the inner robe enshrouding the color of the outer robe, with three rainbow ties, there is a deep mystery in it about the energetic body and energetic dimension, the arising of the Glory Body and Emanation Body from the Body of Truth.

Now, any flowers may be used, but always among the flowers there are roses, "Spanish essence flowers," which are especially sacred to the Celestial Maiden. Along with these, there are also sacred herbs or medicinal plants included, usually from the land in which one lives, although at times a global selection of herbs can prove to be a powerful prayer remembering Earth Mother and your relations everywhere. Here, in the Americas, sage, cedar, sweet grass, lavender, tobacco, corn, copal, and such are sacred among indigenous peoples in our land, so some of these are often included in our sacred bundles.

Everything is collected in a sacred manner, with proper respect and offerings, and what is bought is also gathered in a sacred manner, purified and uplifted, rightly received. When everything is gathered, and it is time to make the sacred bundle, we do so in a ceremonial fashion, with invocations of the Spirit and Powers. Laying everything out, we perform a smudging ceremony, clearing the space, and we call upon the Mother and the Powers. We speak what we are doing, citing our intention, and as we put the bundle together, we pray for ourselves and for the people, praying for the blessings and grace of the Divine Mother to be poured out upon all our relations.

On the outside, bound in the ties, we also include some sacred feathers, and we might make fetishes to put in the ties binding the bundle. The type of feathers, color of beads and other things we use to create the fetishes all correspond to invocations of spiritual powers and prayers we are including in the bundle. When all contents inside the bundle are completely covered and lightly bound by the ties, the bundle is complete. We'll then pray that the Winds or Powers, and the angels and spirits, carry the blessings the Mother gives into all directions, into all realms, worlds, and universes, to all our relations. Then we abide in holy meditation, communing in the Divine Mother, chanting a sacred chant of the Mother and cleaving to her. We may also perform a Wedding Feast, and when all is said and done, we will smudge the sacred bundle.

Usually the sacred bundle is made within a day of the sacred ceremony. The most powerful time to make a sacred bundle is at dawn or sunset, corresponding to the east and west of the Sacred Circle, and to walking between worlds—day and night—the ordinary and the sacred. Once made, this bundle is sacred and holy, and must be dealt with as such, and when you carry the bundle, you will want to walk in a sacred manner, walking in beauty and holiness. The bundle is as your energetic being and life offered to the Holy Mother-Bride, upon which her blessings will come to rest, and it is a sacred talisman of your prayers and the weave of spiritual powers they invoke as blessings for the people. The making of the sacred bundle, of course, is a completely creative and inspired affair in craft and prayer. By nature, it is a sign of the path of enjoyment in the Mother and devotion to her, invoking her grace, remembrance of life abundant in the Great Mother, *Imma Gadol*.

Passing the Bundle

The Ceremony of Passing the Bundle is often performed when an aspirant asks a person of knowledge and power to perform it with them, but at times the Ceremony of Passing the Bundle is performed as the focus of a sacred ceremony in circle, in the continuum of the solar rites, usually at winter solstice in the Feast of the Mother and Child. The pattern of stars on the outer robe of the Celestial Maiden are even interpreted by some mystic Guadalupanos as those of the night sky at winter solstice over Mexico.

Essentially, in this sacred ceremony the person of knowledge and power, the seer and wonderworker, will invoke and embody the emanations of the Holy Mother-Bride and in union with the Sky-Dancing Maiden, as the Sky-Dancing Maiden, they will receive the sacred bundle from you, as from the spiritual warrior and shaman, Juan Diego. Thus, as you go to the sacred ceremony you hold the view of going to the Holy Mother-Bride to meet with her and bring her the sacred flower essences, seeking to give yourself to her and seeking her word of blessing and empowerment. When you pass the sacred bundle you open your heart and mind to the Divine presence and power of Our Lady moving with, in, and through the person of knowledge and power, the *tzaddik*, the righteous one. So also, as you pass the sacred bundle, you abide aware of your call by the Divine Mother, standing in your truth and standing in your power as a spiritual warrior, as a light-bearer, healer, and peacemaker, placing yourself into the service of the Holy Mother-Bride. It is a communion of divine and holy being with divine and holy being, all in the Virgin Mother, the Forever Whole and Perfect Maiden.

As we know in our experience, a true shaman is a walker between worlds, a person of spiritual knowledge and power, who is able to embody and channel various aspects of the Divine Presence and Power, the Divine Light and spiritual forces. In moments of Light Transmission, they become as the Spiritual Sun, an emanation of this Light-Presence and Light-Power, reflecting the Human One of Light that is within us. Seeking a blessing or spiritual empowerment, we approach them with this awareness, and corresponding to our awareness of the presence of divine and holy being is the blessing and empowerment we receive.

As an emanation of the Holy Mother-Bride, receiving the sacred bundle from us they will give a speaking inspired by the Mother Spirit in the power of the moment and they will bless the sacred bundle. In their speaking, we may receive guidance in our journey in this life or we may be given a sacred task to perform, and when they pass the sacred bundle back to us, they will pass the blessing and empowerment the Divine Mother has inspired. When we receive the sacred bundle returned to us with the Celestial Maiden's blessing, we receive it as from her, and we give praise and thanks to the Holy Mother-Bride, worshiping in her Divine presence and power, rejoicing in her grace and glory. We depart in the company of Mother God, the *Shekinah* of the Supreme, and she goes with us from that Heaven Earth Place.

Offering the Sacred Bundle

In order to fully receive and integrate any blessing or empowerment, or any knowledge and power we are given, we must share and give what we have received. It is in giving that we receive in full. Therefore, having received this blessing and empowerment we must go out and create Sacred Circle, the Mother's Circle, and we must invoke the Divine Mother and Powers, and make an offering of the contents of the sacred bundle, praying for the people and doing spiritual work for the people in service to the Holy Mother-Bride. This we do where and how we are inspired, following the impulse of the Mother Spirit, generating the sacred heart of love and compassion, the power of her Heart-Womb. Most essentially, it is for the *tikkune*, healing, of the peoples that we pray, and for the outpouring of the blessings and boons of Our Holy Mother upon all our relations. When we have done this, we take the cloth and cords forming the bundle home with us and we cut the cloth into strips, making prayer-ties from the cloth.

In another sacred ceremony we go to a sacred prayer tree. Such a tree is one that has died and crossed over, whose spirit has gone into the spirit world, but the physical form of which continues to stand erect in this world, in a place of positive energy in the land. If such a tree is consecrated as a sacred prayer tree, prayer ties or prayer flags are hung on it.

If no such tree is consecrated, a ceremony doing so is recommended. First, a smudging ceremony will be performed and a calling in of the Divine Powers, and the sacred tree will be baptized and anointed, usually with a generous quantity of blessed water and holy oil. Then the practitioner will begin to walk around the sacred tree sun wise, and they will do so while praying and chanting. They will pray that the sacred tree have a good spirit to take prayers in ascent to Sky Father. They will call down blessings upon the sacred tree, and ask the sacred tree to be a messenger of prayers and blessings for the people and the land. Once this is done, the practitioner will speak the essence of the Gospel, and will speak of the Pleroma of Light, above and below, and they will give a small discourse about prayer. Finally, with prayers, they will tie these strips of cloth and cords from their prayer bundle onto the sacred tree, letting the great winds carry the prayers and blessings out to the people and the land. This completes the Ceremony of Passing the Bundle, the spiritual empowerment on the Mystical Path of Guadalupe.

A Practice: Self-Empowerment Ceremony

If you know a person of knowledge and power, a *holy tzaddik* or shaman that you can visit and ask to enact the Ceremony of Passing the Bundle with you, that is good and is ideal. The exchange of sparks between two people gathered together in the Divine Mother and the Blessed Name of the Spiritual Sun is very sacred and powerful. Together they can bring in, hold, and anchor greater spiritual power for the people and the land, as is taught in the Scriptures.

Everyone, however, may not be able to visit a person of knowledge and power, but that does not preclude them from performing this sacred ceremony and receiving a blessing and empowerment from the Mother Spirit. A self-empowerment ceremony can be done.

First, a shrine or altar dedicated to Our Lady is built in your home. Taking up a continuum of self-purification and prayer, in the same way as for the traditional ceremony, you will make a sacred bundle. The Ceremony of Passing the Bundle is performed at the shrine or altar with prayer and meditation, setting the sacred bundle on the altar of the Mother, and praying for her blessing and empowerment. When you retrieve it from the altar, know that the Holy Mother-Bride has blessed and empowered you.

This self-empowerment ceremony is completed in the same way as the traditional Ceremony of Passing the Bundle. The self-empowerment ceremony is used when we do not know a person of knowledge and power to whom we might go to perform this sacred ceremony with them, or when life circumstances preclude our visiting them. Naturally, if and when we can visit a person of knowledge and power to perform this sacred ceremony with them, we will. If we know a person of knowledge and power but we cannot visit them, we may ask them to pray for us when we perform the self-empowerment, and likewise, if we have performed the self-empowerment, but later have an opportunity to visit, we will ask them to perform this sacred ceremony with us, seeking to further ground and embody something of this expression of Light Transmission.

Always in our spiritual work we seek to bring in, hold, and anchor the Light Transmission in our physical body and in the physical world, to the greatest possible extent. This is the intention for the play of empowerments and sacred ceremony in the tradition, the physical expression of the movement of spiritual power in the world. Actual ceremonies of empowerment are not just about our own spiritual empowerment, but they are manifestations of the Body of Vision and Divine light in the world for the people and the land, all our relations. We enact them for ourselves and for the people, and always for the glorification and honor of the Divine Mother in our generation.

The Giving of the Sign & Seal of Grace

When the Most High Holy Woman told him what he was to do he went straightaway, as before, to the bishop's palace. He carried the sacred bundle with the utmost care, walking in beauty and holiness along the way, and delighting in the rich fragrances of the flowers of Our Lady. When he arrived at the palace the servants of the bishop came out to see him. He requested an audience with the bishop, but the servants ignored him, and when he did not go away, with ill intention they tried to cast upon him the evil eye, but to no avail. They became curious about the bundle he was carrying. He had been waiting for a very long time so patiently, with his head down, holding the bundle with great care, and speaking only if and when spoken to; so they came close, trying to sneak a peek. He recognized that he could not hide completely what he had, or else they would take it from him by force, so he allowed them some glimpse, and they were completely dumbstruck by the sight and fragrance of flowers in the midst of the dead of winter.

The servants attempted to take the flowers away from him. Three times they tried and failed, because every time they tried to grasp them, the flowers they saw would transform into the Divine Image of Our Lady somehow imprinted upon the cloak.

The servants went to the bishop and reported what they saw, and the bishop realized that Juan Diego had brought the sign he had requested, and ordered that Juan Diego be brought to him right away.

When Juan Diego went in, he bowed down as before and recounted everything to the Right Reverend. He said to the bishop, "Sir, my lord, Speaker for Your People,

I have completed the sacred task you gave to me. I went to tell the special and holy person who is my patroness, the Celestial Maiden, Saint Mary, Precious Mother of Teotl-Dios, that you requested a sign, some kind of proof, in order to believe me about her call for the building of her Holy Temple on the Sacred Mount, the place where she asked you to build it. I told her I gave you my word that I would bring back a sign, a proof of her desire, the sacred task that you placed into my hands. She swiftly and happily honored your wish for a sign so her desire might be carried out.

"Today, in the dark womb of the morning, she told me to come and see you again. I requested a sign of her so you would believe. She acted immediately, honoring the request that you gave me.

"She sent me to the top of the Holy Hill where I had met with her before, and told me to pick the several kinds of Spanish flowers blooming up there. So I did. When I had done so, I brought them back to her and she received the bundle into her arms and took out the flowers, then she restored the bundle and passed it back to me, and told me to bring the bundle to you, and to open it only before you. Even though I realize that the top of the Hill at Tepeyacac is not a place for such flowers, and that it is all overgrown with what seems like weeds and other wild plants, my heart did not go from its place in her, I did not doubt. I ascended the Sacred Mount in complete faith and trust, and gathered in her precious treasure for you and for the people.

"When I arrived at the top of the Holy Hill, it was, indeed, the Place of Flowers, the Heaven Earth Place. There were several flowers of Spanish-essence glistening with celestial dew and I picked them in a sacred manner right away, giving the appropriate offering and respect. She asked me to give them to you from her to manifest her desire. I am doing it so that through them you can have the sign you wanted. Understand that my word and my mission are true. Here they are. Please, receive them!"

Juan Diego opened his white cloak, and, as the many lovely flowers fell to the floor, the precious representation of Our Lady, the Forever Whole and Perfect Maiden, appeared imprinted upon the cloth, just as it is to this very day at the place of her Sacred and Holy Temple at Tepeyacac. This is the Divine Image which has become known as Our Lady of Guadalupe.

The journey of Juan Diego from the Holy Hill to the bishop's palace is a journey from the Heaven Earth Place into the dominion of the demiurge and archons, and it is as though he is going from the Land of Light into the Shadow Land. He is a messenger, a prophet, from the Light Realm bearing the Divine Light into the world of shades and shadows. Profoundly, it is as a journey into the underworld, or into Hades and the abodes of hell, a journey that he makes three times, reflecting the three days of the Spiritual Sun, the Messiah, in the abodes of Hades, the grave.

Indeed, when we awaken and become aware of the energy dimension, the Light Realm within and all around us, the world as we have formerly known it is like a shadow land, and a realm of darkness and death. The way of the dominant culture, the unenlightened society, is like a living death or deep and fitful sleep. We can look and see that it is a dark and hostile realm, a realm of falsehood, a realm alien to the Land of Light. Here we are not speaking of nature as it is, or this good earth as it is, or humanity as it is in the Divine Mother. By the darkness, we mean the world of humankind built upon the illusion of separation, the ignorance devoid of the Holy Spirit, the world of the mental and vital being bound up in the ego's lusts, greed, violence and hatred. All of this is desire's dominion, to receive for self alone.

Truly, apart from the power of the Holy Spirit, the Mother Spirit, we cannot see, hear, feel, taste, smell, or know the world of the Divine Spirit. We are almost completely unaware of the world of the spirits and angels, or world of great cosmic powers and archangels, or the world of the Divine Emanations, the Land of Light. In such a state, blind, deaf, and dumb in the Spirit, it is as though we are among the living dead in a land of death, like a walking corpse or zombie. When we receive the Holy Spirit, however, reintegrating our energy being and material being, embodying our soul and spirit, and opening our interior senses, it is as though we are raised from among the dead to stand among the living ones, the immortals. We receive the life and light, the presence and power, of the Spiritual Sun. In this we may know and understand that the true resurrection is not simply in some future time, but is meant for this life. The reception of the Holy Spirit is the reception of the Divine Life, the soul being awakened and raised up from death to a vibrant life in the Divine Mother.

Of course, in the midst of this awakening and reintegration, we look and see the purpose of this place, this world, this life, and we know that the world is sacred as it is, that all life is sacred, for it is the womb of the Holy Mother giving birth to awakened souls, solar beings. When the Spiritual Sun arises in us, naturally the shades and shadows vanish. What is unreal, illusory, is revealed for what it is when we experience the revelation of the Real, the Divine Light and Truth.

Now we may say that in the process of awakening and reintegration, we must nourish and protect the Holy Child in us; like Juan Diego with the sacred flower bundle, we must be careful not to expose the holy child to dark and hostile forces until it is mature and viable. But when it is time, the Spiritual Sun will burst forth blazing if we live the spiritual life and attend to our spiritual essence. The indwelling Messiah will mature and emerge, insusceptible even to the greatest power of the ignorance, the demiurge.

Here you will note in the story that the Celestial Maiden instructs Juan Diego to show what is in the power bundle to no one else but the bishop. When he goes to the bishop's palace, he does not cast his gaze around and does not speak unless spoken to, and although allowing some indirect glimpse of the wonder he brings, he does not allow a direct gaze and does not allow the bundle to be taken. We may also notice that with the proper, mindful care, the power bundle that he carries protects itself, as shades and shadows—the bishop's servants—cannot grasp on to it so as to take it from him. This reflects the nourishing and protection of the Holy Child in us until it is mature and strong, until it becomes a Sun, a Holy Star. This mindfulness and protection is necessary in the way of working wonders, or magic, and in the way of dream.

As we know, dreams are very powerful. There is great manifesting power in them, and people of knowledge and power teach us that we should always interpret our dreams in a positive fashion, even when they seem to be something of an ill omen. Our interpretation of dreams is prophetic, and things manifest according to our interpretation of our dreams. Likewise, people of knowledge and power tell us that we should be very careful with whom we share our dreams, teaching us that we should only share them with true friends and those who are in the Spirit. Others could catch hold of the power of our dreams and speak a strange or negative interpretation, or in jealousy they might not wish our dreams to be fulfilled and might hold ill-intention, undermining the goodness and fulfillment of our dreams.

The same is true for our spiritual works or wonderworking, our prayers, meditations, and sacred ceremonies. In faith we abide confident in the success of our spiritual works, trusting in the Mother Spirit to accomplish the wonder and, like dreams, we are very careful to whom we speak of such things, tending to keep them private, secret, sealed from all influences that might taint, hinder, or obstruct the movement of spiritual power, the flow of Divine Grace.

When we are led by the Spirit and Winds to speak of our dreams and visions, or to speak of our spiritual works, then we will speak of them, but unless we are led to, we will remain silent. We are in a secret labor of invisible, spiritual assistance, and we only reveal our spiritual works when there is a clear and conscious reason to reveal them. This reflects the play of the conception and gestation of a child in a mother's womb; the child is birthed and revealed when it has come full term in due season. So also is the play of dreaming and wonderworking, the fruit of the labor of many in the Light Continuum, revealed in the time of the Mother.

The attempt of the servant-priests of the bishop to "cast the evil eye" on Juan Diego is an important teaching to us all. It is not so much about what others might do, as about what we do when we direct negativity at others, or fall into a negative energy exchange with others with ill-intention towards them. The "casting of the evil eye" is a psychic assault. Any time that we give way to negative thought and emotion towards another person, or we give way to ill-intention, which becomes negative speech about them or negative actions towards them, we are in a negative exchange of energy and it is, in effect, a psychic assault, the evil eye.

An essential practice in the Mystical Path of Guadalupe is paying attention to our energy and seeking to avoid enacting psychic assaults or entering into negative exchanges of energy. If we abide in the Mother, taking up the spiritual life and attending to our spiritual essence daily, we will not need to worry about anyone who might be engaging in a psychic assault against us because we will be immune to psychic assaults. Rather, our concern will be with our own energy and ensuring that we do not act from the violent inclination, or from a state of imbalance and ignorance. We are to walk as light-bearers, healers, and peacemakers. We are to walk in beauty and holiness, fully responsible in Christ for our own energy.

Now, there is great power, great light, in the bundle that Juan Diego carries to the bishop and, until he is with the bishop, it is in a state of flux. Only when the sacred flower bundle is opened before the bishop is the Divine Power in it fully manifest in spacetime, fully anchored in this world. This reflects the continuum kept in the wonderworking art when a blessing or empowerment is to be passed, or when there is a labor towards a moment of Light Transmission. While there is a continuum of prayer, meditation, and sacred ceremony, generating energy and holding a higher vibration, the spiritual power remains in flux until the instant of transmission. Only when the transmission happens is the Divine Light or Divine Blessing made manifest, fully anchored in this world. We may say it is only fully anchored, embodied, when the one who received what was imparted has integrated it, resulting in a greater capacity to share.

The fruition of this movement, the integration of this Light Transmission, of course, is the building and consecration of the Holy Temple at Tepeyacac, which becomes the dwelling place of the miraculous Divine Image of the Holy Mother. In this respect, the sacred bundle of flowers is like a light seed of a palace of light. In the creation of her Divine Image on the cloak, the Mother herself has fashioned an image of the sacred heart, the object of devotion in her Holy Temple, the true foundation of sacred space.

Here we may say that we are the true living temple of the Divine Mother and the Spiritual Sun, and when she calls to us and reveals herself, we enshrine her Divine Image in our hearts. Taking up the spiritual life and practice of her Mystical Path, we put on her Divine Image, walking in her beauty and holiness, wearing the Body of Vision. If we walk with the Mother in this way, wherever we go is her dwelling place, the Heaven Earth Place.

The Holy Temple of Our Lady of Guadalupe stands on Tepeyacac and the miraculous Divine Image she fashioned is enshrined there to this very day. It is a very sacred, holy, and powerful place of spiritual pilgrimage, and those who make the pilgrimage receive a special blessing and empowerment. Yet, by nature, although dwelling there in a special way, the Mother does not remain only in her temple on Tepeyacac, but she goes with her faithful children everywhere they go, dwelling in them and dwelling in their homes, and dwelling in her great temple, the great outdoors and the whole of this good earth, her Divine body.

The reception of the sacred flower bundle by the bishop completes the story of the revelation of Our Lady of Guadalupe, a seed implanted that does, indeed, flower, bloom, burst forth in flame, the passionate faith in Our Lady lighting off like a wildfire. One oral tradition teaches that there is a second secret meeting when Juan Diego returns to the Holy Mother to convey the success of his sacred mission, to worship in her presence and commune with her. In this meeting, it is said that many prophecies were spoken by the Holy Mother-Bride. It is likely Juan Diego met with her in private many more times and found repose in her sacred heart when he met his responsibility to death. Likewise, her revelation continues with all of us who are faithful to her, in the telling of her story, the sharing of teachings and practices drawn from her original revelation, in her appearances in our dreams and visions, and in our ongoing communion with her and worship of her. In truth, the story of her revelation has no end, for she is Mother God, the One-Without-End, the infinite and eternal; all creation is her Divine Revelation.

A Practice: Sanctuary of Her Lap

The Holy Mother-Bride continues to reveal herself to all who seek her sanctuary. When we contemplate Mother God, *Imma Elohim*, the image of this holy sanctuary becomes the Virgin

Mother with her Holy Child enthroned upon her lap, and so among devotees of the Holy Mother we often speak of the sanctuary of grace as "sitting in the Mother's lap." There is no better place to be! *Hallelu Imma!* Praise the Mother!

Consider this: If I am sitting on the lap of the Virgin of Light as a child of light in repose in her light and love, where is there any *klippah* or barrier? In the very instant I am sitting in her lap, communing with my Mother, there is no more darkness, only her and her child, one Light-Presence and Light-Power. I am hers and she is mine, and in holy communion we are inseparable from one another, the same in essence and nature, and in substance, Light Upon Light. In this instant of union I am her and she is me. I am her Living Presence and Power, and she moves with, in, and through me and becomes manifest as me. There is nothing but *Imma El*, the Gracious Mother, the Compassionate Mother, the Loving Mother, her good grace and glory manifesting as all.

In her wisdom, in her understanding, all is self-liberated as it arises, and so the Holy Child of the Woman of Light is taken up in divine rapture at the very instant of birth, all according to the will and desire of the Supreme. And here we may say that in this perfect repose of the great natural perfection, there is nothing to be liberated, and therefore there is liberation! Of course, sitting in Mother's lap is a method of primordial meditation and primordial contemplation. No method, just being, aware of Mother Wisdom, the Virgin of Clear Light. I'm sitting in her lap, abiding in the bornless nature of being. In this we experience the sinless nature of the Messiah, and we know the true nature of redemption in the grace of the Risen Christ.

In Christ, in the Virgin Mother, all is redeemed, all will be redeemed, for all was redeemed from the very beginning. All sin and death are illusory, never having substantially self-existed. In form, or in formlessness, the truth of bornless being is the same, and recognizing this, we abide in the Heaven-Earth Place, the Mother's lap. We walk in heaven upon the earth, and we transcend the heavens when we pass into cessation, reintegrating with the Clear Light Continuum at the fruition of life. This is called the Way of Perfection.

In the meantime, until we recognize and realize our Innate Perfection in the Risen Christ, in the Virgin Mother, according to the wisdom of perfection, we take up the play of the Way of Transformation. As for the arising of any self-negativity or insecurity, who is there to be negative or insecure? Where is there any real shadow in the Holy Mother? In everything, with everything, and through everything, the Light of the Virgin, the Light of the Messiah, is being revealed where God, the True Light, is concealed! We bring all into the Holy Light and recognize the Holy Light in all, and drawing out that Holy Spark from within the husk of apparent darkness, darkness is dispelled; ignorance is brought to an end, and peace and joy are restored, the peace and joy of the Risen Messiah.

All is the Holy Mother-Bride, and we receive all as the Holy Mother-Bride. Even trial and tribulation, temptation, and darkness, are her sacred dance, and we dance with her in complete self-abandoned ecstasy, letting Divine Passion, Divine Grace, carry us wherever she wills, wherever she desires, knowing all in the Holy Mother-Bride. There is only the Holy Mother-Bride, no other, asking us, "Are you not in the fold of my garment?"

Sacred Play in the Mother

When the Celestial Maiden gave a sign for Juan Diego to take to the bishop, she fashioned an image of herself upon the sacred ayatl, the Sacred Cape. Created in a mystery, as all creation is created in a great and holy mystery, the sacred flowers in the bundle left an imprint of her Divine Image on the cloth of Juan Diego's cape, and this is the Divine Image enshrined to this day in her Holy Temple at Tepeyacac. As you might imagine, her Divine Image becomes a source of deep contemplation in the Mystical Path of Guadalupe, as well as an object of devotion and vehicle of Light Transmission.

The choice of cloth as the medium of the image reflects the Weaving Mother, she who weaves the fabric or tapestry of creation, and symbolizes the Great Matrix of All. As weaving among indigenous peoples has traditionally been a sacred art of women, this choice also symbolizes the sacredness of womanhood, the physical origin and foundation of life and society. The cloth the Divine Mother uses, of course, is Juan Diego's ayatl, his cloak or cape. This is the outer garment that protects from the elements, and during prayer and sacred ceremony with a shaman it can become like the mantle of the prophets or like a prayer shawl. Thus, it represents the Mother's protective presence and devotion, and it may represent a talisman of transmission of something of her Divine Presence and Power. As a personal item of the vision bringer, Juan Diego, it represents the Mother's deep love for him and blessing upon him, and her love for all her devotees and her blessing resting upon them all.

This cloth, of course, is very fragile and impermanent, as is life, and it suggests the preciousness of life, reminding us of how delicate life is. It reminds us of the impermanence of life and its passing, dream-like quality. It also sets the stage for a further display of the miraculous. That the image has endured and remained vibrant is nothing short of an ongoing miracle, a cause of holy awe. The imprint itself, a finely detailed representation on coarse material, is also miraculous. It is meant to invoke wonder, a sense of the mystery. With faith, the ayatl to this day generates hope and love.

Indeed, the Mother preserves her Divine Image, and so she preserves and sustains our life. In life's natural fruition we go to her, returning to her heart-womb from which we have come, the Land of Light, which is her Body of Glory, and her Divine Silence, her No-Thingness, which is her Body of Truth. In effect, in that the Divine Mother fashions this Holy Image, it is her Body of Emanation extended beyond the time of her initial revelation, a material and energetic emanation of her Divine Presence and Power.

If this image is viewed from several hundred feet away it has a startling appearance, like an image of the vagina, the gate of life. This points our attention to the sacredness and holiness of our origin, and to the sacredness and holiness of womanhood, the play of desire, love, and sex. Unlike what we find in patriarchal religions, womanhood and the dynamism of desire, sex and the sensual, the body and the earth, is not cut off or minimized. All life is exalted and we are encouraged to recognize the innate goodness of all life and of all aspects of ourselves, spiritual and material. The vaginal appearance of the image on the sacred ayatl directly implies the dynamism of the Divine and Sacred Feminine joined as co-equal with the Divine and Sacred Masculine.

The great and unimaginable creative force of woman is implied by this image, as is the truly miraculous power of procreation that exists between women and men, the power through which humankind continues from one generation to another and is able to evolve and fulfill its destiny. In terms of a Supernal Realization and the generation of more refined bodies, or even a new species of being that might embody a greater influx of the Supernal Energy-Intelligence, it is through women that this will occur, much like the prophecy of the Woman of Light in Revelation, who gives birth to a very different kind of humanity in her Holy Child who is taken up in divine rapture. In this regard, if we are to speak of the Second Coming, the Age of the Holy Spirit or Sixth Sun, it will come into being through the embodiment of the Divine and Sacred Feminine, the true reception of womanhood as the Holy Mother-Bride.

Now we know that there is an angel or child beneath Guadalupe in her Divine Image, and this reflects the birth of a more refined humanity or new species emerging from the present humankind. It is the labor of the Divine Mother as Nature and the Good Earth to strive towards the generation of higher, more refined and intelligent forms of life. It is an evolution towards an ever greater actualization of knowledge and power, an evolution towards the embodiment of the Highest of Life, Divine and Supernal Being.

In this angel or child there is also a prophecy of the incarnation of souls from among the elder races, "older souls" if you will, who come with a greater energetic being and intelligence, and innate spiritual knowledge and power from their evolution and illumination in former lives. According to those who know the tradition, these messengers of the Divine Mother and Comity of Stars have already begun being born among us. They will continue to be born among us to help us pass through this Dark Age and to help usher in the true New Age, the Age of the Holy Spirit.

Always there has been the incarnation of souls from among the elder races or star people, as well as the incarnation of powerful spirit beings, but at certain times in the evolution of humankind on earth there is a greater influx of these souls of power and knowledge. According to the prophecy, one of the greatest influxes of these enlightened souls will transpire at a critical point in this Dark Age. It is a form of radical divine assistance to help see us through our great evolutionary crisis. This influx has already begun, but the greater influx has yet to transpire, though perhaps that time is drawing near.

This speaks to practices on the Mystical Path of Guadalupe that seek to draw souls from among the elder races into incarnation, practices of a sexual mysticism akin to those found in the Holy Kabbalah, the mysteries of the *arayot*. It speaks to the raising and education of children in families that take up the spiritual life and practice, children being taught the sacred ways from early on in life and being raised to be authentic human beings, having love and compassion for all their relations, and an understanding of their duty and responsibility as human beings.

We will speak about these practices when we take up our sacred discourse about the mysteries of the "Pollen Path" later, but here we can say that when a woman and a man wish to conceive a child and wish to draw in a soul from among the elder races, they will purify themselves and take up a continuum of prayer, meditation and sacred ceremony, invoking the Divine Mother, and calling upon the Great Spirit and Powers to help them. When they take up their love-play they will consecrate it and offer it up as worship to the Divine Mother, the *Shekinah* of the Supreme. When they engage their love-play they will inwardly identify themselves with the Divine Feminine and Divine Masculine, and they will embrace one another as the physical embodiment of the Beloved in space-time. In this way they will generate a radiant energetic field or matrix with a very high vibration that may attract a soul from among the elder races.

Even apart from the various spiritual practices that might be incorporated by a couple, if and when love-play is offered up as worship of the Great Mother, *Imma Gadol*, and the couple holds the conscious intention of conception and drawing in a luminous soul as their child, they may very well attract a soul from among the elder races or star people through the Divine Grace of the Mother. Such is the way with the Holy Mother-Bride, even in the simplest forms of worship the grace of the Mother's Force enters into play and wonders transpire!

Now, the angel or child also has another meaning, representing the world of spirits and angels in which a seer and wonderworker, or a shaman, labors for the people. This speaks of the field of magical workings with spirits and angels as an integral part of the worship of the Divine Mother, an active labor of invisible spiritual assistance seeking to bless and heal people, tending to their spiritual and material welfare. The angel also suggests the need for us to seek to bless and uplift the world of spirits and angels, and to know and understand the interpenetration of the spirit world and material world. We need to learn to remember and pay attention to our dreams, and yet more, to awaken in our dreams as conscious agents of the Holy Mother-Bride.

Here we may note that in patriarchal religions, although we are taught to venerate those who had Spirit Power in the past in the form of dreams and visions, mystical experiences, and wonders or miracles, the practice of mysticism and wonderworking has become forbidden to us, and we are relegated to idle forms of prayer and ritual in which there is little or no real spiritual power. When the Divine and Sacred Feminine is denied, rejected, and cut off, the mysticism and miracles of spirituality are also cut off. When the Divine and Sacred Feminine is restored and is included in our spiritual life, however, the mystical and magical dimensions of spirituality are restored. With direct spiritual and mystical experience, true spiritual power is restored not only to our spiritual leaders, but to all of us. The Divine Mother comes to restore the mystical and magical elements of spirituality, and so her worship is mystical and magical, truly wonderful.

When we perform the wonderworking art to bless and help the people, playing as a Holy Child in the lap of the Divine Mother, it is in devotion to her and worship of her. To the extent that we embody and channel her Divine Presence and Power in this play, she worships herself and glorifies herself as she works wonders with, in, and through us, and it is all delightful, wonderful!

The Mother-Bride imprinted on the sacred ayatl is her standing upon a crescent moon. At times this moon may be represented by the horns of a bull. This is full of multi-layered meanings. First, it is the new moon, and implies that the new moon is especially sacred to Our Lady. Her outer robe is the starry night sky, and on the new moon the stars are most visible, most radiant and glorious. The new moon is also a very magically effective time, a time when we may set wonderworking into motion, the movement of spiritual forces coming to fruition on the full moon, riding upon the astral tide. Devotion and the play of wonderworking following the cycles of the moon is a central way to worship the Celestial Maiden. This also speaks to the very powerful movements of spiritual forces through women in the natural cycle of their bodies, and to special spiritual works that women can perform following the path of their internal moon cycle, or menstrual cycle. Far from the stigmas of "impurity" or "uncleanness" and "weakness" that patriarchal religion projects upon the time of menstruation, a woman's moon time holds particularly powerful opportunities for acquiring knowledge and working with the spirits. Spiritual practices surrounding a woman's moon cycle are an integral part of the Mystical Path of Guadalupe.

Now, the crescent moon suggesting the horns of a bull is significant. It represents the Divine Feminine and Divine Masculine joined together, something of the mystery of the Sacred Marriage, but it also points to the direction north, the Kerub with the Face of an Ox, and to Archangel Uriel, the "Light of God." This alludes to the principle of manifestion and embodiment, the Earth element, and it points to the knowledge of the interplay of star gates and earth gates, and to the generation of a Second Coming that consciously interacts with the Comity of Stars.

North is the direction of the new moon and winter solstice, times sacred to Our Lady of Guadalupe, and it corresponds to the Midnight Sun, the Divine Light hidden in every particle of matter. In the Supernal Realization that she represents and ushers in, this Hidden Light is revealed and released. This is the esoteric meaning of the Woman of Light's holy child that St. John beholds taken up in divine rapture (Revelation 12:5). This great and holy mystery is connected with Archangel Uriel, who is especially associated with the revelation of Guadalupe, appearing in the midst of the Dark Age as the herald of an Age of Divine Illumination fully embodied. We know that Guadalupe corresponds with an emanation of the Woman of Light, but in her association with the new moon and winter, she also corresponds with the Dark Mother and Bride, an emanation of the Black Madonna, as reflected in her emphasis upon healing so well-known with the Black Madonna.

All of this hints at a fierce edge within Our Lady of Guadalupe. She is, indeed, sweet and bright to those who love her, but she also has a very fierce and protective side; she is the Great Mother and Holy Bride, bright and dark, the fullness of the Divine and Sacred Feminine.

The robes of Our Lady are radiant with Solar Light, like the Body of the Woman of Light, but rather than wearing a crown of twelve stars, the outer robe of Guadalupe is the whole starry night sky. Specifically, her outer robe is the starry night sky of the new moon and winter solstice, and it is deep space, infinite spaciousness, encompassing all realms and worlds, throughout all dimensions of space-time or the universe. Like the Woman of Light, Guadalupe stands upon the moon, but the Woman of Light corresponds with the full moon, while Guadalupe corresponds with the new moon. The Woman of Light corresponds with summer solstice and is Mother Day-Sky. The Celestial Maiden corresponds with winter solstice and is Mother Night-Sky. Yet we know and understand they are inseparable from one another, both being emanations of the Great Mother, *Imma Gadol*.

The inner robe of Our Lady may be understood to represent the Land of Light, Pleroma of Light, within and behind the Comity of Stars. In this robe, if one looks closely at the image on the sacred ayatl, there are many sacred symbols forming the patterns in it. We can point out a couple of the symbols that are most significant.

First, on one of her sleeves there is a spider's web. This alludes to her emanation as Spider Woman and Weaving Woman, but it also speaks to cultivating our capacity to listen, to be open and sensitive, and to feel deeply, an awareness of energy and vibration as we see with spider people and their weaving of amazing webs. It may also speak to the creation and use of spirit-catchers and dreamcatchers, magical talismans resembling spiders' webs that trap or catch harmful spirits and bad dreams. A practice of making dreamcatchers is also very common in dream practices on the Mystical Path of Guadalupe.

In the folds of her garment down by the crescent moon there is also the image of a serpent with a human tongue. This alludes to her emanation as Serpent Woman, but also to the mastery of the serpent power or desire energy at the heart of the Mystical Path of Guadalupe, a subject elaborated in Chapter 5.

In the collar of her inner robe, near her throat, there is the symbol of an egg or circle with a cross in it. This alludes to the gnosis of the Spiritual Sun or Solar Being—*Logos*—and it alludes to the creation of Sacred Circles and to the calling in of the Powers in the worship of the Divine Mother. It also indicates our labor to extend the Light of the Cross—Sacred Tau—into all realms, worlds and universes of the Entirety.

As an egg-shape with a cross in it, this also holds other meanings. This is the shape of the energetic body. The cross within this energy body implies the radiant holy breaths and the power of the Spiritual Sun, the Messiah, whose actualization and realization of Solar Being in the Mother restores the self-generating capacity of the energetic body. This figure also implies the restoration of a secret oral tradition, both within the Toltec and Christian streams, a tradition of True Gnosis and Light Transmission. There are many other symbols in her robes and many other teachings about them, but these few, perhaps, indicate something of the great wisdom and power contained in this Divine Image.

Now, when we look at the position of her body, her hands are held in a gesture of prayer. She is praying for the people and blessing the people, and this is our spiritual labor in her, to effectively pray for the people and bless the people, all our relations. Her hands and arms held in this position also cover her breasts, reminding us of the great nourishing and life-sustaining power of the Divine Mother and womanhood, a power to be adored and revered in our worship of the Mother.

As she holds her hands in this position, her torso and head are turned slightly to the right. Her gaze is directed downward. This is a position of one of the energetic meditation practices taught in the Mystical Path of Guadalupe, and at the same time it represents the Holy Mother-Bride watching over all her children and listening to their prayers.

In a manner of speaking, just as she is the object of our meditation, we are the objects of her meditation. When the silence in us touches the Great Silence that she is, she speaks in us and blesses us, and we know her most intimately, experiencing Union with the Holy Mother-Bride.

This reflects the vast range of spiritual practices in the Mystical Path of Guadalupe, from very active forms of prayer and sacred ceremony, song, and dance, and sacred sexuality, to very deep contemplation and meditation: a full spectrum of the spiritual life that weaves the sacred and mundane together in a seamless way. We worship her in movement and in repose, and in all things and in all activities of life.

This discourse reflects an initial contemplation of the Divine Image of Our Lady of Guadalupe, and along with the contemplation of the story of her revelation to Juan Diego, the contemplation of her Divine Image is a common practice in her Mystical Path. Needless to say, this contemplation of Our Lady spans our whole life, for it is a journey into the endless depths of the Great Mother, the gnosis of Mother God and the Spiritual Sun, her Holy Child.

As has been said previously, it is good to build a shrine to Our Lady in our homes and to have an image of her as an object of contemplation and meditation, a focal point of her Divine Presence and Power. As you gaze upon her Divine Image, she will speak to you and teach you of her mysteries, and she will reveal to you that you are her Holy Child, a Solar Being, an emanation of the Human One of Light, that you too are in the folds of her garments and in her heart-womb, just as Juan Diego and all your relations are. *Hallelu Imma Gadol!* Praise the Great Mother!

Tending the Holy Shrine of the Divine Mother

If you have built a shrine to Our Lady of Guadalupe and set an image of her upon the altar, tending the altar and placing offerings upon it is a good way to worship the Holy Mother-Bride.

In representations of Guadalupe it is not uncommon to find various symbols emphasized from one version to another, like the example cited above of the oval and cross near her throat on her inner robe. This symbol is very rich with meaning, as previously mentioned. Certainly there is the suggestion of the Mother speaking the Living Word, the *Logos*, the Christ, the power of the Spiritual Sun, but this symbol also represents the Powers of the Sacred Circle invoked in her worship. Likewise, it is something more. The oval or egg-shape is quite like the appearance of the outer dimension of our energy body. The cross suggests the union of heaven and earth, energy and matter in us: the reintegration of our energetic and material being, an integral state of being in the Holy Mother-Bride. So placing emphasis upon this symbol at her throat can have great significance. The addition of a crown in some images of her isn't surprising. After all, she is called a queen, princess, and noblewoman in stories of her revelation. She is crowned for her nobility.

Now, the original image and the story of the revelation is her message to us, like her "Gospel" or "testament," so the original image holds a special place, the foundation of the tradition for us all. Yet, in the Divine Mother, it's not about literalism and the development of dogmatic creeds and doctrines that come with literalism. Rather, it is about our individual perceptions and experiences of her, our own direct spiritual and mystical experience of the Celestial Noblewoman.

By nature, there must be many images and many stories of the Divine Mother, many perceptions, and all of them are equally valid and real to the perceiver because it is their experience. This is the very nature of the Holy Mother-Bride, the Great Matrix; she shape-shifts and assumes all manner of forms, all manner of various emanations, all of which are her Divine Presence and Power.

One image isn't "right" and another "wrong," not even the original image versus all the others that have been inspired over the centuries. Each bears something of the truth of Our Lady, a true perception and experience of her reflected and expressed in the creation of the image. This reflects an understanding of reality among indigenous peoples and devotees of the Divine Mother that is very different from the way of the dominant culture. We may give some examples of this.

Let's say that there is a sacred dance and sacred ceremony, and let's say that eagles were seen to come and circle above. One person sees two eagles and another sees three eagles, and afterward both share their experience. Among indigenous peoples and devotees of the Divine Mother there would be no argument as to who was "right," and there would be no contradiction between the two perceptions. That's what each person saw and that would be accepted as the truth of their experience.

In a similar way, if there were a person who did not see the eagles, for them the eagles were not present. Naturally, though, that does not mean eagles weren't there in the experience of others, and they would not dismiss the experience of others. In fact, when they hear that eagles were present, then in hearing this and accepting the witness of their friends, they also experience something of the sacredness and spiritual power of eagles showing up, although their experience of what they noticed was different.

Here we may say that in our example, among indigenous people and devotees of the Divine Mother, a lot of personal meaning would not be projected into the eagles showing up. It would be viewed as an integral part of what happened at the sacred event, free from the silliness of thinking "eagles showed up for us" or "eagles showed up for me." Eagles just showed up like all of the rest of the people who came to the sacred dance and ceremony, and their energy or power became part of the sacred event.

Our experiences with the Holy Mother-Bride are much like this. They are our experience of her and they are an integral part of what has transpired in our journey; our own perceptions and experiences of her are how we know and understand her. From one to another, these perceptions are not more or less true.

If and when it is possible, naturally we would like to find an image that resonates with our perceptions and experiences of the Holy Mother-Bride, one that might touch us in a special way, inspiring greater devotion. This is really our method for selecting an image of the Celestial Maiden.

Extending her image on her altar are symbols of the five elements. Perhaps there are other sacred objects representing various attributes of the Divine Mother, as well as perpetual prayers offered up to her through these symbols.

Along with these sacred items there are offerings, the most common being candles, incense and flowers. Many different kinds of incense can be used, but copal and rose are especially sacred to her, and all sweet flower essences express something of her Holy Delight. Other offerings may be of many forms: various foods, especially fruits and sweets, sacred feathers and stones, sacred herbs, anything that seems good as an offering or symbol of a prayer to her.

Tending her altar is an activity of worship, and in tending to her altar you attend to your spiritual essence. Making offerings of light, incense and flowers, praying to her, communing with her and gazing with love upon her image, are even greater worship.

When you have offered up your praise, thanks, and your prayers, rest your mind on her Divine Image, as in the practice of Primordial Meditation with an Object. In this method, one just places the mind on the image and leaves it there, letting consciousness progressively merge with the image. Listen to her speaking silence, or *Hashmal*, in your heart. This is a delightful meditation of communion with the Holy Mother-Bride.

In a similar way, you can also envision and gaze upon her Glory Body, resting your mind upon the envisioned Divine Image, just as upon the image of her on the altar which is as her Emanation Body. This can be an even greater delight, especially in the fruition of Union when you merge your mind, heart and light-body with her Glory Body. Detailed practices of this intention—Union with Our Lady—will be described later on.

If you wish to gaze upon her on the subtlest level, her Truth Body, then rest your mind in its own intrinsic nature, and let that No-Thingness you are rest in the No-Thingness she is. This is the most intimate communion with the Holy Mother-Bride.

There are many ways to worship the Celestial Maiden. Gazing upon her Divine Image, sitting before her shrine, and visiting with her, are all forms of meditation and worship of her. There is the way of jubilation, worshiping before her shrine with music, song, and dance. There is worship through the generation of the Sacred Circle, calling in the Divine Powers, and performing spiritual work for the people. There is also the way of offering up love-play to her, a joyful celebration of life abundant in the Holy Mother-Bride, her joy being your joy, and your joy being the worship of her. Our worship of the Sky-Dancing Maiden is both in repose and movement, and it is a creative affair, creativity itself being worship of Mother God.

Magical Worship of the Divine Mother

The offering of flowers, candles and incense are the most common form of prayer to Our Lady of Guadalupe. We offer flowers because of their beauty, and because they are the sign of her presence and power. Flowers symbolize our aspiration to facilitate the coming of the Age of the Holy Spirit or Sun of Flowering. We offer candles because of their light and in remembrance of the light of the Spiritual Sun shining from the Mother and the stars shining in her robes. The sweet fragrance of incense reminds us of the Mother's sweetness. Incense also speaks of the transformation of matter into pure spirit, the ascent of spirit as in the rising smoke.

When these things are offered up, imbued with the energy of our prayers by conscious intention, passionate emotion, vital energy, and the sound-vibration of our voice, they are talismans of our prayers received by her. As long as they endure on her altar or in her shrine, they continue to speak our prayers before the Divine Mother.

It is good to offer flowers, lights and incense daily upon her altar and to tend to your spiritual essence and a continuum of prayer and meditation in her presence. Any and all flowers are sacred to her, though roses, "Spanish-essence flowers," are especially sacred to Our Lady of Guadalupe. Likewise all sweet smelling incense is sacred to her, various fragrances of resins and flowers, though, as mentioned before, copal and rose are especially sacred. In our lineage, spikenard, frankincense, and myrrh are also offered because they correspond to the Holy Bride of Christ. In the Mystical Path of Guadalupe, the offering of candles becomes something of a wonderworking or magical art. There is an entire art of what may be called "candle magic." In the simplest form of this art a candle is held and caressed, and imbued with our energy as we pray. Then it is set upon her altar or in her shrine and it is lit and offered to her as our prayer. As we pray we consciously focus our vital energy into the candle, and lighting it, we offer our prayer to the Holy Mother-Bride.

When there is a need for greater energy we will purify and consecrate the candle through sacred ceremony. We may perform a smudging ceremony to purify and consecrate the candle, as is the way of indigenous peoples in our land, or we may baptize the candle with holy water drawn from living waters and anoint the candle with holy oil. Once purified and consecrated in this way, we will put our energy of prayer into it, light it, and offer it on the altar of the Celestial Maiden.

The anointing of a candle invoking a wonder by the grace of the Sky-Dancing Maiden can be taken further by selecting a fragrance of oil that corresponds with the intention of our prayer. Along a similar line, this play of candle magic can be drawn out by selecting candles dedicated to certain kinds of prayers, such as the Mexican seven-day candles that can be found in ethnic foods sections of most grocery stores, or by choosing candles of colors that correspond to our theurgic intention in prayer. In our tradition we use the correspondences of the *Sefirot* of the Tree of Life taught in the Holy Kabbalah.

As an example, if we are praying for strength, courage, power or protection and such, a red candle might be chosen. If we are praying for spiritual blessings a blue candle might be selected. When we are praying for money or love for a person, a green candle can be used. If we are praying about study and knowledge, or about travel and magic power, or refinement of desire, an orange candle might be chosen. When we are praying for purification and healing, we might choose a white or yellow candle, and so on. Of course, the attributes of colors can be many and diverse. For example, pink is associated with the Mother's love, her heart womb, and with healing, the union of white masculine and red feminine energy, reintegration, restoration of hope, and many other attributes including the Supernal Light of *Tiferet*, the Spiritual Sun in *Atzilut*. So the list could go on and on.

Coupled with a sacred ceremony of purification and consecration, we can also use a sacred rattle or drum, and use song or chant to put the energy of our prayers into a candle. Likewise we can call upon the Spirit and Powers of Sacred Circle, or we can invoke corresponding Divine Names, archangels, angels, and spirits, as we put our energy of prayer into the candle. In the Mystical Path of Guadalupe, quite naturally we often call upon her various emanations, those named and those not named in the story of her revelation, invoking her power in the form we need for the spiritual work that we are doing.

We may also use sacred feathers or a sacred staff while we are putting our prayer energy into a candle, holding the candle with one hand and the sacred tool in the other, letting gestures and movements be coupled with the sound-vibration of voice, invoking spiritual powers to fulfill the needs for which we are praying.

When further power is needed, we may place flowers or various sacred objects around the candle when we offer it, or we may make fetishes that we set by it and offer up with it, using things that correspond to the prayers. In some cases, we might write a person's name or include their picture by the candle, or we might engage in some sacred art and make some symbol or design corresponding with the prayer. It often becomes a very creative process, understanding that the more energy we put into the process, the greater the power of the prayer. The greater the need, the more difficult the circumstance, or the more radical the wonder, the more merit or energy we will seek to generate as we take up spiritual works for people, all as the Mother Spirit inspires us.

When even greater power is needed, we may create a flower bundle or power bundle to offer up with lights, placing various flowers, sacred herbs, and other sacred objects in it as a prayer for someone. Praying and offering up a candle, we might also make a power bag or medicine bag that is offered up with the candle. In either case, after being offered on the altar of the Holy Mother-Bride with a candle, what we have made will be given to the person in need, passing spiritual power to them by way of a talisman. Sacred stones, shells, feathers, and such offered with a prayer candle, can also be given to people as wonderworking talismans when we pray and do spiritual work for them, passing the spiritual power to them.

When we have prayed and performed spiritual work for a person, and we have consecrated some talisman, we will listen to the Mother Spirit and Powers. According to the inspiration we receive, we will give instructions to the person about what to do with the talisman to bring about the answer to prayers or the wonder that they are seeking.

On occasions when great power is needed, once we have offered up a candle or candles for someone, we may go out on a walk of power. Going into the great outdoors we may create a Sacred Circle, invoke the Spirit and Powers, make offerings, and perform sacred ceremony and pray further for the person and their need, invoking the full force of the Continuum to help them.

An altar or shrine dedicated to the Holy Mother-Bride is a Heaven Earth Place, a place of flowering. It is a place of spiritual alchemy, wonderworking, and magic. Our worship of the Divine Mother is magical, invoking the flow of her abundant blessings and boons for the people, the fulfillment of their desires and dreams, all in the Celestial Maiden.

The greater wonderworking or magical power is not in an isolate prayer or ritual, but rather it is in the daily continuum of worship, prayer, meditation, and sacred ceremony we keep. The more we pray, meditate, and perform sacred ceremony, and take up spiritual works for the people, the greater the power in any single prayer or ceremony, for the force of the Continuum kept flows through all our prayers and ceremonies. They are made powerful and effective in this way, all through the grace of the Divine Mother, the *Shekinah* of the Supreme.

Of course, it is not we who heal and perform the wonders, but it is the Holy Mother-Bride who accomplishes everything—Mother God and her Powers. We merely cooperate with her and we serve as conscious agents and co-creators with her, becoming channels or vehicles of her Divine Presence and Power, invoking, holding and grounding spiritual power for the people, all our relations. We labor for the people with, in, and through Mother God, as midwives in her giving birth, as messengers of her word, and as bearers of her blessings and boons. So she moves with, in, and through us as we become open and sensitive to her as we cleave to her in an active and dynamic surrender, actively attending to our spiritual essence every day and actively engaging in spiritual works for the people.

This is the way we worship the Great Mother, *Imma Gadol*. Here we may say, this way of worship is known and understood by little children. It is known and understood by our true and natural being, our being as we are in the Divine Mother.

Spirit Catchers

In the Mystical Path of Guadalupe all sacred objects are consecrated by way of prayers and invocations of the Holy Mother-Bride. In this case, making or acquiring a dreamcatcher to be consecrated as a spirit catcher, we would invoke Our Lady in the form of Spider Woman, calling upon her power to bind and banish displaced energies. If we are performing spiritual work for a person who is experiencing the displaced energy of hungry ghosts, we might also call upon her in the form of Underworld Woman, invoking her power to draw the spirit of the dead to its proper abode.

Now, it is fine to buy a dreamcatcher that is already made if we are not inclined to make one ourself, but we must add our energy to it, and as part of the consecration we will add things to it, including some fetish. What we add to it will depend upon the kind of hostile spirits we are seeking to bind, and it is something of an intuitive and creative art, but in whatever way we alter the spirit catcher, as we do so we will weave energy and prayers into it, speaking our intention to the Mother God as we do. If we know the way to do so, we might even enter into union with Spider Woman, channeling her presence and power, and, weaving energy into the spirit catcher as she weaves it, we may become Spider.

Usually some sacred stone or crystal will be added, along with something of some angel or angels of Earth Mother that correspond with the spiritual work that we are doing. As an example, we might use a black stone like obsidian, which tends to absorb negative energy, having a natural purifying affect. Perhaps we might use feathers of one of the fly-catching birds, or we might add the owl feathers for sight into the hidden dimensions, or a raven feather for the trickster quality. Who knows? In any case, we will build up the magical power of the spirit catcher, weaving prayers and invocations into it as we do.

Once it is finished, we will purify and consecrate it in the Shrine of the Holy Mother-Bride in the way typical in our tradition: It will be smudged and then purified with holy water, and anointed with an appropriate oil of consecration. We will make offerings to the Holy Mother-Bride in the form of Spider Woman, praying for her power to be in the spirit catcher. Our prayers will include prayers of enchantment and illusion to draw the spirits into the trap. When this is so, we will offer prayers to bind them within the trap, or to make it a door into their proper realm so that entering it, they are banished and bound back into their abodes.

We may also go out and create a Sacred Circle to consecrate a spirit catcher, or we might go to Grandfather Fire, if there is a need for greater power. Spirit catchers are best consecrated during the latter part of a waning moon, around the time of sunset. Often, when we pray like this we will use a sacred rattle or drum, generating energy with our prayers, and we may also use a sacred feather or some other appropriate sacred object. We may use gestures with our hands to direct energy into the spirit catcher, praying and invoking being a creative affair.

Once consecrated, we will then lay the trap, hanging it in the place the problem occurs, or instruct the person for whom we have made it to do so. Then, each day near sunset we will pray for the spirit or spirits to be ensnared, trapped by the spirit catcher.

When we know that the spirit or spirits have been caught in the trap, we will remove it and tie it up in some cloth of an appropriate color. Then we will either bury it in Earth Mother, or we will burn it in Grandfather Fire. If we bury it, we will choose a desolate place, one where it should not be found by anyone.

It needs to be said, however, that entering into engagements with dark and hostile spirits, or negative displaced entities or energies, requires strong faith and a significant development of one's interior life, especially if one starts doing such things for individuals other than oneself. The arts of exorcism in any of their forms are intended only for experienced initiates; we do not recommend them for the novice, but rather would recommend that they get the help of someone having the gifts of an exorcist if they are experiencing a problem. Spirits are very real in their dimensions, and so also are their powers.

Naturally, there are other ways to bind and banish dark and hostile spirits, all depending upon the situation and what's most skillful. This method works for a localized problem in a space; it does not work, for example, for situations when the spirit or spirits are displaced in a person's energy field. Some other methods would be required. Likewise, this method tends to work for spirits with weaker power, spirits that are more annoying than outright harmful. More powerful spirits will require other measures, most likely ones far more skillful and forceful. In any case, this ought to give some idea of the creation and consecration of a spirit catcher.

Sacred Tools in the Worship of Guadalupe

The play of the wonderworking art and healing art is integral to the worship of Guadalupe, a profoundly mystical and magical worship. Naturally, all of the sacred tools used in the wonderworking art may be taken up in the worship of Our Lady. There are, however, several sacred tools that are especially common in the Mystical Path of Guadalupe as practiced in our lineage.

The first is the sacred outer garment, a shawl, poncho, or cape, remembering the outer garment—the sacred ayatl—in which Juan Diego bundled the miraculous flowers. This sacred garment is usually very colorful, though at certain times one that is more plain or even dark colored might be used. It is colorful to celebrate the great beauty and glory of the Celestial Maiden and the remembrance of her path as a path of enjoyment, the Pollen Path. Bright colors are attractive to the spirits and angels, and naturally uplift our energy. The outer garment is a symbol of her presence and power with us in our worship and spiritual work, and represents walking in beauty and holiness, in a sacred manner.

Along with this outer garment, very colorful shirts are also often worn with something of the same intention, and sometimes a special hat or scarf is worn. Putting on such things represents walking between worlds or walking with the spirits, and they are symbols of our energy body or light body.

There may also be a special cloth bag for carrying sacred tools, because in the worship of Our Lady and the spiritual work we do for the people; we often go on treks into the great outdoors and have need to carry sacred tools and offerings with us. Within this bag there will usually be a small bag holding a basic offering in case we have need to collect objects for spiritual work in a sacred manner, a bag holding corn meal, tobacco or some other sacred herb to offer.

Juan Diego was a person of knowledge and power, a shaman, and often on walks of power a shaman will walk with a sacred staff or walking stick. According to the oral tradition, Juan Diego carried a sacred staff. Thus, the sacred staff becomes a central sacred tool in our worship and spiritual work. It represents our knowledge and power, the knowledge and power the Mother Spirit grants us, and it represents standing in our truth and standing in our power, all as ordained by the Divine Mother, the *Shekinah* of the Supreme.

The staff represents the union of sky and earth, heaven and earth, and it represents the serpent power uplifted and redeemed; likewise, when calling on the Spirit and Powers it acts like a lightning rod, channeling and grounding spiritual power. Some staffs are very plain, ornamented only with fetishes tied onto them, while others may be more elaborate, having sacred symbols and animal powers carved into them, and some may even be brightly painted. In the case of a more elaborate staff, though, we must be careful because we do not want all of our knowledge and power displayed upon it, lest it become a symbol of the ego rather than a symbol of the power of our true and natural being, the power of our Holy Star. More elaborate staffs usually have fetishes tied onto them as well, which allow the power of the sacred staff to be changed to reflect the powers we are drawing upon for special spiritual works.

One of the principle emanations of Guadalupe is Snake Woman, the rattlesnake usually representing her. For this reason, sacred rattles are very common in her worship, used as a way of prayer and a way to move spiritual power by sound-vibration. We may chant, sing, or otherwise pray out loud with the sacred rattle, or we may just use the sound of the rattle itself as our prayer, holding a conscious intention or heart-wish. We may use the sound of the rattle and vocalizations that have no specific meaning but are inspired in the moment, holding a conscious intention or heart-wish, just as when we use the sound-vibration of the sacred rattle alone. Using a sacred rattle and staff together is a powerful way of sacred ceremony and wonders can transpire through it.

Another emanation of Guadalupe is as Earth Woman, and Infernal Woman, the Woman of the Underworld. In the tradition, Earth Woman has a resonant heartbeat, and that heartbeat, her rhythm, is represented by a sacred drum. The sacred drum is used in worship and spiritual work in much the same way as the sacred rattle.

Guadalupe also appears as Eagle Woman, so sacred feathers are also very common tools for prayer and sacred ceremony in her worship, feathers uplifting our prayers and energy to Sky Father and Grandmother Deep Space. Eagle, vulture, owl, and raven feathers are especially sacred to her, as well as hummingbird and Blue-and-Gold Macaw feathers.

Eagle feathers invoke great influxes of spiritual power—Supernal Light—and they uplift energy and vibration. Vulture feathers represent alchemical transformation, rebirth, and healing, and abiding in peace. Owl represents the angel of death and sight into the hidden and the darkness, secret knowledge and wisdom. Raven represents the transformation of shape-shifting and knowledge of powerful wonderworking or magic. The hummingbird in Aztec and Toltec tradition represents the spirits of great ancient warriors who died in glory and honor. Hummingbird feathers are often put into power bags or tied in fetishes for strength, courage, and protection. The Blue-and-Gold Macaw in Aztec and Toltec tradition represents the power of the Spiritual Sun that shines in Sky Father and are very holy and sacred, like those of the eagle.

The eagle that is most sacred in the Guadalupe Path is the Golden Eagle, the eagle that represents her Holy Child, the Messiah, the Spiritual Sun, which is the snake-eating eagle, representing mastery of the serpent power. The Bald Eagle is also very sacred to her, representing the Divine and Sacred Feminine, being the fish-eating eagle, the "fisher eagle," with all that implies in

Christian mysticism. As Eagle Woman, she is also "Bird Woman," so naturally all birds are sacred to her, and all manner of sacred feathers are used in her worship.

As much as the Sacred Circle of Guadalupe, we also invoke the Bird People Circle in her worship: eagle to the east, owl to the west, hawk to the south, and raven to the north. When we take up a sacred feather, or a feather fan, and the sacred staff in a circle, it becomes a very powerful invocation and movement. Likewise when we pray with a sacred feather and sacred rattle, it can also create a powerful ceremony.

Now Guadalupe is also known as War Woman and so a power shield is also often made and used in sacred ceremony, the shield having symbols of power painted on it. This is taken up in sacred ceremonies for strength and protection, and serves to guard against fierce and dark spirits. Sometimes a spear will also be made and used with the shield in spiritual works of protection or guardianship, but when the power shield is taken up the sacred staff becomes like a spear, so often a spear isn't needed. Just the power shield can be used with the sacred staff.

The smudge pot is an important sacred tool in the Mystical Path of Guadalupe, a large shell or clay pot for the burning and offering of smudge or incense. It is a significant sacred tool used in smudging ceremonies to purify or banish, as well as to sanctify. Along with these, there is often also a sacred blanket or sacred rug to be spread out representing holy ground, a place to sit to pray and meditate, and to hold and anchor spiritual power. Naturally, a power bag or "medicine bag" consecrated to the Holy Mother-Bride is often worn; that or one might find a rustic, sacred cross representing the Spiritual Sun and power of the Sacred Circle. These are the most essential sacred tools used in the worship of Our Lady of Guadalupe. Of all of these sacred tools, perhaps the most key are the staff, rattle and smudge pot, for with these alone a very passionate worship and powerful works of wonder can be done.

Now we can speak something more of the sacred staff. This is a very powerful sacred tool. It is like the emanation of the Celestial Maiden when carried by men, and like the emanation of the Spiritual Sun when carried by a woman. It is the Divine consort, balancing our energy and uplifting our vibration. In essence, it is a rod of great power. When we walk with it, we walk in the company of the *Holy Shekinah*, the Divine Presence and Power. When we uplift it, the spirits see us and hear us and come to us, and when we strike or touch the earth with it, we ground or anchor the spiritual powers invoked. The sacred staff is very holy and is always dealt with in a sacred manner, for when it is moved, so also are great spiritual powers moved.

The Mystical Path of Guadalupe is clearly a shamanic path, the way of spiritual warriors and shamans. Although we are all not necessarily shamans, or seers and wonderworkers, we can all benefit from the wisdom of the shamanic path and spirituality. We can all seek to live as spiritual warriors, and sojourn the Mystical Path of Guadalupe. We can all take up a mystical and magical spirituality, and seek to draw upon the spiritual gifts and spiritual power that the Holy Mother-Bride has given to us.

Here and there in the journey of the Mystical Path of the Celestial Maiden some sojourners do, indeed, come into being as seers and wonderworkers, or as shamans, people of knowledge and power. These individuals, however, are not taught to be shamans, but rather they are born shamans and called as shamans, being taken up by the Spirit and Powers in service to the people.

Rather than being taught to be a shaman, they are taught how to cope with their spiritual gifts and how to manage the influx of spiritual power and the spirits. These individuals usually become the apprentice of a spiritual benefactor to learn the ways of a shaman in full. The spiritual power and gifts are already with them, and through their apprenticeship they acquire the knowledge and understanding of how to use the spiritual power and gifts. Naturally, these individuals are compelled to immerse themselves in the Mystical Path far more deeply than most of us, for contact with the sacred and the spirit world is very natural and spontaneous for them, and with little effort on their part they tend to walk between worlds. The unpredictability and uncertainty of the sacred and the spirit world is "normal" to them, and so they are inclined to pursue it much further than most of us.

In the Mystical Path of Guadalupe, however, there is nothing hierarchical about these spiritual leaders. As with every role to which one might be called in life and given the talents to perform, their role in community and the world is not better than any other, though it is certainly honored and respected and given its proper place. In the Mystical Path of Guadalupe, shamans are viewed as spiritual midwives, helping to facilitate the spiritual life of the people and taking up spiritual works for the people; but like a midwife, their role isn't "center stage," rather the center and focus of their spiritual work is the Holy Mother-Bride and the Divine Child to whom she is giving birth.

Indeed, the Mystical Path of the Celestial Maiden is not isolate to the shaman. It is a path for all of us who feel called to it. There need be no apprenticeship to sojourn this path, just a heart filled with love and devotion to the Holy Mother-Bride. If you open your mind, heart, and life to the Sky Dancing Maiden, she will instruct you in her ways of worship and spiritual works. If you find that the spiritual gifts and power of a shaman are given to you, then perhaps you may wish to seek out an apprenticeship in the ways of the shaman, or the seer and wonderworker, cultivating and refining your desire, and seeking to meet and fulfill your destiny. In the Mother's Way it is all a question of our natural desire and why we are here in this life. There is no hierarchy in this. It is simply a matter of our true enjoyment.

Self-Purification in the Guadalupe Path

The smudging ceremony comes from many Native American traditions. Essentially, the smudging ceremony is a method of purification of people, sacred objects, and sacred space. The idea of smudging, however, isn't isolate to Native American traditions, but the offering of incense and the smoke it produces is viewed in many wisdom traditions as having a purifying and sanctifying effect, making people, objects, and spaces sacred, opening the way for prayer, meditation, and sacred ceremony.

Among indigenous peoples, smudging is something usually done before sacred events as a method of preparation for sacred ceremony. This is also true of the use of smudging ceremony in our tradition. For us, however, this becomes a way of prayer, meditation, and sacred ceremony itself, often marking the main movement of a ceremony creating Sacred Circle, calling in the Spirit and Power, and praying and communing with the world of spirits and angels. Smudging is a ceremony for purification and sanctification, but it is also a way of offering, "feeding the spirits," as it were, and of worship.

In a smudging ceremony, sacred herbs are burnt in a smudge pot, large seashell or clay bowl, or they are burned upon a stone, and often a sacred feather or feather fan is used to move the smoke and energy, though just as often we may move the smoke and energy with our hands. In many Native American traditions the most common sacred herbs used for smudge are sage, cedar, sweet grass, and lavender. These are sacred herbs used in this land, but other sacred herbs may also be used, including resins such as copal, or various fragrant flowers such as jasmine or honeysuckle. In mystical Christian traditions, of course, rose, frankincense, and myrrh are common, as is spikenard.

Now, in sacred ceremonies for prayer and meditation there is often an offering up of sacred herbs or incense in worship, representing the idea of a holy sacrifice or an exchange of energy between the spiritual and material world. Quite apart from the idea of purification and sanctification, the smoke or energy released is viewed as an offering of devotion and prayer. This is part of the smudging ceremony in our tradition, but smudging includes the intention of purification and sanctification, as well as *tikkune*-healing, the smoke or energy of the smudge being viewed as having a purifying and healing power akin to that of the living waters in which we bathe during baptism or water ceremony. Because of this purifying and healing effect in a smudging ceremony, the smoke touching the air of a space, an object, or a person, makes that space, object or person sacred and holy. This "touching with smoke" is the basic intention of the smudging ceremony.

Sweet fragrances are used because their energy resonates with luminous and divine spirits. On one hand, fierce and dark spirits are repelled by the sweetness of the smudge, while simultaneously the smudge attracts luminous and Divine spirits. This is reflected in the effect of the sweet fragrances on ourselves; sweet fragrances tend to be pleasing and uplifting, inspiring more luminous thoughts and emotions, peace and joy, and naturally dispelling or banishing negativity. As is well known, the power of smell and fragrance reaches very deeply into our memory and has a very powerful effect on consciousness, and so it is with the world of spirits and angels as well.

The great power of a smudging ceremony, however, lies in our sacred intention, and in our capacity of concentration—*kavvanah*—and passionate faith—*devekut*. Smudging is only fully effective through awareness, when exercised with great care and attentiveness. In everything dealing with the sacred, it is through this awareness that we draw out the spiritual power and blessing. As we perform or participate in a smudging ceremony, we go within and center, focusing ourselves upon our sacred intention to purify, sanctify, and heal. We cleave to the Divine Spirit with passionate faith in its power to purify, sanctify, and heal us, the smudge being the talisman of that Divine Power.

When we wish to enter into a sacred ceremony or sacred space, seeking to experience the spiritual dimension, we set the ordinary and mundane aside and hold the conscious intention of becoming open and sensitive to the sacred, the world of spirits, angels, and the Divine. So it is when we are smudging or being smudged. We leave the ordinary or mundane behind us, focusing on what is luminous, sacred, and Divine. Once we have smudged or have been smudged, we then maintain our focus on the sacred, what is spiritual, throughout the sacred event or ceremony, holding, and anchoring the sacred and spiritual power for ourselves and for the people.

When we light the smudge at the outset of the smudging ceremony, we first give thanks and praise to the Divine and to the Powers. We offer up the smudge to the Divine and the Powers, calling in the Spirit and Powers to the smudging ceremony, becoming aware of the Presence and Power of the Divine and the Winds in the smudge.

The order of the calling in of the Powers will vary depending upon the spiritual work that we are doing, but the most common order of invocation is to Sky Father and Earth Mother, the Holy One, in the remembrance of the Spiritual Sun and Holy Spirit. Then we will offer the smoke and call in the Powers of the east and west, north and south. Then we will begin smudging. Another common order for the invocation of the Powers follows the Sacred Circle in a sun wise or clockwise direction. Occasionally, in spiritual works focusing on the Divine and Sacred Feminine, or on the "path of spirits," the invocations may go moon wise or counterclockwise. When we are doing a special spiritual work that requires the powers of a specific direction first and foremost, after invoking the Holy One, we may begin by invoking the Divine powers of that direction, and then invoke the others in an order corresponding to the spiritual work we seek to do.

Here it may be said that in spiritual works of those walking "contrary," or when we take up the power of the "trickster spirit," the invocations and movements are performed in the opposite order to the sacred intention. This, however, requires the special call and talents of those who work strongly with the trickster spirit, or requires a call by the Spirit and Powers in dream or vision to do so. The place of the contrary or trickster spirit corresponds to the emanations of the Divine Mother as War Woman and Infernal Woman, but most especially to Infernal Woman, the Old Wise Woman, or Crone.

Most often we will first smudge the sacred space or Sacred Circle, then the sacred objects and then the people. At times, however, this may be reversed, so that the people are smudged first, then the sacred space and sacred objects.

To smudge the sacred space or Sacred Circle, usually we will go sun wise waving the smudge as we walk the Sacred Circle. Then, often, we will walk the pattern of the holy cross in the circle waving the smudge as we go, east to west and south to north. Then we will smudge our sacred tools and the altar, or the sacred blanket or rug and all that's on it. Following this, we will smudge all of the people gathered for the sacred event or sacred ceremony.

When we smudge ourselves or another, first we pass the smudge in a sun wise circle around the face, and then we pass it down the front of the body and back up to the heart. At this point the person being smudged will draw the smoke with their hands to the face, head, shoulders, and heart, rather like drawing water to wash our face. Then the smudge is passed sun wise around the whole body, down the left side and up the right side, and then it is offered so that the person can step over the smoke with each foot, first the left foot and then the right foot. Next, the backside of the person is smudged, going down from the head to the feet and up to a point level with the heart in their back. This completes the smudging. A gentle tap on one shoulder may be used to signal the completion of the smudging.

This is a complete smudging for a sacred event, such as sacred dance or sacred ceremony. At times, however, a simpler ceremony of smudging may be used to swiftly clear the energy of a person, object, or space when the spiritual work to be done does not require a larger amount of energy, such as sacred discourse or prayer when there is a need to clear energy between people and mark the transition in a simple way.

Now, often in the Guadalupe Path a smudging ceremony itself may be extended as the vehicle of prayer, worship, and wonderworking. Having performed the purification and sanctification, a sacred rattle, drum, staff, or other sacred tool may be taken up for prayer and the moving of spiritual power and, along with the smudge, other offerings might be made as spirits and angels are invoked for the spiritual work and worship being performed. As the smoke of the smudge continues to rise, the spiritual power or energy is directed towards the sacred intention, whether that might be protection, healing or blessing.

When a smudging ceremony is drawn out to become a larger spiritual work, usually we will use a smudge stick that will last for a longer period, or continue adding smudge to the smudge pot throughout the sacred ceremony. We will let the smudge stick burn in full, and all the while we will pray and meditate. If and when there is a need to close the Sacred Circle before the smudge stick has burned in full, perhaps because the spiritual work being performed requires a swift movement, then we will remain in that place as a silent witness or watcher until the smudge has finished burning.

Essentially, as long as the sacred smudge burns and the smoke rises, spirits and angels are attracted; they are happy, and so they may listen and hear our prayers and share their spiritual power with us to help answer our prayers. In the Mystical Path of the Celestial Maiden, as you may have noticed, we speak often of the world of spirits and angels, for it is primarily through the world of spirits and angels that we relate with the Divine and through which the Divine responds to our prayers. The world of spirits and angels represents a mediating principle between the Divine and human worlds. Thus, most spiritual work we perform for people is accomplished through the spiritual power of spirits and angels, what are called *Tzavaot* in the Holy Kabbalah. Smudging ceremony is especially powerful in working with spirits and angels—*Tzavaot*—the hosts of our Earthly Mother and Heavenly Father.

As we have taught elsewhere, there are other ways to smudge. We can also smudge with sound-vibration, using a sacred rattle or drum, and we can smudge with energy or Light Power, using our hands or a sacred object and passing the energy or light around the person in the same way as with the smoke. We may also smudge with holy water or living water and a sprig of hyssop or branch of cedar, or we can do so by way of an anointing with holy oil.

Generally speaking, though, in the Mystical Path of Guadalupe, smudging with sweet fragrant smoke is most common, honoring she who is Flower Woman and Sacred Herb Woman, the Celestial Maiden. Her sign of Spanish-essence flowers reflects the principle way of making flower or scent offerings in devotion to her and naturally invoking her Divine Presence and Power. Smudging is a common way of prayer and worship in our teachings of the Mystical Path of Guadalupe.

The Sacred Fire in the Guadalupe Path

It may be rightly argued that our unlocking of the secrets and mystery of fire in prehistoric times is at the very heart of human development and evolution, both spiritual and material, sacred and mundane. Since that time, in one form or another, fire has been at the center of our lives, and among the most ancient of human activities is the fire-keeping and sitting around the sacred fire. We have sat around the sacred fire to enjoy its light and warmth, to keep company with one another, and to cook our food. We have gathered around it for sacred storytelling or spiritual teaching, for sacred dance, prayer, meditation, and ceremony. In our lives, the fire flickers between the completely sacred and the completely mundane, and to this day, though we have gained a certain mastery of fire, nevertheless, it remains mysterious, dangerous, and very enchanting in our experience. Nothing can give nor take life quite like fire.

Indeed, it is no wonder the Divine has often been likened to fire, or that the *Holy Shekinah*, the Divine Presence and Power, is often associated with fire, as at the burning bush beheld by the ancient Israeli shaman, Moses. Fire has many qualities like those of the Great Spirit or God: *The LORD our God is a consuming fire* (Deuteronomy 4:24); *I baptize you with water for repentance. But after me will come one who is more powerful than I, whose sandals I am not fit to carry. He will baptize you with the Holy Spirit and with fire* (St. Matthew 3:11); *Suddenly a sound like the blowing of a violent wind came from heaven and filled the whole house where they were sitting. They saw what seemed to be tongues of fire that separated and came to rest on each of them* (Acts 2:2-3); and *Jesus said, Whoever is near me is near the fire, and whoever is far from me is far from the kingdom* (St. Thomas, 82).

In the tradition, of course, we view fire as very sacred, and so it is in many wisdom traditions around the world, including the Aztec and Toltec traditions. Sitting around the sacred fire and making offerings to the fire are also an integral part of the Mystical Path of Guadalupe drawn from Aztec and Toltec influence in the tradition. If you were to encounter a person of knowledge and power in such traditions, a holy person or shaman, and you had a question about your path in life, or some question about your dreams or destiny, they would likely say, "Go and ask Grandfather Fire," or "Go talk with the Sacred Fire." Saying this, they might share with you how to build and tend a sacred fire, and how to talk with the sacred fire, or they might invite you to a gathering around a sacred fire, or might offer to go out and sit around the sacred fire with you. It is from the sacred fire that they would encourage you to seek your answer, from the presence and power of the Great Spirit, the Creator.

The way of building and keeping a sacred fire, and of sitting around the sacred fire, can be very simple, weaving the ordinary or mundane with the sacred in a rather casual fashion, or it can be very elaborate and very ceremonial. What is intriguing, though, is that in the experience of the sacred fire, the sacredness and power of the fire are the same, whether the ceremony is simple and casual, or more formal and elaborate.

We go to the sacred fire as a way of vision quest and everything we learn about vision quest can be applied to going to the sacred fire; but even apart from the usual preparations for a vision quest, we can go to the sacred fire for a vision or to talk with the fire, because it has a natural power of purification and sanctification. So when we have a need for a swift word of the Divine Spirit in our lives, or some guidance or insight through dream or vision, we can go to the sacred fire to pray and to gaze. We need only go with sacred intention, walking in a sacred manner. We go to the sacred fire as a way of vision quest in the Guadalupe Path, but we also go to the sacred fire to make offerings and to worship, to commune with the Divine Mother and Powers in the sacred fire. We may enact a version of fire-offering ceremony, invoking the Sacred Circle of the Holy Mother-Bride, the sacred fire becoming as the presence and power of the Celestial Maiden in the center of the Sacred Circle.

We also go to the sacred fire for wonderworking, to pray and perform spiritual work for the people. This usually combines invocations of the Spirit and Powers, and various angels of our Heavenly Father and Earthly Mother, with offerings to the sacred fire. In other words, there are many reasons we go to the sacred fire, and there may be many ceremonies surrounding the sacred fire. The play of the sacred fire is a very common spiritual practice in the Mystical Path of the Celestial Maiden.

We can certainly commune with the sacred fire in a fireplace or wood-burning stove in our home, but the true place and full effectiveness of the sacred fire is experienced in the great outdoors beneath the night sky, with a fire pit in Earth Mother, one dug with the intention of building and tending a sacred fire, or one purified and consecrated with that holy intention. There, we are naturally in touch with earth and sky, the elements and winds. As we sit around the sacred fire, we are in touch with the spirits of our ancient ancestors, and with the spirit world that holds special power in the wilderness and the nighttime.

In the great outdoors, the sacred fire naturally manifests a Sacred Circle, whether or not we go to greater lengths to trace a circle or gather stones to form a circle. When a sacred fire is lit, there is a Sacred Circle manifest by its radiance, and the sacred fire stands in the center of the circle, in the God Place. When a more formal Sacred Circle is to be traced on the earth or created with stones, then the Sacred Circle is created before the fire pit is blessed and the initial material for the fire is placed into it.

When we dig a fire pit, or we purify and consecrate one that already exists, always we pray and ask permission to build a sacred fire in that place. We pray to Sky Father and Earth Mother, and to invite the Powers, seeking their blessing, and we ask the spirits of that place for their permission and blessing. When we are praying and asking, we give some offering and we hold the heart-wish that all people are blessed by the sacred fire and our sacred ceremony. Once we have done this, we will dig or prepare the fire pit. As we do so, most especially we keep Earth Mother and the spirits of the place in mind, digging or preparing the fire pit in a respectful and mindful way, with full attention and devotion in what we are doing.

If stones are to be gathered to place around the mouth of the fire pit, they are gathered in a sacred manner. If there is already a fire pit with stones around it, then we will honor and bless the stones that are there. We will form a mound with the earth that we dig out of the pit. The mound is usually placed to the north, and often it is made into a sacred mound, especially in more elaborate ceremonies. When we dig a fire pit, usually we will place the earth back into the pit when we are finished with the sacred ceremony. On occasions when a fire pit is already in place and there is no earth to make a mound with or return, we might make a small mound of stones, and afterward those stones may be placed into the pit.

Once the fire pit is prepared with due attentiveness and care, it can be purified and consecrated. Living water might be sprinkled in it, along with some holy oil, or some salt might be used, and some offering is given to the spirit of the pit. Then the initial kindling and wood is set into place in a sacred manner, and some initial offerings are placed in with them. Whatever is to be used as fuel for the sacred fire should be gathered in a sacred manner; often, the fuel for the sacred fire will be put in the south or the southwest. Everything must be done in a respectful way with prayer and a good heart.

Before the sacred fire is lit, the sacred ground is usually allowed to "settle" for some hours prior, and typically a smudging ceremony is performed, smudging the sacred space, any sacred tools, and all who come to sit around the sacred fire. Sometimes, however, the fire itself is used for smudging by placing a significant amount of sacred herbs in it, in which case there is no smudging ceremony before lighting the sacred fire.

When a sacred fire is lit, it is lit with prayer and sacred chant, and sometimes sacred rattles or drums may be sounded. When there is a gathering to sit around the sacred fire, usually a fire-keeper is chosen and it is their sacred duty to light and keep the fire going. At times they may have a helper. In some sacred ceremonies, however, the person of knowledge and power leading the sacred ceremony will start the sacred fire, and then the fire-keeper will take up their sacred task of tending it.

Once the sacred fire is burning, some initial prayers and invocations will be spoken, chanted, or sung. The Spirit and Powers will be called in, and the worship and spiritual work will begin. As has been said, this could all be done in a very casual way or a more formal way, depending on what is to be done around the sacred fire.

Teachings or inspired speech are often given around the sacred fire, and when this is happening, here and there the sacred discourse may break into prayer, meditation, or simple ceremonial invocations and gestures. Very often such discourses may include a play with the spirits and wonderworking, teaching mysteries on an experiential level.

Sometimes blessings or spiritual empowerments might be shared around the sacred fire, or healings might be performed; the sacred fire can inspire many things, many spiritual movements. Sometimes the focus may be on offerings, prayer, and worship. Sometimes there is drumming around the sacred fire, and so also the use of the sacred rattle. There may also be sacred dance around the sacred fire, dances that call in, hold, and anchor spirit powers.

Always, with any or all of these movements, there is sitting and talking with the sacred fire, and there is gazing into the sacred fire. The sacred fire is the center and focus of the ceremony, and the mind, heart, and gaze continually return to it. Whatever sacred ceremony is done, whatever transpires, all is inspired by the sacred fire, as by the Holy Spirit. In a manner of speaking, it all comes from the Sacred Fire of the Divine, the Holy Spirit of the Divine.

Sitting around the sacred fire might often be a gathering, a group worship engaging spiritual work, but just as often, a fire ceremony may be initiated by an individual. As with a group, an individual may perform this sacred ceremony in a simple or elaborate way, drawing from the teachings that have been given. In the simplest form we go outdoors and build and tend a sacred fire in a respectful and mindful way, all as feels right and good to us, all as we are inclined and inspired to do. We sit by the sacred fire and talk with the fire. There needs to be nothing complex about it. We are communing with the sacred fire, aware of the sacredness and spiritual power of the fire, listening and hearing, looking and seeing, the Divine Presence and Power in it.

As you might suspect, the art of ceremony with the sacred fire, or the art of "sitting around the sacred fire," is something we are usually taught by example and experience, going out with a person of knowledge and power to learn the ways of the sacred fire. More than through words, it is usually taught through shared experience. Ultimately, though, it is a creative spiritual art; we just have to come to know and understand the power of the sacred fire and Sacred Circle, and how to open ourselves to the sacred or spiritual dimension.

If Our Lady is Flower Woman, understanding the Nahautl word for flowering or blooming is also the word for "bursting forth into flame," then she is also Fire Woman, Mother of the Sacred Fire, Bride of the Spiritual Sun. This sacred fire is in our Mother's heart and belly!

The Pot of Fire: Awakening the Serpent

The awareness of the serpent power, or what has been called "kundalini energy" in Hindu schools of thought, occurs throughout many wisdom traditions around the world. Virtually everywhere that spirituality ventures into the mystical and magical there is knowledge of this divine power in us. Essentially, it is a Fiery Intelligence and an evolutionary force that manifests as desire-energy, the most basic form of which is sexual energy.

This divine power is rooted in the base of the spine, and it lies sleeping in the belly. In the case of most ordinary people, it is largely a latent or dormant power, the barest thread or spark of it sustaining life and being expressed in desires and dreams of the mundane, material world. If and when this great force awakens, however, it brings luminous dreams and visions, a development of consciousness beyond the body, and spiritual knowledge and power, wonderworking or magical powers. In and of itself the awakening of the serpent is not enlightenment, but it is a force that can be directed towards enlightenment and that facilitates the enlightenment and liberation of the soul, the fulfillment of our destiny.

Naturally, the awakening of this great power is an integral part of our spiritual development and evolution, and many would say that it is an integral part of our future development and evolution on a material level, holding the potential for the generation of a new species of humanity, one far superior to the present human life-wave on earth. Basically speaking, this is the true force or power of consciousness in us, and thus as we seek to ascend into higher states of consciousness, we also seek to awaken this spiritual power, the force driving our ascent in consciousness and all our spiritual works.

Although some Eastern schools teach methods to force the awakening of the serpent power, in our tradition we do not seek to force its awakening, but rather it awakens in a natural and spontaneous way through the spiritual life and practice. Specifically it awakens through the blessings and grace of the Divine Mother, through an influx of the Mother's Force from above that sparks the Holy Fire of the Serpent below.

Indeed, what we find is that by simply taking up the spiritual life and practice with the intention of awakening this Fiery Intelligence, this spiritual power awakens in us, more or less. Drawing upon this divine power, it increases and awakens in full, all in a very natural and spontaneous way, purely through the conscious intention for its awakening. We do not need to force its awakening, but rather we merely need to be open to the possibility and create the conditions in which it can awaken. When we do this, the Holy Mother-Bride kindles this power of herself in us, and she uplifts and reintegrates this divine power in us with the Light Continuum, the Divine Presence and Power above and everywhere below.

Although we do not take up spiritual practices to force the awakening of the serpent power, we can and do take up practices that serve to create the necessary conditions in which this great power can awaken. Likewise, we take up practices that draw upon this spiritual power, understanding that as we use the spiritual knowledge and power we have, more will be given to us. Using our knowledge and power naturally generates greater knowledge and power.

We have spoken elsewhere about the cultivation and refinement of desire and our dreams. This in itself is a practice that tends to activate the serpent power. Becoming lucid in dream and generating out of body experiences are also practices for the awakening of this Fiery Intelligence. So, too, is the practice of sacred sexuality, as well as many of the practices of the wonderworking and healing arts in the Guadalupe Path. All of them may serve to create the necessary conditions for the awakening of the serpent power.

Perhaps the most essential way to spark this holy fire in us is through passionate devotion, or *devekut*: cleaving to the Divine, passionately yearning for direct experience of conscious union with the Divine. This, in and of itself, can awaken the serpent power in a natural and spontaneous way. The very prayer for direct knowledge and experience of the Divine, and for union with the Divine, is an invocation of this awakening, for it is by this great power that such knowledge and experience comes.

In many Sophian practices, of course, we focus upon the heart center or the Spiritual Sun envisioned within and behind the heart. Likewise we focus upon the brow or a sphere of white brilliance in the center of the head. We may do this in some practices of the Guadalupe Path, but primarily, in the Mystical Path of Guadalupe, we focus on the "pot of fire," the serpent power in the belly, and the generation of the "inner heat." In other words, we work in our spiritual practices from the belly, joining the power of the belly to our heart, motivated in our spiritual works by the love and compassion of the Divine Mother.

Here and there in practices given for the Path of Guadalupe a secret key is taught for a natural and spontaneous awakening of the serpent power: The Centering and Grounding Practice. In this, we focus upon our breath and draw up the power of Earth Mother with our inhalation, offering it up to Sky Father with our exhalation. Then we reverse this, drawing down the power of Sky Father and the Spiritual Sun through us and into Earth Mother. This is a practice that often facilitates the awakening of the serpent power, not by force, but rather through a conscious intention and an active prayer for Divine Grace.

When this practice is taken up for the awakening of the Fire

Snake, we breathe in the power of Earth Mother, drawing it up to our belly and holding it there. Then we breathe it out the top of our head as an offering to Sky Father. When we breathe in the power of Sky Father and the Spiritual Sun, we breathe it into our belly, holding it there, and then breathe it down through the base of our spine or our feet into Earth Mother. The focus of gathering and holding the Divine Power is in the belly, and we will do this practice often in devotion to our Father-Mother, the Holy One.

Another practice very similar to this will later be detailed in the Union with the Celestial Maiden practice. We envision her before us, joining our breath with her breath, allowing her to breathe with, in, and through us, and then we draw in her energy through our breath and hold it in our bellies, as though in her womb. Then we hold the breath and, generating the force in our bellies, we breathe that force into her as a sacred sacrifice. She, in turn, breathes it back into us again, and so the practice goes on, breathing with the Celestial Maiden. When we have breathed with her in this way, generating the pot of fire, we then merge ourselves completely with her as in the standard practice, passing into union with the Holy Mother-Bride.

After some practice this naturally tends to generate a profound experience of an inner heat that purifies the subtle, energetic body, as well as the physical body. With this inner heat, we find a natural and spontaneous movement of the serpent power occurs, activating this spiritual power.

In the case of men, of course, with such practices they will want to pay attention to preserving their vital energy and not releasing their seed, or lightning strike, too often; holding their vital charge is integral to the generation of the pot of fire with men. In a similar way, in the case of women, drawing out the spiritual power of their moon cycle becomes important, using the power that is in it for the generation of the pot of fire until it blazes forth like a great Solar Being in their belly.

There are many other powerful practices associated with the pot of fire in the belly we will detail later, such as belly cords. The creation of belly cords in healing work can naturally lead to the generation of the pot of fire and inner heat, and this practice can extend beyond healing, for if and when we want to commune with our relations, the spiritual essence of beings, we can do so by the creation of belly cords and an exchange of energy with them.

As an example, suppose I come upon a great rock and wish to commune and exchange energy with the rock. First, I will ask the rock if I may commune and exchange energy with it, and then, if the spirit of the rock is willing, I can extend a light cord from my belly to the rock, feeling it, "listening and hearing" in my belly, and exchanging energy with the spirit of the rock. Afterwards, in one way or another, I would then make an offering and give thanks, thanking the rock for the exchange, and thanking Sky Father and Earth Mother for the great communion of life. Even aside from the generation of belly cords, we can center our attention on our bellies and feel and commune with others on a belly level, and this too may create the conditions for a natural generation of the pot of fire, the awakening of the serpent power in the belly.

Now in the subtle, energetic body there are seven main interior stars or centers: the root, navel, solar plexus, heart, throat, brow, and crown, and there is also an eighth star above the head, the Supernal or Supramental Center. We can and do center ourselves in these interior stars for different spiritual works, but in the Guadalupe Path we always begin with the belly or womb, and then draw the serpent power up from there to the corresponding star for the intended spiritual work. When we need to push force or energy by a movement of will, seeking to bring about a wonder in that way, we will lift the Fire Snake to the solar plexus with conscious intention and move the energy through that star. If we are seeking to uplift or restore a Spirit-connection, or in healing works, or for a deeper spiritual communion, we may uplift the Fire Snake to the heart. To place the serpent power in sound-vibration or our speaking, we may lift it to the throat star. If we wish to open our sight into the World of the Holy Spirit, or into the world of spirits and angels, or we seek to invoke lucid dream and visions, we will uplift the Fire Snake to the brow star or the center of the head. If we seek to experience consciousness beyond the body or union with the Divine I Am, we might lift the serpent power to the crown at the top of our head. Always, however, we will first focus on the belly and generate the pot of fire, and then uplift the Fire Snake from its abode in the belly.

If we work continuously in this way in our spiritual life and practice, the Mother's Force will move and we will experience the pot of fire and inner heat; her grace will awaken the Fire Snake in us. Once stirring, the more we draw upon this great power in our spiritual work for the people and the land, and in our worship of the Holy Mother-Bride, the more it will awaken and move, and the more spiritual knowledge and power we will acquire.

Here we may speak an open secret: The sound of the sacred rattle can be used to generate the pot of fire and inner heat, and so also the sacred rattle may be used to uplift the Fire Snake to various interior stars. When a person of knowledge and power works wonders with a sacred rattle, this is what they are doing inwardly, stirring and moving the Fire Snake.

If you wish to use the sacred rattle in this way, take up the rattle and breathe into your belly, holding and generating the energy there, and as you do this envision a rattlesnake formed of fiery light coiled in your belly, and envision that Fire Snake awakening and rattling, and raising its head, perching to strike. As you continue to rattle, and it is rattling in you, envision its head pointing upward and envision that it begins to ascend upward, its head going to the interior star you intend to move the spiritual power through, while continuing to rattle its tail in your belly. Let your breath become the breath of the Fire Snake and let its energy fill and pervade you, becoming focused in the interior star through which you are working. Alternatively, all of this can be done with a simple and clear conscious intention; the visualization and breathing merely serve to facilitate concentration, *kavvanah*.

A sacred drum can also be used, but the meditation is different. As you drum, draw up Earth Mother's great power into your belly, and envision the Sky-Dancing Maiden magically appearing in your belly, dancing there as you drum and chant or sing. As she dances, see her aura blazing with fiery light like the sun, and envision that light shooting up the three channel-ways to the interior star you intend. A sacred feather and holy staff can also be used in a similar way to stir, uplift and direct the Fire Snake, all with clear and conscious intention. There are many ways.

Sitting around the sacred fire and speaking with Grandfather Fire, let the sacred fire before you be in your belly, and ask Grandfather to help you kindle the sacred fire in your belly and the inner heat that comes with it. Commune with the sacred fire before you and within you, and you will know and see the sacred fire that is hidden in everything.

Gazing at the stars, as into the robes of the Queen of Heaven, the Body of Grandmother Deep Space, ask for her blessing and light. Envision rays of light shooting down from the stars and pouring down through the top of your head. Breathe the light of the stars into your belly and let a holy star shine there in your belly. Then, bring that light to the interior star through which you wish to work through a conscious intention, bring that light for spiritual work or worship you intend in the Divine Mother. These are some simple ways in the Mystical Path of Guadalupe of working with the Fire Snake.

Perhaps the most essential way to work with the serpent power is to go within and live within, opening to the Divine Light from above, holding the conscious intention of receiving an influx of the Mother's Force, and of awakening the Fire Snake in the belly. Worship the Divine Mother in this way, engaging in an active and dynamic surrender to her, cultivating and refining your desires and dreams. Wait upon the Mother Spirit, and in due season she will awaken the serpent power in you, her Divine Presence and Power in your belly. Indeed, this is her presence and power in our bellies, she who has asked, "Am I not right here who is your Mother?" She is within and all around us, though at the same time she is transcendent of all that appears!

This serpent power, once awakened, can be moved to any part of the body and transmitted through any part of the body. If put into the voice, the voice may transmit it; if put into the eyes, then a mere glance can impart it; if put into the hands, then with a touch it can be passed. In these ways it can be put into all manner of objects as talismans of blessing, or it may be passed from person to person, being to being, blessing and uplifting. Very often the initial sparking, stirring, or awakening of the serpent power may come through an initiation or an empowerment given by a person of power.

As we might expect, frequently sharing the company of a person in whom the Fire Snake is awakened may spontaneously awaken the Fire Snake in us, for this holy fire tends to ignite itself by proximity and contact. It leaps like a wildfire, self-generating! We do not force the stirring of the Fire Snake, however, but rather we rely upon the Holy Mother-Bride and her timing. Until it is due season, the premature awakening of the Fire Snake could be very unwise, and rather than something luminous and joyful, it could be dreadful and sorrowful. This is a fierce and volatile power, and it is a power for good and evil alike. In it is the power to create or destroy, the power of life and death and everything in between.

It is through the Mother's Force, her Divine Grace, that we awaken this power, and it is through her Force, the Light from above, that the serpent is uplifted and redeemed, reintegrated with the Divine Presence and Power above, and everywhere below. Awakening it, we may use it to manifest our true dreams and our destiny, to perform good works for the people and the land, and to worship the Holy Mother-Bride in spirit and truth. Awakening it, if we are willing, the Mother Spirit and Powers will guide us and show us what to do with this great power.

It is a great sacred power, very mysterious, mystical, magical, powerful, and unpredictable; in it there is great beauty and great danger. We approach it wisely with holy awe, wonder, and humility. When it awakens, and when it is uplifted, we will need make no great claim of ourselves. The Mother will have done this thing, and it is her Divine Presence and Power. We will need to make no great claim, for the Mother Spirit will bear witness by way of her signs and wonders, gestures of her compassionate heart and undying love for her children.

In this regard, we will take a lesson from the Thunder Beings who once tried to put themselves off as the Creator. They are bound to remain as they are until the end of time, unable to show their faces, no longer having bodies, but abiding for all time in between heaven and earth until eventually they may reincarnate in another great cosmic cycle. While they are very powerful and they have a very significant place, they are destined to learn humility, bound to their present incarnation until the end of this great cosmic cycle. Human beings can be much like them, putting themselves off as God. We, too, must learn humility as we come into power, and learn how to manage the great power of the Creator in us, living in surrender to Mother God.

We are wise to purify and prepare ourselves for the awakening of this serpent power in us, seeking to shed our ego, letting go of egoistic desire and fear, and restoring ourselves to the love of the Divine and all our relations. If we prepare ourselves in this way, when the Fire Snake awakens, it will heal, empower, illuminate, and liberate us. The *Holy Shekinah* will take up our person and life, and the true desire of our holy soul will be fulfilled in the Divine Mother. In this, perhaps, you may know and understand the way of awakening the serpent power in the Mystical Path of Guadalupe.

Belly of Earth Mother Practice

If you want the Holy Mother to kindle the pot of fire in your belly, lie upon Earth Mother with your belly on her, and extend a belly cord into the secret center of Earth Mother. As you breathe in, envision her holy fire rushing up into your belly. As you breathe out, offer your energy to her, and so in this way be fed by your Holy Mother as when you were in the womb. When you arise, bring this fiery light to your heart and worship in the presence of the Holy Mother-Bride and Spiritual Sun.

This is a way of energetic purification, as well as generating the pot of fire, and it is also a practice that shamanic healers will use with people, having them do this practice during a healing session. This is a simple practice, but very powerful. There is great purifying and healing power in Earth Mother.

Sun In The Belly Practice

Go out and greet the dawn, smudging yourself and worshiping the Celestial Maiden and the Spiritual Sun. As the sun rises, give salutations and breathe the light of the sun into your belly, holding the energy there and envisioning the ignition of a solar sphere in your belly. Then let this fiery light be uplifted to your heart and brow, and abide in communion with the Sky-Dancing Maiden and the Sun within the sun, giving offerings, praise and thanks to the Holy One and *Shekinah*. This is also a healing practice for oneself or another in need of healing energy.

Awakening the Fire Snake

If we wonder if the serpent power was known to Aztec and Toltec peoples, or if its awakening was an innate part of their tradition as much as we may see in Eastern wisdom traditions, we may merely ponder the image of the plumed or winged serpent associated with Quetzalcoatl in Aztec and Toltec tradition. If we wonder if the serpent power was known in early Judeo-Christian tradition, in a similar manner we might ponder what Yeshua says to Nicodemus in the third chapter of St. John, where he speaks of the uplifting of the Messiah like the serpent uplifted by Moses in the wilderness: *And just as Moses lifted up the serpent in the wilderness, so must the Son of Man be lifted up, that whoever believes in him may have eternal life* (v. 14-15). We need only inquire into the Hebrew word for the serpent in the Garden of Eden, nechash—נחש—and the Hebrew word for the anointed of God, Messiah—משיח—which share the same gematria in Hebrew: 358. According to Kabbalah, Hebrew words or phrases of equal sum imply one and the same spiritual force.

In the Guadalupe Path the focus for the awakening of the serpent power is in the belly, the generation of the "pot of fire," for the central aim in the Guadalupe Path is the reintegration of our energetic being and material being, drawing down the Mother's Force, the Supernal Light, fully into the body, fulfilling our desires, spiritual and material.

Consider now the outer garment of the Mother-Bride appearing as Guadalupe. She is robed in stars. Let these stars be both the macrocosm of the heavens we see at night and the microcosm of the interior stars within our subtle body. Outside and inside, the Mother-Bride is one, within and all-enveloping. Essentially, the seven main interior stars or centers of our subtle, energetic body represent the manifestations of our consciousness-force at different levels of being, intersecting with various dimensions of being, and with the realms, worlds and universes within those inner or metaphysical dimensions. The navel star or belly corresponds with the astral or dreamtime, the inner dimensions nearest to the material dimension through which all influxes and influences of spiritual forces enter into the material dimension. Thus, this interior star is key to the integration of our energetic being and the more subtle dimensions of our being with our material being, and it is also central to actual spiritual works or wonders affecting radical shifts in the balance of forces and the material world.

Now, although we may focus on the awakening of the Fire Snake in the belly, we seek to bring about this awakening by way of an influx of the Mother's Force, the Light from above. Unless the three lower stars are joined to the upper stars, the lower root, navel, and solarplexus stars will represent the bestial nature and egoistic condition. In effect, surface consciousness and its play of egoistic desires and fears is the experience of feeling separated, cut off from one's deeper spiritual being and essence. Our aim and focus is to bring the Mother's Force down into the belly and in this way to awaken the Fire Snake sleeping in the belly.

The key to our reception of the Mother's Force, the reception of the Holy Spirit, is our passionate devotion to the Holy Mother-Bride, our cultivation of our passionate love of her and the refinement of our desires that naturally come from that Divine Passion. The Divine Mother affirms our desires and dreams, and she promises the fulfillment of our desires and dreams, the granting of blessings and boons. However, it is not the misguided desires of our ego that she affirms; rather it is the true desires of our heart and soul, our true and natural being, our true human desires and dreams. So we focus in the Guadalupe Path on the awareness of our true heart's desires, the cultivation and refinement of our desires, the union of our belly with our heart.

The knowledge and power of the heart in devotion and surrender to the Divine Mother illuminates and informs our belly; and the knowledge and power of the brow guides the belly and directs our desire-energy towards the fulfillment of our true dreams and visions, our destiny. In our focus on the awakening of the Fire Snake in our belly, it is not that we repress or abandon this great power in the belly, but rather, awakening it in the belly, we draw it up to the heart and brow, and to the crown, the Holy Star of the Divine I Am.

This is the development and evolution of consciousness beyond the body, but at the same time it is an influx of consciousness into the body. Our holy soul, the fullness of our energetic being, becomes incarnate, embodied. Heaven and earth meet and embrace in us. It is a non-dual self-realization in which heaven and earth, the Light Land and material dimension, are joined, inseparable from one another.

Although we focus on the awakening of the Fire Snake in the belly on the Guadalupe Path, it may, in fact, spark and awaken in any of the interior stars or centers. For example, in the experience of the Mother's presence, it is not uncommon for a sparking in the heart, the heart bursting open with the boundless love and compassion of the Mother, with a joyful outpouring of compassionate tears. In a similar fashion, it is also not uncommon for a sparking to occur in the brow star or center of the head and an experience to unfold of the opening of sight into the visionary dimension, the World of the Holy Spirit.

The serpent power can spark and awaken in any of the interior stars. When it does, it invokes a corresponding spiritual and mystical experience. As another example, if it sparks in the solar plexus, all of a sudden a person may acquire certain spiritual gifts, or magic and psychic powers, distinct abilities of wonder-working and knowledge of hidden things. Likewise, if and when awakening in the heart, it may spread and move up and down simultaneously. The serpent power may also awaken from the top to the bottom, beginning with the crown and moving down to the root, or it may awaken from the bottom to the top, beginning from the root and moving up to the crown. Each of these movements in the awakening of the Fire Snake represent very different spiritual and mystical experiences.

Once the serpent power awakens, the aim is to allow the movement of the serpent power evenly throughout all of the interior stars for the activation, actualization, and realization of the full spectrum of our being-consciousness-force, our holy soul.

First, of course, the serpent power needs to be awakened and we find that a focus on its awakening in the belly to be the swiftest and easiest way. Generally speaking, from the very outset we can all connect with the belly. When we receive the Mother's Force from above, the serpent in the belly is her Divine Presence and Power in us, and our desires become as her desires, for we gain the knowledge of ourselves in her and she in us.

In a manner of speaking, these interior stars are our life or existence in various dimensions and worlds, from the material dimension and world to the Supernal dimension and worlds. It is the play of meta-dimensional being, akin to what we behold in the Hebrew Divine Name for Mother, *Elohim*, and all of her various emanations or manifestations. We are, indeed, her children, fashioned in her meta-dimensional image and likeness.

Root Star

The root star at the base of the spine corresponds to our physical or material body and life in this world, and with all of our basic needs for survival. This star corresponds to the energy of matter composing our bodies and the world, food, shelter, clothing, the instinct for survival, and procreation. Our capacity to ground energy and to individuate our body consciousness is the intelligence of the physical body. The elemental force of the earth and the direction north in the Sacred Circle are also attributes of the Root Star.

The body that arises and the world in which it appears are inseparable from one another, so while the root represents a vehicle for individuation in an infinite plethora of life-forms, it also represents an underlying unity of all life, all bodies, completely interdependent and interconnected with one another.

Although we may speak of our material being as somehow distinct from our energetic being, and of the need for the reintegration of our material and energetic being, in truth, every level of our being or existence is energetic, including our physical or material being. Basically speaking, our physical or material body is a vortex of matter-energy-light in a vast ocean of matter-energy-light: pure energy, light, or spirit manifest in material form. Mass is energy, as modern physics affirms. This is the truth of our being, our existence, even on a physical or material level. As we receive the Divine Light from above, the Holy Spirit, we can recognize and realize our energetic being, and naturally in this recognition is the realization of all reality as dream-like, a radiant display of the mind, consciousness or soul, all as an expression of our energetic being.

Navel Star

The navel star corresponds to our astral body and astral worlds, and to the dreamtime. Corresponding with emotions, pleasure, and sexuality, movement, change, and polarity; it is the play of duality and opposition necessary for individuation and self-realization, socialization and exchanges of energy, nourishment, and nurturance. The navel star is the power of clairsentience and is attributed to the elemental force of water and the direction west in the Sacred Circle.

This is the dynamic center of life and vital energy, the lower vital, which, when joined to the higher vital in the heart, becomes the vehicle of self-actualization and self-realization. When joined to the heart, the navel, or belly becomes like a womb through which we conceive, gestate and give birth to something of our true and natural being, our holy soul. Yet, when divorced from the intelligence of the heart, it is the "belly of the Great Beast," a play of extreme selfishness, egoistic desire and fear, bound up in cosmic ignorance, self-consumption and self-destruction.

This is the energetic center through which we are able to become aware of the subtle energetic dimension within and behind the physical or material dimension, and through which we contact and interact with the world of spirits. In spiritual work affecting changes or shifts in the material reality, this interior star is key, a principle center of focus.

Solar Plexus Star

The solar plexus star corresponds with our mental body and the mental world, the ordinary mind or surface consciousness, the force of personal will or power, the transformation and delivery of energy. In this star is the knowledge and ability necessary for works of magic or wonderworking arts, alchemy, psychism, all intellectual pursuits, metaphysical, and spiritual metabolism, technology, and humor. It also corresponds to the elemental force of fire and the direction south in the Sacred Circle.

When the solar plexus is joined to the heart, the mental consciousness becomes illuminated and inspired; the solar plexus then acts as the receiver and transmitter of the spiritual influxes and energy from above. In this illumination, all human endeavors assume their true purpose and meaning, generating a true and righteous humanity in balance with Creator and Creation. However, when cut off from the heart, this star is the "head of the Great Beast," and our life is bound up in the titanic power of egotism, the play of dominion or power over others in selfish consumerism and selfish ambition that potentially knows no end, no satisfaction.

Religions preaching a revelation of love but enacting holy wars and inquisitions are an example of the *klippah* of this center when divorced from the heart and upper interior stars. Reviving a pure spirituality of direct experience, founded upon the awareness of Sacred Unity, is the redemption of this center, its restoration to its rightful place in submission to the Divine.

Here we may remind: When your will becomes God's will, God's will becomes your own. The Divine Presence and Power of God moves with, in, and through you. This is the true virtue and power of this interior star.

Heart Star

The heart star corresponds with our higher vital body and the higher vital worlds, and it corresponds with our true intelligence: faith, hope, and love, and the knowledge, understanding, and wisdom that come with them. Corresponding with the radiant holy breath that kindles the Fire Snake, with affinity, empathy, unity, true relationship, connectedness, devotion, and healing, this star is the seat of true spirituality and genuine mysticism. It is depth of feeling, active compassion or charity, redemption, or salvation, balance and harmony. The heart star corresponds with the elemental power of air and the direction east in the Sacred Circle.

In the heart star we recognize and realize our innate unity with all our relations and begin to enter into communion with the Divine. Humankind struggles to come to the heart and to ignite the heart star, as it is the place where we begin to become a true human being and begin to realize the divinity within our humanity. The heart is the seat of the indwelling Messiah, the Human One of Light in us, our true and natural being as we are in the Divine Mother. This is the place of true self-knowledge, and specifically the knowledge of our purpose in this life. This star is the center of our true desires and dreams.

The heart star joins the three upper interior stars with the three lower interior stars, and thus this center is the key to the actualization and realization of the full spectrum of our being-consciousness-force or holy soul. It is the gate through which we access our spiritual essence which abides in the heart and crown stars. Although we may be incarnate in a human form or body, until we are able to open the heart—going within and living within—as yet we are not a human being. The heart is the true life and being of humanity, the "true measure of a woman or a man."

Throat Star

The throat star is the first of the upper interior stars in ascent, corresponding with the foundation of the karmic continuum, the "memory" that binds to the past, but that also anchors to facilitate the development and evolution of the soul-being. This is the center of sound-vibration and communication, speaking, and potentially may correspond with the the Greek principle for the living Word, or *Logos*. From this star, one vibrates chant, prayer, and speaks the force of the Body of Vision. Along with media, creativity, and telepathy, the throat star corresponds with Divine prophecy, the force of the element of space in the depth of depth (the downward direction in the Sacred Circle), and the entirety of the Sacred Circle below, what is manifest.

This is the center that initiates the actualization of the intelligence of the heart and that gives expression to the spiritual inspirations and influxes that come from within and above. It is the distinct divine power described in Genesis 2:19 of the human one naming creatures. As *Elohim* spoke Creation into being in Genesis saying, *Let there be*, so the Human One—Adam—named every creature. The throat star is the active power of prophecy, speaking what shall come to pass or speaking the Word of God, communicating the knowledge, understanding, and wisdom of the Holy Mother. With the power of this interior star we give voice to all creation in our prayers and sacred chants. This star is the active power to uplift all to the Creator.

It must be said, however, that when speech is dominated by the three lower interior stars, when the bestial nature remains unredeemed, speech becomes vain and futile, and is the cause of great bondage, great sorrow, and suffering. Unconscious or negative speech is the manifestation of the great co-creative power in us to maintain habitual patterns of the past, the karmic conditioning that keeps us bound to the ignorance, the demiurge.

Brow Star

The brow star corresponds to our spiritual body and the spiritual worlds. In the heart we come into contact and communion with the world of angels, the world of souls, with the great cosmic forces and archangels. This is the center of cosmic consciousness, the peak of mental consciousness, and it is the center of sight into the World of the Holy Spirit. Corresponding with light, color, seeing, envisioning, creative imagination, clairvoyance, divine vision, and divine thought, the brow is the "seat of the Gnosis Mind," the Divine Mind. The brow star corresponds to the force of the space element in infinite expansion, the circumference of the Sacred Circle nowhere to be found, which is the Sacred Circle in the ideal realm. The depth of above, the upward direction in Sacred Circle, is also attributed to this star.

This is the center of Divine Illumination, the full actualization and illumination of the mental being and consciousness, and it is the center of spiritual knowledge, understanding and wisdom. Yet it remains within the subtle dualism of the mental being and consciousness. As the ceiling of cosmic consciousness, apart from the full breakthrough to the Supernal and union with the Divine I Am, Supernal or Supramental Being, the illumination of the brow is not Supernal.

This center is the guiding or directing principle of the interior stars below it, receiving and interpreting the Divine and Supernal influxes from above, facilitating their actualization and realization. It is the center that translates the Divine potential into the actual, providing the Body of Vision to be worn, spoken and enacted.

The full clarity and force of the intelligence of the heart comes into being when it is joined to the brow star, the center within the head. The illumination of Divine Gnosis this center brings is the heart liberated from the subtle *klippot* of vital sentimentality in its faith, hope, and love. This is the center of illumined spirituality and the actualization of our full capacity as co-creators, consciously directing our evolution, fulfilling our soul's destiny.

Crown Star

The crown center corresponds to the "seat of the Divine I Am" and to the threshold of the Supernal or Supramental Consciousness; it is the place of the full generation of the Solar Being and Threefold Body. This center corresponds with our True Will, the force of silent volition, the essence and nature of mind or consciousness, which is Supramental. The crown corresponds to transcendence, deep meditation, repose, enlightenment, and liberation. In a word, Supernal *Habad:* Knowledge, Understanding, and Wisdom. Pure Radiant Awareness is Non-Dual Gnostic Awareness. This center corresponds with the center of the Sacred Circle or "seventh direction" as well.

The crown is the interior star of True Gnosis, Messianic Consciousness. Abiding in the holy womb of the Primordial Mother, Mother Clear Light, the womb of profound emptiness, the womb of infinite spaciousness, bringing all thought and desire into cessation, this True and Holy Star ignites and blazes forth in full glory. It is in the brow that we experience direct knowledge of God, and it is in the crown that we experience conscious unification with God. In this we may know and understand the distinction between the brow and crown.

Transcendent Star

Of the transcendent star beyond we can only say that it is our spiritual essence.

Essentially, in the Guadalupe Path we seek to bring the Light of our Holy Star or Divine I Am, the Force of our Supernal Being in the Divine Mother, "down" into the belly and root, and we seek to uplift the serpent power to the brow, and ultimately to the crown. This, of course, as has been said, is accomplished by Divine Grace: the Light-Presence and Light-Power. This is the force of the Messiah and Holy Spirit in us: the Holy Mother-Bride.

Now, if you want deeper insight into the interior stars or centers in your energetic body, you can contemplate their basic correspondences and meditate directly upon these centers. If you want insight into your energetic being for healing and personal growth, then look and see where there is balance and imbalance in the corresponding areas of your life, and where energy flows freely and where energy is blocked. This is a practice for self-knowledge in the Path of Our Lady Who-Wears-The-Starry-Robe, and in this way we will understand how to cultivate and refine our desires, our person and life.

With a knowledge of the basic correspondences of the interior stars, as given above, taking up contemplation of the correspondences and meditating directly upon each interior star is far better and more productive than reading many books talking about the interior stars or "chakras." As with learning about the directions or Powers of the Sacred Circle, knowledge acquired through direct personal experience is what will truly illuminate and empower us.

Coupled with the contemplation of the basic correspondences, you can also contemplate the correspondence of the interior stars with the *Holy Sefirot* of the Kabbalah, the Tree of Life, for these interior stars are the direct expression of the Seven *Sefirot* of Construction in us, and the correspondences given to the *Sefirot* are connected with the interior stars.

The root star corresponds with *Malkut*, but it is given the celestial attribute of *Binah*, Shabbatai or Saturn. The transcendent star corresponds with the three Supernals in Sacred Unity: the Holy One.

Navel star—*Yesod*
Solar plexus star—*Hod*
Heart star—*Netzach*
Throat star—*Tiferet*
Brow star—*Gevurah*
Crown star—*Hesed*

Apart from the correspondence of archangels and orders of angels by way of the corresponding *Sefirot* and celestial attributes, there is also a correspondence of the archangels of the Sacred Circle to the interior stars. Alternatively, at times, Metatron is ascribed to the crown star and Hua to the brow star.

Root Star—*Archangel Uriel*
Navel Star—*Archangel Gabriel*
Solar plexus Star—*Archangel Michael*
Heart Star—*Archangel Raphael*
Throat Star—*Archangel Sandalfon*
Brow Star—*Archangel Metatron*
Crown—*Archangel Hua*

Contemplating the basic and extended correspondences of the interior stars, and meditating upon them, cleave to the Holy Mother-Bride and open your mind, heart, and life to her. Her Divine Force may enter into you from above and she may reveal deep mysteries of these interior stars and the generation of the Solar Body to you. In such contemplation, however, pay attention to feeling and intuition more than thought and thinking. Contemplation and meditation is among the practices that may create the conditions in which the serpent power is awakened, uplifted and redeemed.

Serpent, Sun, Moon, Stars & Winds

The Channel-Ways

The interior stars are linked together by three channel-ways, a central channel called the stellar channel, or the "Milky Way", and two channels that run alongside it, crisscrossing at the centers. The left channel is called the lunar channel and the right channel is called the solar channel. Essentially, these channels form an image like the famous caduceus, the common symbol for medical practice.

From these three main channel-ways an entire network of channel-ways extends throughout the subtle energetic body, like a matrix or web of light, and along with the seven main interior stars there are many secondary stars or centers, vortexes of energy formed by the currents of subtle energy moving through the channels. Until the serpent power is awakened and made to flow through these channel ways, only the slightest amount of this spiritual power moves through them, along with the power of the inner winds or radiant breaths. In most ordinary individuals the interior stars are only partly ignited or partly opened, or may look rather like sparks instead of stars, being in effect "closed." The actual ignition or opening of the interior stars comes with the awakening of the Fire Snake and its full movement through the great matrix of channel-ways.

Now, the Holy Names of the Celestial Maiden and her Divine Image point to the Holy Mother as the entire external cosmos, physical, and metaphysical: the Serpent Woman, the Force, Spider Woman, the Matrix, and so on. But they also allude to this interior cosmos within the subtle energetic body, the microcosm as well as the macrocosm. This energetic body, the egg-shaped sphere, the light body in it, the matrix of channels and the stars or vortexes—all of this is the presence and power of the Celestial Maiden manifesting as us. The serpent power is the force that activates this energetic being in us, the inner winds or radiant breaths feeding the Fire Snake, as it were, kindling it until it blazes forth.

As has been said, the serpent power can awaken and move in any number of ways, igniting in any of the interior stars. The most common way, however, is from the bottom to the top or top to bottom, and awakening and being set into motion, it can flow through any or all of the three main channel-ways.

When the serpent power is made to flow up through the stellar channel it leads to various states of illumination or higher consciousness. If and when drawn up to the brow and brought into repose a state of gnosis mind is engendered, and when brought to cessation in the crown, the actual breakthrough to Supernal or Supramental consciousness may occur. When the serpent power is made to flow through the solar channel it gives strength to the physical body and becomes spiritual power directed outward towards the physical or material world. When it flows through the lunar channel it gives strength to the subtle body and spiritual power is directed into the world of spirits and angels, and into dreamtime.

In the Guadalupe Path and the Sophian Gnostic tradition, the aim is to have the serpent power flow through all three of the main channel-ways at one and the same time, for our intention is an integral self-realization. Although the initial breakthrough to Supernal Consciousness may take place by a directing of this great power up the stellar channel or central channel, Supernal Realization requires a movement through all of the channel-ways, the reintegration of our whole being with the *Supernal Shekinah*. It is a movement of the serpent power through all three main channels that we hold as our conscious intention when we are praying for the awakening of the Fire Snake.

When the serpent power is made to flow through the three main channels, naturally and spontaneously it will flow through the entire matrix of channels and will ignite the secondary interior stars: six in the torso, six in the legs and six in the arms. Of these secondary interior stars, those in the feet and the hands are most essential. We may channel and transmit spiritual power into the earth through our feet, and we may direct this power into others by the laying on of hands.

When we receive the influx of Supernal Light from above and the serpent power flows through this matrix, the body of light is generated in full, the Solar Body and Solar Being, and if we are able to look and see a person in the energetic dimension, they resemble something like a blazing sun or star, a great light in the world. This is our being in the folds of the Divine Mother's robes, our being as we are in the Holy Mother-Bride, forever whole and perfect, self-begetting, self-generating: a bornless, energetic being.

The Twin Forces

There are two forces or currents of the serpent power: descending and ascending. The descending force is rooted in the white father seed in the crown. It is a gentle, cooling and illuminating force. The ascending force is rooted in the red mother seed at the base of the spine. It is a fierce and hot force that is very unpredictable, but also quite empowering. We focus on the reception of the Light from above and the awakening of the Fire Snake in the belly through Divine Grace, for the Light from above brings with it the descending force, which tempers and guides the ascending force, the Fire Snake proper.

In a Western "kundalini yoga" this is very important, for if the ascending force is awakened apart from the descending force, it can be extremely fierce and dangerous, leading to serious energetic imbalances, psychic, or mental-emotional dysfunctions, and even illness in the physical body. This is reflected in the many accounts of individuals who tell the tale of the awakening of the serpent power prematurely without proper training and preparation, recounting terrible and even hellish experiences, even insisting that everyone should leave the Fire Snake alone based upon their own distorted experience.

In Eastern methods of "kundalini yoga," a complete retreat from ordinary life is an integral part of the practices, as is typical of Eastern schools of thought. Practitioners will focus upon transcendence, and liberation through transcendence, allowing for periods of significant imbalance and dysfunction during a prolonged process of integrating this great spiritual power. This, however, is not the way in Western practice, nor is it the way in the Mystical Path of Guadalupe, for we remain active in ordinary life while taking up the spiritual life, and we cannot afford such abreactions in consciousness. Unlike Eastern methods, we do not force the awakening of the serpent power, but we rely upon Divine Grace, and we focus on the reception of the Divine Light from above, letting that Holy Light of the Spiritual Sun ignite the "pot of fire" in the belly. We rely on the descending force to balance and guide the ascending force, and in our methods this happens in a natural and spontaneous way as an expression of the boundless compassion of the Holy Mother.

The serpent power, as with everything sacred, is indeed very mysterious, mystical, magical, powerful, and unpredictable. In a word, this is dangerous. The image of the rattlesnake for this great power reflects this unpredictable nature. However, liberated from ego-cherishing, egoistic desire, and fear, we are no longer the doer. We rely upon the Mother's Force and her compassion and need have no concern for the danger, for we abide in the sweet embrace of the Holy Mother-Bride, surrendered to her. This active and dynamic surrender is the key, allowing the Divine Passion of the Mother to carry us wherever she desires.

Inner Winds, Radiant Breaths

In our experience of Sacred Circle we encounter the Four Winds and a secret "Fifth Wind," the Spirit of the Spiritual Sun: the Messiah. These Winds are the powers of the directions, personified by the archangels or kerubim that stand in the directions of Sacred Circle. These Winds also occur in our subtle body so that we may speak of five Outer Winds and five Inner Winds, the same forces moving the microcosm—the human one—as in the macrocosm—the world or universe.

These Winds are the elemental forces of consciousness and are spiritual powers in themselves. Such are the Powers of the Great Spirit and consciousness that forms and sustains all that appears, inward and outward. These Sacred Winds or Radiant Breaths kindle or feed the Fire Snake, as surely as an actual wind stokes a sacred fire in the great outdoors.

Acquiring an awareness of the Inner Winds and the knowledge of how to direct them can prove very helpful in the awakening of the Fire Snake. When they are joined to the serpent power, they become as great powers of the Fire Snake, wonderworking powers as we see with great Jewish shamans like Elijah or Yeshua. Indeed, when the Fire Snake is fed by these winds and joined to them, they may be unified with the Great Winds of the Sacred Circle and great wonders can be performed.

The Four Inner Winds have their abode in the heart, solar plexus, navel and root stars, the Secret Fifth Wind having its abode in the upper three stars, the crown, brow and throat. These are energetic currents within and behind our physical breath, a radiant holy breath within breath. We become aware of them and catch hold of them through practices with breath during prayer, meditation, and worship. There is something of an open secret about how we become aware of them. While breathing in certain patterns, we focus on the rise and fall of the diaphragm instead of directly on the breath itself, seeking to feel and become aware of the energetic dimension of our breathing.

The Heart Wind (or all-pervading wind) corresponds with an equal and even inhalation and exhalation, with no pause between them. Smoothly breathe in and smoothly breathe out.

The Solar Plexus Wind (or upward-moving wind) corresponds with an inhalation, holding the breath, and then an exhalation. Breathe in, hold, and then breathe out.

The Navel Wind (or downward-moving wind) corresponds with an inhalation, exhalation, and holding of breath. Breathe in, breathe out, and then hold the breath before the next cycle.

The Root Wind (or equal-abiding wind) corresponds with an inhalation, a holding of breath, an exhalation, and another holding of breath. Each action is of equal duration. Breathe in, hold, breathe out, and hold.

The Secret Wind (or jar breath) corresponds with a tapering breath, beginning inhalations and exhalations gently, letting them become more forceful in the midpoint, and then tapering them off to become gentler at the end just as at the beginning of the inhalation or exhalation. Gently breathe in; strongly breathe in; gently breathe in. Gently breathe out; strongly breathe out; gently breathe out.

As we breathe in these patterns to become aware of the energy current, we focus on the rise and fall of the diaphragm, as well as extending the equal lengths of time holding, breathing in, or breathing out. Once we catch hold of the energetic currents, we will no longer need to focus in this way.

When we take up this practice with breaths or inner winds in the Guadalupe Path, we enter into union with the Holy Mother-Bride and let her breathe our breaths. She is breathing with, in and through us, empowering us. That, or in Sacred Circle we will let the Spirit and Powers take up these breaths, facing the direction and invoking the Power corresponding to the inner wind we are working with. Often a sacred rattle is used during these breath practices, the rattle helping with the energetic recognition.

Much could be said regarding these energetic breaths or inner winds and their powers. If you are familiar with the great winds in Sacred Circle, as you might suspect they share the same attributes or correspondences. However, before anything is communicated in the oral tradition about these inner winds, first an aspirant must become aware of them and glean their own insights from experience. Only then will a woman or man of knowledge and power share something more of their understanding of these radiant breaths, the inner winds.

Once a person is aware of these breaths and catches hold of them, like the serpent power, they can be directed through any of the channel-ways or interior stars, or directed and focused anywhere in the subtle energetic body, allowing the transmission of their spiritual powers. In this regard, you might recall Adonai Yeshua breathing the power of the Holy Spirit upon his disciples in the upper room following the resurrection, empowering the disciples as apostles, true people of knowledge and power. From the awakening, uplifting, and joining of these inner winds with the serpent come great abilities for a woman or man of power. By this union of inner winds with the serpent power, they can impart this great spiritual empowerment to others as well.

Essentially, awakening and uplifting the serpent power, and actualizing the full force of these holy winds of the Spirit, a person becomes like a generator of great power for the people and is able to share and transmit spiritual power to others, able to channel the blessings and grace of the Divine Mother, as in the sacred ceremony of Passing the Bundle and other spiritual works. Their prayers and invocations become very powerful and very effective.

Here we can say, the serpent will breathe these winds; the Mother will breathe these radiant breaths. She will accomplish all manner of wonders through them, with, in, and through us.

In fruition, the presence and power of the Celestial Maiden emanates and manifests as the woman or man of knowledge and power, the seer and wonderworker, the shaman.

This, coupled with what has been shared previously, represents the essential teachings on the awakening of the serpent power in the Mystical Path of Guadalupe, the Serpent Woman.

A Wedding Feast in Our Lady of Guadalupe

An altar is built to the Holy Mother-Bride for this Wedding Feast. It is adorned with whole roses and rose petals, with all manner of offerings, and the bread and wine is set upon it. Naturally it is ideal if this form of the Wedding Feast is performed outdoors in a Sacred Circle.

This, of course, is only an example of a Wedding Feast of the Holy Mother-Bride. More often than not, most Wedding Feasts of the tradition are performed in the power of the moment, impromptu as it were. In fact, it is in the power of the moment that this example is written based upon a Sophian way of sacred ceremony and basic patterns of invocation.

The Ceremony:

O Virgin of Light, Celestial Maiden, we call upon your Holy Name: *Imma El,* Mother God, Matrix of all. We give all praise to You and we bless You.

O Grandmother Deep Space, Birther of the star realms and countless worlds, we call upon your Holy Name: *Imma Gadol,* Great Mother. Womb of all, we give all praise to You and we bless You.

O Spider Woman, Weaving Woman, Mistress of the light web in endless space, we call upon your Holy Name: *Imma Elohim,* Mother of the Powers, Fashioner of all. We give all praise to You and we bless You.

O Eagle Woman, we receive your Holy Emanation in the east,

the womb of the dawn, and we pray to You: Come with inspiration and illumination in your wings, and draw our soul in ascent with You into Sky Father, Our Heavenly Father, that we might receive the influx of Supernal Mercy, Supernal Grace.

O Snake Woman, we receive your Holy Emanation in the west, the womb of twilight, and we pray to You: Come and stir the pot of fire in our bellies and awaken your serpent child in us, that we might be empowered with knowledge, understanding, and wisdom to walk between worlds and to bring about the Great Transformation.

O War Woman, we receive your Holy Emanation in the south, the place of the righteous warriors, and we pray to You: Come and grant us the courage and strength to overcome the Four Enemies, and empower us to open the way to the Sun of Flowering and to bring true peace.

O Infernal Woman, we receive your Holy Emanation in the north, the place of the in-betweens and elder races, and we pray to You: Come, grant us the vision of the Ancient of Days and of the End-Of-Days, and reveal to us the mysteries of the Sun at Midnight—the dark radiance of primordial glory that shines in the great void of chaos.

O Noblewoman, Forever Whole and Perfect Maiden, Holy Mother of the Serpent-Sun, we receive your Holy Emanation in the secret center, and we pray to You: Give birth to your Holy Child in us and let us burst forth into flower-bloom-flame, on fire with your Holy Spirit, shining as Holy Stars with your Presence and Power.

O You Who Come From The Land of Light Like A Fire Eagle, we invite and we welcome You, and we pray: Send forth your Holy Emanations and let this be the Heaven Earth Place of Promise, the place of the Holy Bridal Chamber.

O Holy Mother-Bride, *Imma-Kallah*, please bless this Wedding Feast.

With holy staff in hand I give salutations to You, and I praise and bless Your Holy Name, and with a sacred eagle feather uplifted I call upon the Powers of the four directions, and height and depth, and Infinite Within. O Sky-Dancing Maiden, let the Winds answer our call and let them bless us. O Woman of Light breathe upon us and bless us, and anoint us with your Supernal Fire.

Spirit of the Light Continuum, Wind of the east, receive us and bless us, heal and illuminate us.

Spirit of Understanding and Wisdom, Wind of the west, receive us and bless us, and teach us the way of reintegration.

Spirit of Counsel and Might, Wind of the south, receive us and bless us, and guide us in the way of the Divine Life.

Spirit of Knowing and Seeing in the Light Continuum, Wind of the north, receive us and bless us, and reveal to us the Great Body of Vision.

O Sky Father, Great Spirit, look and see your Holy Child, the Spiritual Sun that shines in us, and let the Sacred Winds fill us and carry us up in the Great Resurrection and Ascension.

O Earth Mother, Great Life, look and see your Holy Child, the Spiritual Sun that Shines in us, and let your Holy Fire rise up and lead us in the way of the Great Liberation.

In the Name of the Spiritual Sun and the Holy Bride, I take up the sacred rattle and walk the circle with sacred staff sun wise, singing, chanting, dancing, invoking the Supernal Grace and Glory of the Land of Light, calling down the Great Thunder of the Mother's Force.

I put on the Body of Vision, the Light Body of the Serpent-Sun, remembering the Son of the Human One uplifted on the Cross, pouring out Holy Fire and Light upon us, opening the way to the Day of Be-With-Us, the Great Aeon of Light and Truth.

Ya-Ma-Ma-Ya Ah-La (chanted)

Mother God, bless us and grant us your boons, heal us and restore our life.

IAO (Chanted EE Ah Oh)

I am the Serpent-Sun, Winged-Serpent, Bornless Spirit. This is my Holy Body, this is my Holy Blood, eating and drinking become and be as I Am, Fire, Light, Pure Spirit.

IAO-OAI (intoned in all directions EE Ah Oh Oh Ah EE)

I stand in the Midst, as in the Great Abyss, radiant with the Great Glory of my Father-Mother, He-She Who-Sends-Me. Behold the fiery light of the True Cross, *Sha-Ta*, and receive the Light of the Living *Elohim*.

O you of height and depth, east and west, north and south, and in-betweens, I pray you be blessed and I pray for the fulfillment of your dreams.

We pray for the blue and the green, for creatures of air, fire, water, and earth, for land and sea, for all our relations: the two-legs and four-legs, winged-ones and finned-ones, and the creeping and crawling ones. We pray for the spirit people and the star people, and for those who dwell within and beyond.

O spirits of the day and spirits of the night, visible, and invisible, come and partake of this bread and wine, my Body and my Blood, and be nourished, satisfied, and fulfilled in the Divine I Am. Come, and let us walk among the stars and let us bring forth the emanation of the Land of Light upon the earth, the time of the Sun of Flowering, Blooming, Bursting-Forth-Into-Flame.

I Am, the Spirit and the Body, the Beginning and the End, the First and the Last. I Am You and You are me. Today we shine as Holy Stars in Our Mother's Robe. The End-Of-Days is come; let us rejoice in the company of *Kodesh Imma-Kallah*, my Mother, my Bride, my Youngest Daughter.

(Partaking of the bread and wine the assembly bursts forth into song/chant, dance, and praise, using sacred instruments like rattles and drums. It is a time of charismatic worship, prayer, and spiritual works for people.)

Let us intone *Hallelu Or Imma, Hallelu Or Kallah!* And let us say, "Amen." This concludes the prayer-ceremony of the Wedding Feast.

 # Healing Arts in the Mother

In Sophian Tradition, the healing way is an essential vehicle of recognizing and realizing the nearness of the Divine. The Order of St. Rafael, named for the archangel whose name means 'Healing Power of God,' focuses on contemplative and ceremonial practices of the healing way. Many of the teachings and practices comprising the Order are summarized in Tau Malachi's *Gnostic Healing*, which presents this healing way from a Kabbalistic perspective. While sharing many principle teachings from the Order of St. Rafael, the healing arts presented here, many for the first time, emphasize a shamanic dimension within Sophian Tradition for those so called by Our Venerable Mother who heals us in this body and life and beyond.

Along with the sign of the sacred flowers the Celestial Maiden heals Juan Bernadino, the spiritual benefactor of Juan Diego, bringing him back from the threshold of death. She is also the Virgin Mother of Yeshua Messiah—perhaps the greatest spiritual healer to walk among us—whose primary earthly ministry was that of an exorcist and healer. This sign of flowers and the healing of Juan Diego's "uncle" represent the two main intentions of the Holy Mother-Bride's appearance, her two key actions: the flowering of our being—the realization of our Forever Whole and Perfect Nature—and our healing. These two, in truth, are one and the same action, for healing is the restoration of our wholeness and harmony of being, our health and happiness. Thus, healing arts are an integral and significant part of the Mystical Path of Guadalupe, for we often turn to her in prayer for the healing of people and take up works of healing in devotion to her.

Naturally, the healing arts taught in the Order of St. Rafael are integrated into the healing arts that are taught in the Mystical Path of the Forever Whole and Perfect Maiden. There is yet another way taught in this Mystical Path, a very shamanic way that draws upon the healing power of the Divine within the light of the sun, moon, and stars, in natural and elemental forces.

Now it must be said, in much the same way that we cannot teach a person to be a seer and wonderworker—a shaman—the same is true of the healer. The power of healing is a spiritual gift given by the Mother Spirit and it is a calling. We do not choose to be healers, just as the shaman does not choose to be a shaman, but rather we are born to be healers or called by the Mother Spirit as healers. We can teach about healing and we can teach ways of healing, how the conditions necessary for healing can be co-created, but we cannot make a person a healer or give a person healing power. It is the Divine Mother alone who makes a person a healer and gives the healing power.

We all have spiritual or magical power, whether or not we are called to be a shaman, and likewise we all have healing power, whether or not we are called to be a healer. Thus, like the wonderworking ways of a shaman, we can all benefit from the study and practice of the ways of the healer, as they are an innate part of our devotion to the Holy Mother-Bride and Spiritual Sun, the Messiah. Whether or not we become a healer among the people, we all have the power to heal ourselves and our own lives. In fact, it is the natural healing power of our energetic being within all that healers are able to activate and draw upon when they perform a healing with us, a power that is within us and all around us in Nature, in the Holy Mother. There is a great need for healing individuals, peoples, and this Good Earth. Whether or not we are called as a healer, it is good for us to perform healing practices to bring in healing energy for the people and the land.

When we take up healing practices, first and foremost we must know and understand that healing is not something that we do as individuals, or something we do by our own power, but rather we are a channel or vehicle of the healing energy of the universe, the healing energy of the Mother Spirit and Powers. This is very important because if we try to heal with our own power or our egos, we will end up draining ourselves of vitality, becoming very tired, feeling nauseous, and may even become sick. Whatever healing occurred by our own power might not last. We may even harm ourselves in performing healings in this way, as well as cause harm to others. Likewise, those who falsely pretend to heal do themselves and others great harm, for they are acting in such a way as to destroy faith and hope among the people.

Instead of something contrived, conjured, or forced, or by using one's own personal energy, healing is something that is done in harmony with the flow of life and the Mother Spirit, drawing upon and channeling the healing power of Sky Father and Earth Mother, the Spiritual Sun and Holy Bride. When we heal in this way, we do not become depleted and tired, at least not to any significant extent, and the healing will be effective, having lasting effects.

Healing is something that should never be forced upon someone, but rather, a person must seek out healing for themselves, and they must understand that they need to be a co-creator of the healing they seek, and that they need to be a participant in their own healing. To seek healing initiates one's own process and path to wholeness and harmony of being, the healer merely serving as a midwife of the Divine Mother in the healing work.

Indeed, healing is about faith and about our relationship with the Divine and all our relations. We are wise to also remember this. That, and all healings are provisional. Once healed, we must tend right relationships with ourselves, our relations, and the Divine, seeking to live in a way that reflects wholeness and harmony, bringing health and happiness to ourselves and to others. Unless we are willing to make necessary changes in our lives, any experience of healing we've received is unlikely to be fully grounded and integrated, and might not last.

In healing we must also have a distinct connection with the person that we are working with. There must be some bond and good energy between us, some feeling of connectedness, or otherwise the healing power cannot pass between us. Likewise, it must also be recognized that some illnesses are not meant to be healed, or that some things are not necessarily a problem. Sometimes our apparent weaknesses are an integral part of our strengths and talents, and the healing that is needed is self-knowledge and self-acceptance, and perhaps a bit of humility.

Although the Divine Mother brings Juan Diego's uncle back from the threshold of death, we must also be very careful about healing work with the dying. All healing is not for the physical body alone, but may be meant to happen beyond the body, in the natural reintegration that we call "death." If we are trying to heal a dying person beyond a palliative level, we may well be increasing and extending their suffering, going against the flow of life and will of the Creator, encouraging them to cling to material life by giving them false hope when it is time to let go. On the other hand, on occasion, very radical healings can and do happen, tantamount to bringing a person back from the threshold of death. But this is not the principle focus when we work with the dying, save by the inspiration of the Holy Spirit. Rather, our focus is the relief of their immediate suffering and their ultimate reintegration with the source of their being, God the Mother, God the Father.

At the outset of a healing practice, before you try to heal anyone else, first you must focus on healing yourself and your life. You must take care of yourself and be in good shape before you can fully attend to the needs of others and care for others. Thus, at the outset you will want to bring yourself into balance and harmony with the flow of life, and seek to bring balance and harmony to your spirit, mind, emotions, and body. Seek to reintegrate the inside and outside, reintegrating your energetic and material being.

As you take up the healing ways, in the process of self-healing pay attention to purifying and consecrating yourself, letting go of negativity and all that is false and unreal. Offer yourself to the Mother Spirit and Powers. As you purify and consecrate yourself, pray to the Divine Mother for the knowledge and power to heal yourself, and for the knowledge and power to bring healing to the people and the land. Tend a continuum of seeking healing—spiritual, psychic and material—and be passionate in your devotion to the Holy Mother-Bride.

Healing is a sacred action. Whether we are serving as a healer or are the person being healed, healing work always begins with prayer, a communion with the Mother Spirit and Powers. Essentially, we begin by giving praise and thanks to the Divine, and by invoking the Divine Mother and Powers to help and guide us, and to show us what needs to be done. This is very important, for although we can speak of methods of healing in general, the actual methods come from the insight and inspiration of the

Mother Spirit and the Powers, and by way of the spirits and angels that work with us in the healing way. True healing is an intuitive art that requires us to be open and sensitive to the Divine Mother and Powers. Ultimately, it is the Divine that teaches and empowers us to work wonders and to heal.

A good healer knows and understands that they cannot heal everybody. A healing work must accord with the Divine Will and the desire of the person being healed, and, there must be a real connection or bond. The Holy Spirit must give a person to us to be healed and inspire the healing. So part of our prayers and meditations at the outset must include looking to see if a healing work is to be done, as well as looking to see what might be done.

Naturally, along with prayer at the outset of a healing work we will also smudge thoroughly, smudging the sacred space of healing, any tools that might be used, as well as ourselves and the person with whom we are working. Smudging is done at the beginning, as well as at the end. We smudge the space, the tools, and ourselves after every healing. Coupled with smudging, we may also make offerings to the Divine Mother, Powers, and the spirits as we start the healing work.

We may make offerings on behalf of the person we are working with, but they also come with offerings, both a gift for the healer and an offering to the Divine. They do not do this because they "have to" or "should," or at the demand of the healer, but rather because they know and understand the principle of receiving and giving, knowing that healing is rooted in their own energy and participation. They do so with awareness and from the heart.

Here it must be said that however it might be justified in much of modern spirituality and the new age movement, at no time should any spiritual work, let alone healing, be sold. The ignorance and delusion of lack behind this is one of the great causes of much illness and disease in our society and people, and the making of a business out of spiritual and healing work only perpetuates this great darkness, this profound ignorance. No, indeed, rather an education must be provided about giving and receiving, loving our neighbor—all our relations—and being aware and responsible for our energy. We must learn to give freely from love, both the healer and the person that is receiving healing. It is good that a person gives as they receive, and in healing work a person is more likely to receive a healing when they give of themselves in return, but it is not a business transaction among spiritual people. Rather, it is an offering from the heart and soul from both sides, a free exchange of energy in connectedness, in love and compassion. This is the basis of true spiritual healing. This is a point that we cannot emphasize enough.

There are many ways of healing, and all of them can be extremely effective; it is all a question of what works, and specifically what works with a given person in their situation. What works with one person, or in one situation, might not work with another, so it is good to know and practice many different ways, rather like building up one's tool belt to have the appropriate tools for various jobs that might be encountered. Essentially, the more ways of healing we know, the more skill we will have and the greater the spectrum of our healing language in the Spirit. When we know many ways, the Spirit and Powers have a better vehicle to work with, in and through.

The Body of Light & Hands of Light

When we are healing, with conscious intention and visualization, we bring our energetic being through our physical being. We envision ourselves radiant with the light of the sun and stars, like the Celestial Maiden. We envision ourselves as Solar Being. We "see" the egg-shaped sphere of light surrounding us, and "see" our body as a light-form within it, and "see" our seven centers as interior stars in that body of light. We see the Divine Light flowing down from above and the Holy Fire rushing up from below. In this way, we have a body of light and hands of light channeling the healing power.

Clapping your hands together several times and rubbing your palms together swiftly is a good way to get the energy of your hands flowing, and to open the centers of energy in your hands. Then, with your hands, you can begin to sweep near the person's body, scanning their energetic body and seeking to feel the flows and blocks of energy there. As you do this you will feel hot spots and cold spots, places where there is too much or too little energy, and you will feel knots and distortions in the energetic body, as well as holes or voids in it. Often you will feel something like cords of energy between the person and others, some of which are very negative and harmful connections. These are the areas you will address in the healing work.

Allowing light and healing power to flow through your hands of light and body of light, you can move energy in the person's energetic body as the Mother Spirit and Powers guide you. You can work with cold spots by laying your hands on the front of the person where the cold spot is and directing energy into it, while you can work with hot spots from the back. Likewise, with sweeping motions, coupled with radiant breath, you can mix the cold and the hot, moving energy between these spots to balance them.

With hands of light you can "reach in" and untie knots, and so also you can reach in and draw out negative and dark energy. Anytime you are drawing out negative or dark energy, flick your hands and fingers several times, as though some substance was stuck on your hands. Cast the negative energy down into Earth Mother with the conscious intention of dispelling it in her great silence and holy fire. In a similar way, when we call upon the Divine Mother and Powers, and the angels and spirits at the outset of a working, there are many luminous beings gathered around us and we can reach out and draw their Light Power into the person, or we can channel it into the person through our light body and light hands. So not only do we perform gestures removing negative energy, but we also place positive energy into the energetic body.

We make our hands talismanic of moving energy as necessary. When we find distortions or blocks, we can smooth out the distortions and direct energy through the blocks, all through laying on hands and intentional gestures. On finding energy cords of negative connections between people, we seek to sever them and facilitate an energetic release, returning to each individual their own energy, and praying for the forgiveness and healing of those involved. The intention is to uplift all into the Divine Light, to bless and heal all in the Divine Mother. With energy cords, however, we must be careful, as there can be cords from actual people or from spirit people, and at times there can be a very intense and powerful interaction going on. When we encounter energy cords and work to remove them, we want to be sure to stay centered in the Divine and be guided by the Divine.

Usually, we join breath with this, breathing the radiant breath of the Spirit with our movements, using the breath also as a vehicle to work with the currents of energy in the person's energetic body. As we are engaged in this laying on of hands and movement of energy with our hands, we may be inspired to make specific sacred signs over the person with our hands, such as the sign of the cross, hexagram or pentagram, or various other symbols, like spirals and circles, or even more complex geometric designs. Essentially, we do what we feel and intuit, all as inspired in the power of the moment.

Coupled with this, we may be inspired to various prayers, invocations, chants, and such, or calling upon various Divine Names and Powers. We may also use voice or sound-vibration to move energy. Along with this, there may be things to be spoken to the person we are working with, affirmations countering negativity, or a word of the Mother Spirit blessing and empowering them. Never, however, is any judgment or anything disempowering spoken during a healing. The person is very open, sensitive, and very vulnerable, and they are to be guarded and sheltered, nurtured and nourished in the Divine Presence and Power. They are to be uplifted.

Naturally, as we work with a person in this way our energetic bodies come into resonance and merge, more or less. It is a very deep and intimate energetic communion in the Divine Presence and Power, as are all moments of Light Transmission. Always it is important to respect and honor the person you are working with, taking this energetic exchange and communion only so far as they are willing and able at that time. Often, several healing sessions may be necessary to resolve an energetic problem or heal the damage in the energetic body, so remember that everything need not and often cannot be done in a single session. Frequently, the energetic exchange of healing must grow and evolve over time in a natural way, as in virtually all other relationships.

In a healing work, as much as coming into resonance and merging with the person on an energetic level, your focus is upon resonating and merging with the Divine Mother and Powers. In this way you will uplift the energy and vibration of the person you are working with, drawing them into some resonance and union with the Divine. This is how healing happens, whatever the method we use.

Hand of Light & Sacred Rattle

In the midst of healing work we may also be inspired to take up sacred tools to help channel, focus, and move energy. One very common sacred tool is the sacred rattle. The sacred rattle can generate and move energy. It can dispel negative energy and invoke positive energy. Thus, in healing practices in the Guadalupe Path, we often take up a sacred rattle in one hand and use our other hand to channel the energy into the person's energetic and material body. It is much the same as the laying on of hands, but using the sacred rattle as well.

Shaking the rattle and uplifting it, we may uplift energy into the Divine Light and bring down influxes of Divine Light. Shaking the rattle and pointing it towards the earth, we may send negative energy into Earth Mother, dispelling it. Likewise, shaking the rattle and moving it about the body of the person we can work with the currents of energy in their subtle energetic body, the sacred rattle becoming like a "rattling hand of light," a hand of sound-vibration.

When a sacred rattle is properly consecrated it can be a very powerful sacred tool for healing, as is well known by shamans from traditions around the world.

The Sacred Drum and Healing

Often a sacred drum is used in healing work, but drumming, unlike the rattling, is usually not done close to the person. While drumming, there is prayer and a calling-in of the needed powers, and sometimes a speaking that becomes something of a guided meditation working with the person for their healing.

At the outset of a healing we might be called to drum, or perhaps at the very end. Once in a while we might be called to do so in the midst. Usually it is a call for specific prayers, the drumming generating energy and sending the prayers.

When we are called to use the drum it is often because there is some spiritual experience the person needs for their healing, and the drumming is used to invoke that experience of the sacred dimension.

Living Waters & Healing

Living waters, which is to say "flowing waters," are known to have purifying and healing power, a great spiritual power. It is well known that Yohanan and Yeshua used baptism or water ceremony as a way to purify and heal people, and that Lady Miryam was known to take people to springs for healing ceremony. The same is true in the Mystical Path of Guadalupe. We will often take people to living waters for healing ceremony, using the pouring of water or immersion in water as a vehicle of the healing power of the Divine Mother.

Although, in these modern times when creature comfort is so highly prized, often people may avoid cold water or the waters of winter. In the Mystical Path of Guadalupe it is understood that cold water can carry an even greater charge of spiritual power and that the effects of the cold can produce some very powerful spiritual experiences. For this reason, cold water isn't avoided, but often is sought out, and water ceremony in winter often proves very powerful and effective for purification and healing. After all, let us remember that the Mother appears in the midst of winter and Juan Diego braves the cold of winter nights and early mornings to have his vision of the Holy Mother-Bride.

The Sacred Fire & Healing

We have spoken previously of the sacred fire and sitting around the sacred fire in the Mystical Path of Guadalupe. Often sacred fire circles are created specifically for healing work, and people may be asked to come to the sacred fire for healing, seeking their own healing and praying for the healing of the people and the land.

At times, water ceremony is joined to gathering around a sacred fire as a way of healing. All manner of sacred ceremonies can be created around living water and sacred fire to bring about the healing of people. In this regard, we might contemplate the baptism of water, fire, and the Spirit of which Yohanan taught: *I baptize you with water for repentance, but one who is more powerful than I is coming after me; I am not worthy to carry his sandals. He will baptize you with the Holy Spirit and fire* (Matthew 3:11). Baptized in living water, sitting around the sacred fire, the Mother Spirit may move to heal and illuminate. In such a sacred ceremony, we are enacting a Body of Vision, a talismanic gesture.

The Stone & Living Waters Healing

Very often individuals suffer from illness because they are holding on to negativity and negative energy exchanges from the past. Sometimes healing is as simple as letting go of the negativity. Taking up a stone and placing the negative energy into it, then casting the stone into living waters, is a way that negative energy can be released and dispelled.

We will go out with the person in need of healing and we will perform a smudging ceremony with them. We will pray with them and ask them to go and find a stone that is willing to help in this sacred ceremony. They will ask the stone if it is willing, and making an offering, they will gather it in a sacred manner. When they return with the stone we will take it and hold it, and we will praise and give thanks to Sky Father and Earth Mother for the stone. We will bless it with the Light of the Spiritual Sun, and give it back to the person. Then we will ask them to tell the stone about what happened to them and about what they have done, and to ask the stone to take the negative energy from them, and thank the stone for taking it on. When they have done this, we will have them go and throw the stone out into living waters, releasing the negativity as they do this, throwing it away to be washed clean by the living waters.

Once this has been done, we will pray with them again, this time for all people and the land, praying that all are delivered from bondage to negativity. This movement may be sealed by a Holy Wedding Feast, or with prayer for the good of the people, and a flower offering may be thrown out upon the living waters. This sacred ceremony can be performed at any time, though on or around the new moon is most auspicious.

Healing Power of Stones

Stones have great healing powers in them, especially crystals. Healings can be performed by laying stones or crystals on or around a person, combined with a laying on of hands, holy breath, and the use of sacred tools like the rattle or drum, or others, like the holy staff or a power stick. Essentially, through a sacred ceremony, the healing power is conveyed to the person by way of the stones or crystals. A person does not necessarily have to be present for a sacred stone or crystal to convey healing power to them. Rather, a ceremony can be performed consecrating the sacred stone or crystal, praying for the person, and then the sacred stone or crystal can be given to them or sent to them as a talisman of the healing power.

Stones resonate with the great power of Earth Mother and tend to ground individuals. This in itself can be healing. Likewise, different kinds of stones carry different power or "medicine," so selecting the appropriate stones can help invoke the energy needed for healing. As you might imagine, the use of sacred stones and crystals is an entire art in itself, much like the use of flower essences and sacred herbs for healing.

Looking Deeper into Healing in the Mother

In our modern society and culture there is a great divorce of the spirit, mind, and body. We tend to live only in our heads and to think of our body as a possession, rather like our cars, SUV's and trucks. We do not realize that our intelligence spans many levels, that our consciousness and intelligence are also in our heart and extend throughout our bodies. Neither do we realize that our bodies are a direct expression of us, as surely as are the mind and spirit. In the midst of this clinging to name, form, and personal history—the egoistic self—we lose touch with our spiritual being and energetic being. In a manner of speaking, we become a mental and vital being disconnected from our body and our spirit.

This is very unfortunate, for our spirit or energetic being and our bodies have a self-healing capacity. The knowledge of how to bring about our healing is in the body and in our spirit and soul: our energetic being. We discover this very swiftly in healing work, for as we are engaged in healing practices with people, touching this or that part of their body, or performing energetic work with this or that part of their body, all of a sudden individuals might burst into tears or begin to recount a traumatic event, a negative energy exchange from the past. The damage on a subtle level has been held in the memory of the cells of the body and in the energetic body; the physical and energetic body both remember the cause of injury. Therefore, they hold the key to healing it.

In healing work, we must learn to listen to our bodies and to the bodies of others. We need to listen to the knowledge, understanding, and wisdom that is in the physical body. By this, we can reconnect the head, heart, and body and draw upon the power of our spirit, soul, or energetic being. The open secret, of course, is that the mind, heart, and body are all expressions of our spirit and soul, our energetic being. They are all expressions of the energy-intelligence that we are, and the truth is that the spirit, soul, or energetic being pervades all. On every level, physical, vital, mental, and spiritual, we are energy-intelligence: We are light.

It is said in the tradition, "The Earth Mother remembers," and our material being and physical body is an emanation of Earth Mother, as surely as our energetic being is the emanation of the Queen of Heaven and Sky Father. Like Earth Mother, our bodies remember and know what has transpired. We must learn to listen to our body, recognizing the great intelligence and wisdom that is in it. Through this recognition, we become attuned to our energy body: our mind, heart, and soul.

Science tells us that humans, animals, and plants descended from a common ancestor. It has been pointed out that hemoglobin in animals is similar to chlorophyll in plants. It may be that our ancestors were single-celled organisms in the waters of primordial Earth Mother when she was a very young maiden. Nevertheless, the fact remains that we have our physical foundation or "root" in something of these most primordial, prehistoric ancestors. In a similar way, evolutionary biologists speak of this when they tell us that humans share much genetic material in common with myriad life forms on earth. The mineral layer of life is even more mysterious, as we are formed from the "dust," the matter, of this Good Earth. We must learn to listen to Earth Mother. We must learn to listen to our body.

Here we may share another open secret well known by shamans, aside from the knowledge and power of healing. If all life on earth is physically related to us, and we learn to listen to our body and to Earth Mother, we will be able to speak and communicate with all of the angels of our Earthly Mother, the rocks and plants and animals, and even the elements and celestial bodies. The whole material creation is spiritual as well as material; all is conscious and alive. Very swiftly in this true and holy communion, the distinction of "animate" and "inanimate" vanishes entirely.

Earth Healing

Earth Mother has great knowledge and power. She has great healing power. Just coming into contact with her, listening to her, and listening to the body, very often healing can take place in body, heart, mind, and spirit. In the Guadalupe Path, healers know and understand this and often draw people out into the great outdoors for their healing. We may recall the prophet or shaman Moses at the burning bush when the *Shekinah* of *Yahweh* appeared to him. He was told to take off his sandals, for the ground upon which he was standing was holy. Earth Mother is holy, not just at the burning bush, but everywhere.

Indeed, Moses beheld a burning bush, but with the influx of the Supernal Light, the Mother's Force, we behold the entire world on fire with spiritual energy, the Supernal Light shining like the sun in the sky from within the secret center of every particle of matter. We know and understand the holiness of this Good Earth and all that is in it, the holiness of the entire Great Matrix of Creation as *Elohim*, the emanation of *Imma Gadol*, the Great Mother.

This is a key to a healing practice. If you want to be healed, let your body come into direct contact with the earth, unimpeded by footwear. You may even go so far as to be completely naked in the wilderness, walking, or lying upon Earth Mother, clad in Sky Father, exposed to the light of the moon, sun, or stars, drawing in the healing power in a physical and spiritual communion. Thus, in the healing way of a shamanic path, a healer may very well ask a person to go walk upon Earth Mother without shoes, or while performing a healing they might ask a person to lie upon Earth Mother. As they are healing they may draw upon the power of Earth Mother, as well as the spiritual influxes of the Divine Light from above. They might also call upon the power of great stones, having a person sit or lie upon a very large rock, listening to the stone and body for their healing.

Joined to this, they might have a person lie in a certain direction or face a certain direction, calling upon the power of that direction, one of the Four Winds, to help heal and make whole, or to help energize and reintegrate. Sometimes they might take a person to the top of a sacred hill or mountain, vertical nodes of Earth Mother's power, where Sky Father and Earth Mother consort with one another, and where the Power of the Holy Winds can be most strong.

At times, they might place a person in a hole dug in Earth Mother and perform sacred ceremony for healing, or they may even cover a person in a hole with earth, leaving only their face exposed, making a healing Earth Mother womb.

There can also be healing power in rock clefts and in caves, which are natural wombs of Earth Mother, though you must pay attention to the spirits of a place. In such places there can be fierce spirits that are not good for healing, or there may be very magical spirits whose talents are good for other forms of spiritual work. Places near springs and water falls can be especially healing, as can some meadows and some groves of trees. Simply holding healing intention while in contact with Earth Mother can bring change.

As you might imagine, healers may often go out on walks of power, praying, and performing sacred ceremony, seeking out healing places so that when there is a need they can take people to them for healing prayer and ceremony.

Earth healing may also occur within Sacred Circles traced upon the ground in one way or another, or formed by stones that have been gathered. Likewise, healings might be performed in or on other sacred geometrical patterns, such as a pentagram, hexagram, cross, or an even more elaborate design.

Here it must be said again that merely going out into nature and walking in a sacred manner can be very healing. So many of us in modern times experience imbalances in our energy and illnesses because we are out of touch with nature and the natural order. Anything we might do to commune in nature, to commune with Sky Father and Earth Mother, the Spiritual Sun and Moon, the stars and elements, and our relations, can lead to healing and wholeness of being. We must repeat: If some healing happens, unless a person is willing to restore a balance and harmony with the natural order in their lives, getting back in touch with the Great Spirit and Powers in Mother Nature, the healing will not last. In this regard, we can only wonder about the future when it is said that the majority of human beings will be living in vast cities. As this happens, unless some points of contact are made with Mother Nature in preserved, open spaces, imbalanced spirits, thoughts, and emotions, and dysfunctional ways of living will increase. In such a toxic context, there will be greater vulnerability to plagues of illness and disease.

Tree Healing

There is healing power in trees. Reaching high up to Sky Father and reaching deep down into Earth Mother, gathering in power from the sun, moon and stars, becoming the roost for birds of the air, they are often channels of great spiritual power. If we approach a tree in a sacred manner, making an offering and asking to commune with the tree, we can embrace the tree and draw in healing strength from it. In a similar manner, if we sit under a tree, touching Earth Mother and drawing down power from Sky Father, we may gain healing strength.

There is a simple practice of communion with a sacred tree and the Holy One, and there can be healing power in this way of communion. In the practice of healing by sitting under a sacred tree, it must be said that you need to be careful in choosing a tree, for some trees are inhabited by fierce spirits and hungry ghosts, especially lone trees that stand in desolate places. Some tree spirits are not friendly and will not seek to help you. As you approach the sacred tree take off your shoes from your feet, for the ground is holy, and make offerings in that place, offerings to the sacred tree and spirits of the place, calling upon the Spirit and Powers there, and go to the sacred tree as to an Emanation Body of the Holy Mother-Bride. Seating yourself beneath the sacred tree, with your back against it, let that sacred tree become as your spine going down deep into Earth Mother and reaching up to Father Sky.

Inhale, drawing up the Holy Fire of Earth Mother into you.

As you exhale, let this power go up as an offering to Sky Father, merging with the Father. Then, reverse this holy breath. Bring down the Father's Power—the Sun's Power—with inhalation. And with exhalation ground and anchor it in your body and Earth Mother. Bring healing power down for yourself and the people, all your relations. Abide, then, centered and grounded, rooted as the sacred tree. Be pervaded by the healing power of the Holy One, the *Shekinah* of the Holy One moving with, in, and through you, and manifesting as you, Forever Whole and Perfect. All causes of illness and disease are dissolved.

A healer may have a person take up this healing practice, and using a sacred rattle or drum, or performing some sacred ceremony, they will facilitate the process of healing with the person in need. This can prove a very powerful method of healing.

Moon Healing

The cycles of Grandmother Moon often determine the times for healing work. With the new moon there is purification and the seeds of new beginning. It is also a time for works of transcendence, awareness of the fullness of the Body of the Queen of Heaven and Grandmother Deep Space, the Comity of Stars. The full moon is a time for energizing and bringing to fruition, wholeness, completion, the play of dreams and visions, and the great play of spirits in the fullness of the astral tide. New and full moon are both powerful healing times, depending on what needs to be done to bring about the healing sought.

New and Full Moons offer many opportunities for combinations with other healing practices as well. Very often a sacred fire ceremony is performed for healing on the new or full moon, much the same as other wonderworking ceremonies around the sacred fire are performed on the new and full moon. When we work with sacred stones and crystals in healing arts, as in other wonderworking arts, it is common every month to bathe the stones and crystals in the light of the full moon, for they are energized and blessed by the light of Grandmother Moon and there is healing power in her light. In a similar way, a healer may have a person bathe in the Moon's light for healing, gathering in the energy of the Moon's light into the subtle body, or they may take a person out upon the full moon for a healing ceremony.

The essence of the new moon is banishing or dispelling causes of illness and misfortune, and the essence of the full moon is invoking spiritual energy for wellness and good fortune. Naturally, if we tend a continuum of sacred ceremony following the cycles of Grandmother Moon, we will tend to experience greater health and happiness, for the Great Spirit will smile upon us through her and we will be blessed and illuminated by her presence and power.

Sun Healing

There are many practices surrounding the sun and healing in the Order of St. Rafael and all of these are also found in the healing arts of the Guadalupe Path as well. There is great healing power in predawn and in the light of the morning sun, so going out to greet the rising sun in remembrance of the Holy Mother-Bride and Spiritual Sun, the Risen Messiah, can invoke healing power.

A healer may give a person instructions regarding this, asking them to go out and greet the sun and pray for healing, giving them a sacred ceremony to perform, such as the blessing of water for healing and Union with the Spiritual Sun for healing. On occasion they might ask a person to join them for a healing ceremony in the light of the morning sun.

Quite often, healers will take up spiritual work alone at predawn or in the early morning light, praying for people, performing sacred ceremony for them, and sending energy to them. In this same time of early day, they will consecrate healing talismans, which they will later pass to the person in need, talismans charged with the healing power of the Spiritual Sun and East Wind, a Wind of Healing personified by Archangel Rafael and the emanation of the Holy Mother-Bride as Eagle Woman.

With sacred staff and rattle in hand, we might greet the rising sun and pray for healing, or, drumming as the sun rises, we may pray for healing, the drum sounding as the heartbeat of Earth Mother giving salutations to the dawn of the Spiritual Sun, the light and life of a new day. A smudging ceremony may be joined to this at the outset, and with it the giving of offerings. Then we may pray and do healing work for the people and the land, sending healing to all who have asked us and to all who are in need. We may also pray for those who will die that day, praying for guardianship, guidance, and full reintegration.

In the healing arts we cannot live in fear of dying and death. We ourselves will walk knowing that it is a "good day to die," if that day is the day for us. Conversely, some healers on the Guadalupe Path will perform prayer and ceremony for healing and life in the morning, and will pray at dawn for those who are being born into the world that day. In the evening, as the sun is setting, they will pray and perform sacred ceremony for those who are dying. Between these gates of sunrise and sunset is noonday when they will pray for the needs of life and the living. On the other side of noonday, at midnight, they will pray for the needs of those in the afterlife. Noonday is for those walking in this world, and midnight is for those walking in the spirit world; sunrise and sunset are for those in between. This is called "the Healing Way in the Path of the Sun," following the Sacred Circle as the sun moves round it.

Now here we may speak of a secret contrary method known to people of knowledge and power who walk with the power or medicine of the trickster. For them, all of this is reversed, for life is in the spirit world and death is in this world. Times of the moon and seasons can be reversed in their contrary walk. Their prayers and sacred ceremonies can be very powerful for healing, for often the cure for illness and disease requires a reverse polarity and the power of opposition that shatters old patterns, engaging a radical shift. Though it can be extremely jolting, like a defibrillating shock resetting the heart beat steady again, such crazy wisdom methods can literally be lifesaving when the contrary trickster walks with the Sacred Heart, knowing and loving the Holy Mother-Bride.

This highly specialized method, of course, can only be used by those who naturally carry presence and power in this way, who have been called to walk this way by the Mother Spirit and Powers in a spiritual working, and who have been empowered by a deep integration with emptiness to do so for that spiritual work. Apart from the Holy Spirit, the contrary method consumes fools. It is a dangerous walk unless a person is walking it in the Holy Spirit.

Spitting Healing Power

The Spirit puts healing words into our mouth, and at times a talisman of healing might be made in a similar way to what Adonai Yeshua shamanistically did for a blind man to restore his sight. You may recall in Chapter 9 of St. John, Yeshua heals a blind man by gathering earth and spitting into it, then wiping the paste upon the eyelids of the man and telling him to go and wash it off in the sacred waters of Siloam. This is a distinctly shamanic form of healing. As it is done in the Gospel, so is it also done in the healing arts of Guadalupe by men and women of knowledge and power.

As strange as it might seem by the standards of the dominant culture, there is another common way of healing among shamans in various traditions using spitting, and it is used in the Path of Guadalupe as well: the spitting or spewing of a fluid from the mouth, usually water or strong liquor. In many cultures, strong alcohol is a common, fragrant offering to spirits, known to have spiritual energy as a consciousness-altering "ally."

By taking a mouthful of fluid, carrying a prayer and conscious intention, a shaman may convey a blessing or spiritual power to a person by spitting or spewing the fluid from their mouth, spraying the person with the fluid. Setting aside the taboos of the dominant culture that are placed on spitting, the experience and effects of this can be very powerful. Along with imparting blessings this way, this is also used for purification and exorcism, and to pass healing power by targeting the place in the body healing might be needed. It can be a way to banish negative energy or to imbue positive energy, and is a very common practice in the healing arts of Guadalupe.

Of course, such a practice is usually only used with initiates, with those who understand and accept the practice, for otherwise it could very well offend and cause a negative energy exchange that is harmful to a person. But when it is acceptable, it is a very powerful method for the transmission of spiritual power, joining the material and energetic dimension together in the action.

Naturally, though, this assumes that a person is a man or woman of knowledge and power, and that they have the gift of communicating spiritual power in this way, as Yeshua did. It is a method taught and inspired by the Mother Spirit and Powers. As we learn to let them take us up in spiritual work, something of this is usually taught through oral instruction and experience, with an actual empowerment.

Sucking Out Darkness, Blowing In Light

This is a common practice of shamanic healing around the world. A shamanic healer may place their mouth on the body of a person being healed and suck out the darkness or negative energy that is causing illness or disease, and they will either devour it with their inner fire and heat or they will spit it out, either spitting it into Earth Mother or spitting it into some container that will "bind" or "trap" the fierce spirit. This movement of energy in the talismanic gesture of sucking out the darkness is accomplished with prayer and conscious intention. Unless the inner fire and inner heat of the belly is fully kindled and active, spitting out the "evil spirit" early in practice is wise, as the healer would not want to take on the negative energy unless they had the actual capacity to transform it.

Coupled with this method, often the shamanic healer will also blow healing energy into the body of the person. After sucking out the darkness, they will blow light into the person's body. They may do this directly, or they may set a sacred healing tool on the body so as to "blow through" the sacred tool, blowing its energy into the person's body. Something similar to this occurs in the Order of St. Rafael using Giving and Receiving Practices, focusing on the Spiritual Sun in the heart. But in shamanic healing practices, our focus is in the belly and we work with the great fire in our bellies as we take up the practice of healing. Thus, all movements of healing energy, like sucking energy and blowing light, have their energetic foundation, or root, in our bellies.

Belly Cord Healing

At times, shamanic healers in the Guadalupe Path will envision the extension of light cords from their bellies to the belly of the person they are working with, and they will perform an exchange of energy much the same as in Giving and Receiving Practices. But rather than drawing the negativity into the Spiritual Sun in the heart, they will draw it into the Great Fire of the belly, and from that Great Fire they will envision healing power going into the person's body.

At the outset of this practice, in order to do this and not deplete their vital energy, they will bring down the spiritual light from Sky Father through the top of their head, letting it shine down into their bellies, and they will bring up the Holy Fire from the secret center of Earth Mother below, drawing it up into their bellies. With these two forces of light and fire, which in truth are one great force, they will channel and transmit through their belly to the person they are working with for healing.

Most often this cord is formed belly to belly, but sometimes these cords are formed from the belly to other energetic centers in the person's subtle body to remove blocks in energy and restore the proper flow. This method is frequently used in conjunction with other methods simultaneously. This is considered a very powerful method of healing and is among the most frequently practiced by shamanic healers in the Guadalupe Path.

The cord is envisioned like a luminous hose formed of fiery light that goes from the navel of the healer to the navel of the person being healed, and at the outset the healer will pray and will focus on their inhalations, sucking out dark or negative energy from the person rather like a vacuum cleaner on the in breath. As they draw in this dark or negative energy, they will envision it devoured by the Great Fire and Heat in their belly. Once this is done, they will pray again and will focus on their exhalations, reversing the direction of the current and blowing the healing power of the fiery light into the body of the person as they breathe out, until the person's body is full of this light, completely pervaded by it.

Laying the Body Down for Healing

At times, when great power is needed for healing, it is not uncommon for a healer to lay their body upon the person being healed. This method is recounted with Elijah (1 Kings 17:17-22) and Elisha (2 Kings 4:27-37). Generating the Solar Body, drawing the full force of Light from above and Fire from below, and opening all of the interior stars in the Body of Light, the healer lies down upon the person, stretching their body over the body of the person, and merges both subtle bodies for the healing.

Along a similar line, hugging or embracing a person to communicate healing power is also very common. When this is done the same internal practices are used as in laying the body down. As in all of the methods of healing in the Guadalupe Path, the focus is in the belly during both of these practices, in the belly and on the fiery light within the breath.

Healing with a Feather Fan

Some of the most common sacred tools used in healing are feathers or feather fans. These tools are brushed and swept over the body, sweeping away negative energy and sweeping in positive energy. The most powerful feather fans for healing are those of the vulture, but depending upon the cause of the problem, fans made of other sacred feathers might be used. For example, if illness is caused by a psychic assault from a human person or spirit person, then Red-Tailed Hawk feathers might be used, or if it is caused by a person being cut off from their spiritual essence, eagle feathers might be used.

Often, when feather fans are used in healing, two fans formed of feathers from both the right and left wings might be utilized. Feathers from the left wing serve to banish negative energy and those from the right wing serve to draw in positive energy, when they are used together. The correspondence of right and left might change in the case of a left-handed healer, however, and very often left-handed people have a call as a shaman and healer. Many indigenous people believe that left-handed individuals tend to have a natural affinity for contact with the spirit world and magic.

Lodge of Healing

On occasion a healer in the Guadalupe Path may make a temporary structure for a healing ceremony. It is usually a simple, primitive structure made of natural materials, such as branches and boughs from a cedar or pine tree, or with limbs and twigs, cloth or sacred blankets. In one way or another, a shelter is made. Often, as part of this lodge, prayer ties are made and attached, as well as power bundles, and it is not uncommon for a special power bag or "medicine bag" to be made for the person to wear when they depart the lodge once the healing work is done. Essentially, the lodge helps to contain and focus healing power, and when called for, can prove very effective.

A sacred blanket or the robe of an animal is laid in the lodge for the person to sit or lie down upon during the healing, and various sacred objects and sacred tools will be arranged there in the lodge, all with the intention of the healing that is needed. A smudging ceremony will be performed around the lodge and within it, and offerings will be made. The Mother Spirit and Powers will be called into it, and it will be consecrated as a lodge or tabernacle of the Holy Mother-Bride.

As needs of individuals are known to a healing practitioner in the Guadalupe Path, that practitioner will go within in prayer, asking of the will of the Mother. If Mother calls for a healing ceremony, so will the practitioner call that individual in need to the lodge of healing. Before entering, the one in need will be smudged outside by the practitioner. Once within it, the healing work will take place as directed by the Spirit and Powers.

After a cycle of workings are accomplished, the temporary lodge of healing is mindfully dismantled. The materials for making a healing lodge will be offered as fuel in a sacred fire circle with the intention of praying for the purification and healing of the people and the land. All materials that were gifted by the Mother and used in a lodge of healing are ceremonially released back to the Mother with healing intention. May She, who is the Forever-Whole-and-Perfect-Maiden, bring forth from within us her power to heal and make whole.

 # Mother & the Serpent

The symbol of the serpent is integral to the tradition of Our Lady of Guadalupe. There is a serpent formed by the folds and patterns of the inner robe of her original image, and beneath her feet in some depictions is a serpent with a human, rather than a forked, tongue. Among her primary emanations is Serpent Woman, corresponding to the West in her Sacred Circle. Likewise, in some traditions surrounding Guadalupe the name of Guadalupe means "She-Who-Crushes-The-Serpent."

The serpent as an angel of our Earthly Mother or "totem animal" represents renewal and transformation, a transformative power, and it also has attributes of fertility or virility, cunning, stealth, and knowledge of the hidden. Aside from arboreal species that dwell in trees, land-dwelling snakes or serpents move close to the ground and therefore also represent a grounding or "earthing" of power. They are considered by many indigenous peoples to be powerful messengers of the Earthly Mother, Grandmother Earth. Serpents live high in trees as well as on land, in water, and many are noted for dwelling in the earth, so they represent the movement of power or energy in all realms and dimensions, power or energy being the essence of the serpent.

The principle serpent associated with Guadalupe, the Serpent Woman, of course, is the rattlesnake. In fact, in Aztec and Toltec tradition, the hands in a gesture of prayer in the image of Guadalupe conceal her "rattle breast nipples," which, when they vibrate and send forth their luminous milk, create the stars that appear in the night sky. The rattler is a pit viper and is venomous; the venom represents great transformative power, a fiery power making all like itself, akin to what is said in scriptures of the presence of *Yahweh*. As a pit viper, it has a special capacity for perceiving infrared thermal radiation to locate, stalk, and follow its prey, indicating sight into the darkness and the ability to see hidden spirits and currents of energy. Its rattle, of course, represents the power of sound-vibration, also implying the great power of silence, which alludes to the Living Word—*Logos*—and the essential arising of all reality from Primordial Space or the Clear Light. It is a snake corresponding with great magic power in the Americas, much like the cobra in the East.

The serpent is also deeply associated with Sophia, Divine Wisdom, and is often a symbol of the Divine and Sacred Feminine. At the same time, it is also frequently a symbol of the Divine and Sacred Masculine. The serpent is radical and dynamic power, and creative power or fertility. On an archetypal and mythical level the "great serpent" is the dragon. As we know in the Holy Kabbalah, some of the greatest and most ancient angels of the order of the Serafim are said to assume the forms of great dragons, and throughout various wisdom traditions, dragons are associated with guardianship, great magic power, hidden treasures, and ancient wisdom. They are likewise noted as great creative and destructive agents.

In Judeo-Christian tradition, of course, the serpent or dragon is most often a symbol of evil and Satan, the Adversary, the tempter and the agent of the "Fall" of the Mother of Life: Eve. On an esoteric level, this describes the activation of the divine potential of creation, free will, and the involution of souls. The serpent symbolizes both evil and good, darkness and light, and represents the power of dualism and polarity necessary for the individuation, development, and evolution of souls. This complex image depicts the generation of the matrix of creation and the true nature of Divine Power manifest as all—evil and good alike—a power transcendent of evil and good.

Such is the true nature of power, of energy: neither good nor evil in and of itself, but becoming good and evil, and everything in between, It is really a question of how power is used and what is manifested by it. In this sense, the serpent is as "The Force" in the modern mythology of George Lucas' film series Star Wars, where the Force has a Light Side and Dark Side, flowing through everyone and everything, and manifesting as everyone and everything. In Hinduism and in Vajrayana Buddhism, this Force is called Shakti and Dakini respectively, and in our Sophian tradition it corresponds with the *Holy Shekinah* and Holy Spirit manifest in creatures and creation, in heaven and on earth. Most specifically, this force is the serpent power, Fire Snake, or Fiery Intelligence, or what in the East is called "Kundalini Energy," an evolutionary force or Divine power in all things.

First and foremost, the association of the serpent with Guadalupe is as this serpent power, the awakening, refinement, and uplifting of which is essential in the process of self-realization, or the enlightenment and liberation of souls. As indicated by the dual nature of this great force, the serpent power is not Divine Illumination, but it is the power through which Divine Illumination or Divine Gnosis is realized. This is the power that sustains and gives rise to all life, to all things, but in most creatures and in most ordinary human beings the barest spark or thread of this power is active and expressed. In most creatures and in most human beings this is a latent potential or dormant power said to be "asleep" and in need of "awakening." Yet this very power is the impulse and force within and behind the development and evolution of all life, the evolutionary power of Mother Nature that has acted on an unconscious level in the generation of life on earth, her force that is becoming conscious in humanity.

This power has been said to be rooted in the base of the spine, there like a "serpent coiled," but as we know, its dwelling or den is in the belly, which is like a pot of great energy or life-force in us, one that we hardly tap into in our present unenlightened condition. The awakening of this serpent power, however, is integral to the dawn of a true New Age, the Age of the Holy Spirit and Second Coming of Christ, the reception of the Holy Mother-Bride or Sun of Flowering. The revelation of Our Lady of Guadalupe heralds the stirring of this great power in us, and is an impulse or call for its full awakening or activation. In essence, the Mystical Path of Guadalupe is akin to what might be called a "Kundalini Yoga" or a "Tantra Yoga," although unlike the very rigid and complex systems of Eastern Traditions for the awakening of the Fire Snake, in the Holy Mother-Bride and Spiritual Sun, in the Mystical Path of Guadalupe, it is a "Yoga," or union, of grace. For in those who adore the Divine Mother and draw near to her, opening their minds, hearts and lives to her, and who take up her Mystical Path, worshiping her, she awakens this Fiery Intelligence in them, and she guides the refinement and uplifting of this great force from the belly to the heart and brow, and to the crown, the top of the head.

Awakening her force is very simple in the Divine Mother. We invite and we welcome her, we open our mind, heart, and life to her, and we ask her to indwell us, dedicating ourselves to her service, engaging an active and dynamic surrender to her, and letting her lead us in the Way. Essentially, we go within and we live within, and we hold the conscious intention of opening to the Divine Light from above, the Mother's Force, and we abide waiting upon her, communing with her. When the influx of the Light of the Celestial Maiden comes from above, we seek to integrate our mind, heart and life with that Holy Light, and that Holy Light awakens, refines and uplifts the Fire Snake. In this, she is our effortlessness, for in truth we have done nothing to awaken the serpent power, but it is she who awakens it in us, and it is she who uplifts it. How we consciously invite and welcome this experience will be detailed below.

In the Divine Mother we do not need to focus upon or force the awakening of the serpent power; the awakening of the Mother's force happens through Divine Grace—the Mother's Force—naturally and spontaneously. We need only open to her and love her, and surrender ourselves to her, moving with her presence and power, and let her presence and power move with, in and through us. We let her Holy Child, the Spiritual Sun, take up our personality and life display. This is our "Yoga," our Way of Union with the Beloved, the Divine, founded upon our awareness of our innate unity and perfection in the Divine.

Now, this serpent power is desire-energy, and in an active and dynamic surrender to the Great Mother we are called to cultivate and refine our desire, to look and see our true heart's desires, our true dreams, and to pursue them in our worship of her, offering up our desires and their enjoyments as an offering to her. In our true heart's desires, our true dreams, is the purpose of our soul, the fulfillment of our destiny. These, however, are not the desires of our surface consciousness and ego, or those imposed upon us from outside of ourselves by the suggestions of the unenlightened society and dominant culture. Rather, they are the desires and dreams of our true and natural being, our being as we are in the Divine Mother.

The title of "She-Who-Crushes-The-Serpent" speaks to the shedding or shattering of false desires and fears of the ego, the unreal desires born of ignorance, all of the abreactions and perversions of desire-energy that prevent the soul's enjoyment and fulfillment. When false desires are dispelled, we may look and see our true desires and dreams, and seeing them we may pursue them in the Divine Mother, knowing her as the Serpent Woman, for she will fulfill those desires and dreams. If you wish to know the best way to awaken and uplift the serpent power, it is very simple: Let desire arise free from self-grasping, attachment, and aversion. In this freedom, follow the bliss of your soul, your energetic being. Live as who and what you are in the Divine Mother. Let all that you do be the worship of her, all as the Sky-Dancing Maiden desires! This is the Path of True Desire.

If we know and understand the principle of enlightened selfishness, we will recognize that the fulfillment of our desires and dreams is dependent upon the fulfillment of the desires and dreams of others. In seeking the fulfillment of our desires and dreams, we will naturally seek to help others fulfill their desires and dreams. We will know that active compassion and love, as embodied in the Mother and Sun, is integral to our fulfillment, and is our greatest joy. The Path of True Desire, or "True Will," is not the path of selfish and egoistic desire, but the refined and enlightened desire of the Spiritual Sun in us, the Human One of Light.

In speaking of desire and the fulfillment of desire, though, we are not just speaking of heavenly desires or the desire for heaven, but we are speaking of earthly desires or the desire for the fullness of life. We are speaking of spiritual and material desires, all in the goodness of the Holy Mother-Bride, the innate good of our true and natural self. We are speaking of an integral realization of a human being woven of heaven and earth, and the manifestation of the Heaven Earth Place, the "Divine sovereignty on earth." In this regard we may echo what has been said by a wise sage: "If it is not here, then it is nowhere; if not now, then when?"

So the Mother says to us, "Am I not right here who is your

Mother?" Around the world religion and its dogmas have arisen to encrust, distort, and pervert true spirituality, pure spirit. And so in religions of the East, just like those of the West, the earth, the body, sensuality, and sexuality, have been denounced as something impure or evil. We are taught doctrines of self-loathing and repression. Here we may say that if Creator has woven us of heaven and earth, and if heaven and earth is the manifestation of one and the same Divine Power, such doctrines are the same fundamental ignorance as those that deny heaven and the Divine, seeking only earthly and material pleasures.

The most basic expression of the serpent power or desire-energy in our experience is sexual energy and the desire for sex. Sexual desire is the root of all life, the great impulse of life, and an innate good. Through sensual and sexual play, souls enter into material incarnation, the vehicle through which souls are actualized and realized, and are able to fulfill their destinies.

Religion tends to propose that the only way to heaven or enlightenment is through celibacy. While it is completely true that periods of celibacy can be very useful and can be called for in our spiritual work, and that some individuals even have a natural propensity to celibacy, it is not the only way to heaven or enlightenment. The real issue is not sex, sexuality, or sexual orientation; it is the conscious direction of sexual or desire-energy, the cultivation, refinement, and mastery of desiring and dreaming. This is self-knowledge and the understanding of energy, and the use of energy or power in harmony with our true self and true desires. The symbol of the serpent associated with Guadalupe, as well as the sign she gives indicating the Pollen Path—the sign of flowers—alludes to the refinement and illumination of the play of desire, the play of the Mother's Power in us.

This play with men and women is different, for men and women carry this Divine Power differently. The ways men and women work with their sexual or desire energy are different, tied to their bodies and how their energy being interacts and moves through their bodies. The currents and cycles of energy in women are directly expressed through their moon cycle or menstrual cycle, and the currents and cycles of energy with men are directly expressed through their generation of sperm and ejaculation. These dynamic movements of energy conveyed by women and men hold teachings of spiritual practices of sacred sexuality and play as worship of the Divine in the Mystical Path of Guadalupe.

Having discussed the symbol of the serpent with Guadalupe, and the basic principle of the awakening and uplifting of the serpent power as an integral part of her Mystical Path, next we can explore practices surrounding the moon cycles of women and the thunder strikes of men, as well as practices of sacred sexuality.

The Pollen Path: Moon & Lightning

The flowers of the plant realm are beautiful and delightful to see, and so also the coming and going of bees, butterflies, hummingbirds, and the like, which serve to pollinate the plants. In essence, we are witnessing a scene of orgasmic bliss, the love-play of the plant realm. When the Noblewoman gives the sign of her grace in the form of flowers, she directly speaks of this pollen path, the play of desire and the delight of life.

The desire of life is in the symbol of the serpent with Guadalupe, representing the serpent power or desire-energy in us. When the image on the sacred ayatl is viewed at a distance, Guadalupe is seen surrounded by a flaming mandorla with a distinctly vaginal shape, suggesting the Gate of Life. The little angel or child beneath her symbolizes the birthing of souls from among the elder races. A new and divine humanity comes from the blessedness of love-play and womanhood in the dynamism of her full glory, power and fertility.

The Divine Mother is spoken of as a Holy Virgin to indicate her innate purity of being, the essence and nature of the soul, her changeless and transcendental aspect. Yet, she is the Holy Mother who has given birth to the Messiah, the Spiritual Sun, and to a new race of humanity, full of sensual and sexual potency, exhaustless creative dynamism and fertility, pregnant with the Divine Potential of all.

Like the Woman of Light from Revelation (12:1), she stands

upon the moon, but it is the new moon, the time of new beginnings, renewal, conception, and initiation, and the time of transition between one moon cycle and another. The moon, often formed as bullhorns or cow horns holds deep symbolism in ancient imagery. The bull implies the dynamism of sacred sexuality in procreation or creative endeavors, and the cow the dynamism of feminine fertility and the power to give birth to new life.

The moon, of course, points to menstruation in a woman's body and suggests deep spiritual meaning in this monthly cycle, as very powerful spiritual forces and life currents are flowing through women, being grounded or earthed by women. Thus, in the Mystical Path of Guadalupe, the moon time is a phase when women may intensify their spiritual practice and spiritual works for the people, taking up more introspective contemplation, as well as prayer, meditation, and sacred ceremony for the people.

Indeed, rather than how patriarchal religions reproach women for being "unclean" or "impure" during their moon time, or the moon time representing some kind of "weakness," in the path of Guadalupe we view women's menses as a time of great power and a sign of fertility. If a woman chooses to withdraw from mundane work and to separate herself or go into a retreat, it is to attend to her spiritual essence and to take up a deeper spiritual work for the people, not to remove herself because she is "unclean." It is a time when women naturally enter into greater psychic and spiritual sensitivity, experiencing deeper connection with the people and the land, and with the world of spirits. In an enlightened society, or at least one that truly honored the Divine and Sacred Feminine, and the blessedness of womanhood, room would be made in the hustle and bustle of daily living so that if and when a woman wished to withdraw and take up spiritual retreat, she would be free to do so. But as with the freedom of choice regarding her body and whether or not to carry a child, it would be a woman's choice, not something imposed upon her.

It is interesting in modern Western societies to see the all-too common struggle of women with premenstrual syndrome. Women initiates in Sophian tradition would propose that this syndrome is directly connected to the repression of womanhood, distorted ideas surrounding menstruation and sexuality, and a lack of teachings about the spiritual or energetic dimension of the moon time and how to work with it on a spiritual level. Essentially, women move great life-power and spiritual force through their bodies, and women have a great manifesting power that grounds in the body, manifesting things in and through their bodies, most miraculously in a woman's capacity to give birth to children. The moon time is a time of a great flow of energy on all levels—material, psychic, and spiritual—and during the moon time when the mental, emotional, and spiritual levels are not tended to, there can be distortions and blocks in the flow of energy, which can play themselves out on a physical or material level in painful experiences such as premenstrual syndrome.

But this is not only an issue of the individual woman's energy, but it is the energy of all womanhood, all humanity, and the entire earth. Women channel and process the psychic and spiritual energy of the whole earth, Earth Mother, taking on the energy of the world. When there is imbalance in the energetic dimension on psychic and spiritual levels, and imbalances in the flow of nature and Earth Mother's energy, this becomes expressed through women and their bodies. Much like the suffering of labor pains for women in giving birth, women tend to take on the suffering of the world, processing what's happening through their bodies. If women hold on to these energies, or are unaware of how to consciously work with them in prayer, they may experience actual physical suffering, even various illnesses or diseases. Thus, what transpires during the moon time is not only an issue of the energy of an individual woman, but also of her environment and the world around her, the energy dimension within and behind life.

In this regard we can't help but consider other illnesses that appear to be on the rise and are associated specifically with women, such as ovarian cancer, breast cancer, and fibromyalgia. May this reflect something of the great oppression of the Divine and Sacred Feminine in womanhood, and the energetic imbalances in our societies and in our environment? As is well known in the spiritual healing arts, the cause of illness and disease is in the energetic and spiritual dimension; they all have their root and cause on an energetic level. This is never to suggest that any fault lies with women or to put the blame of such suffering upon women. Far from it! Rather, it is to propose that a soul incarnate in womanhood has taken up a very sacred task and duty, and that, far from being the "weaker sex," as put forth by the ignorance of patriarchy, women represent a strong sex, assuming the role as a channel of life and matrix of great spiritual power or influxes in their incarnation. Indeed, on many levels women would rightly be called the stronger sex!

An excellent example of the strength of women is seen in the level of sensual and sexual dynamism between women and men. When a man climaxes in love-play, he loses his charge of vital energy while on the other hand, a woman loses nothing, but rather generates even more vital energy. When his force is expended, hers is just beginning to be set into motion. Here we must note how the irony of sensual and sexual strength in women is complicated by patriarchal religion with all kinds of strange ideas and dogmas of sinfulness. After all, if men typically can't keep up on a sensual and sexual level with women, it would be hard to assert the "superiority" of the male gender over the female! The same strength of a woman's moon time is further degraded by patriarchal, religious teachings that the mensus create a state of "uncleanness" or reflect some sort of "weakness." In much the same way this can be true of other flows of energy on psychic and spiritual levels. Women are energetic dynamos, generating and grounding incredible influxes of energy or power, all connected to their capacity to conceive, gestate, and give birth, the capacity of the Mother of Life.

Now, the moon time is, indeed, a time of purification and a transition on an energetic level. During menstruation, a woman is shifting from one moon cycle to another, releasing energy held on physical, psychic, and spiritual levels in one cycle and receiving the influx of new energy and generating the energy of another cycle. It is a powerful time to take up spiritual work for the purification of the people and the land, and for shifts in her own energy. As a woman engages in self-purification and theurgic work for shifts in her own energetic being, she purifies and shifts the energetic being of the people and the land, enacting a spiritual labor in sacred priesthood.

Menses is a time of great transformative and healing power, and during this time a woman is rather like a "spiritual magnet," attracting all manner of spiritual forces to herself. She has many spirits at her disposal to take up spiritual works for the people, all her relations. In that all kinds of spiritual forces are attracted, naturally, spiritual discernment is necessary during the moon time; it is not necessarily a good idea to channel and bring in all spiritual forces that present themselves. Likewise, it becomes especially important to keep thoughts, emotions, speech, and actions positive, to bring in and channel luminous and positive spiritual forces for the people. As in the midst of love-play, when seeking to bring a more luminous soul into incarnation, the state of mind and heart during the moon cycle is very important. The moon time is a very powerful time, but as we know, power can be manifest in many different ways, some good and some not good. Truly, this is a time of incredible responsibility, much like when a woman is carrying new life in her womb.

Thus, during their moon time, women initiates of the Mystical Path of Guadalupe attend to their spiritual essence and seek to manifest a completely positive energy field, and typically speaking they will extend sessions of spiritual practice and add sessions of spiritual practice, seeking to pray and meditate more, and to take up sacred ceremonies for the people. They may take up all manner of ceremonies in harmony with the moon time, reflecting works that are performed on or near the new moon in the continuum.

Naturally, women initiates pay close attention to their moon time. They pay close attention to feelings, intuitions, dreams, or visions that may come just before their moon time begins, understanding that very often the Mother Spirit and Powers speak to them at this time. They also pay close attention to feelings, intuitions, dreams, or visions that come during their moon time to know how to direct their spiritual work, and they will pay attention to creative inspirations that come immediately following menstruation. In a way, it is much like a monthly vision quest for sisters, and, in part, that is how sister-initiates view the moon time, seeking the new Body of Vision at this time of renewal and transition.

Women initiates also pay close attention to shifts in their moon cycle, which reflect shifts in the energy of the environment around women. Such attunement can be prophetic. For example, women involved in more intense energetic work of spiritual community often observe shifts in their moon cycle when there is a greater influx of divine energy or Light Power, their moon time kicking-off, as it were, to help process, channel, and ground the new influx of energy for the people. In other words, women often know in their bodies when there is a greater influx of energy or spiritual power, for their moon time begins to allow them to channel and anchor that power. When this is the case, naturally, they will work with that spiritual current as their moon time continues, laboring for the people in the Continuum, as well as integrating the spiritual empowerment they have received.

Unlike many traditions, in the Sophian tradition, which deeply honors the Divine and Sacred Feminine, women are not isolated from the sacred ceremonies of the group or community during their moon time, but they are welcomed and encouraged to participate, bringing the great power of their moon time with them to the works of the Continuum. There is even more reason for them to come to sacred ceremony during this phase of their moon cycle, save in the case of a ceremony that might produce undue physical stress upon the body or spiritual workings to which they do not feel called at that time.

When suffering or pain arises during the moon time, women initiates view it as a call to Giving and Receiving Practices for the people, or other works consciously taking the suffering of others into their own suffering, praying for the liberation of all beings from their bondage to sorrow and suffering, and praying for the healing and illumination of all their relations. In this way the suffering and pain that arises is not without purpose and meaning, and very often women experience relief and healing as they take up this spiritual work. Indeed, many women who experience great suffering and pain in association with their moon cycle have experienced relief and healing when they learn how to take up spiritual work during this time. There are women initiates in our Sacred Circle who can bear witness to this, having experienced relief and healing by consciously working with the influxes and currents of energy. Intensifying one's spiritual practice and work during the entirety of their moon time is a central part of women's practices on the Mystical Path of Guadalupe.

Similar to works of the moon time, the practice of holding or releasing sexual energy is also significant, for men as well as women. Men's awareness of the cycle of potency generated in their subtle body is directly tied to the physical generation of sperm; paying attention to when they release or hold this charge of energy can be used for the sake of spiritual works for the people. Generally speaking, women tend to a period of celibacy every month in conjunction with their moon time, and men in relationship with women can also use this time to generate greater force and potency in spiritual work, withholding themselves from the release of energy outwardly. Likewise, men can choose to take up periods of celibacy, much like fasting, to build up a greater charge of vital and spiritual energy for theurgic or magical works.

Essentially, women do not have the same need in this regard because they do not give away or lose energy in a sexual encounter; a woman would have to go to very extreme lengths to discharge and lose energy through sexual encounters. Men, on the other hand, give away or discharge their energy every time they ejaculate, as reflected in their bodies' response. Not only that, but men go up out of their body into another dimension, becoming open and sensitive to other dimensions beyond the physical, unlike women who become completely present in the body and physical-energetic environment. The climax of a man is called a "thunder strike" or "lightning strike," reflecting this radical discharge of energy. Because it takes time for a man to recharge and regenerate this energy, it is important that he learns to pay attention to how often he discharges this energy when he seeks to take up spiritual work. If this energy is discharged too often, typically speaking, he will not be as potent in spiritual and magical working; he will not have the full charge of his vital, psychic and spiritual energy.

Here it must be said that there is no religious, moral judgment in cycles of men holding sexual energy. There is no greater moral superiority in celibacy, neither is an active sexual life or fatherhood less Spirit-connected. Witness the falsehood and devastating consequences of religions imposing celibacy upon its leaders. Celibacy is neither called for, nor natural for most, but only serves to create distortions and abusive perversions in desire-energy and sexuality. We ought to learn from the mistakes and grievous consequences that we have witnessed! No, indeed, there is no issue of morality in this whatsoever, but rather it is simply an awareness of energy and spiritual power in the experience of men, a conscious experience of manhood.

The only exception to this radical discharge of energy is with a realized man who has awakened, refined, and uplifted the serpent power in full. When this is the case the masculine and feminine are joined in him, and he is self-generating, a very intense generator of energy, rather like a power plant, fully connected to an exhaustless source of energy, an infinite ocean of Light Power. Such a man may, in fact, outwardly release physical energy without sustaining any significant loss of subtle energy, save in the biological function of the physical body and its generation of sperm. As for the rest of us men, however, paying attention to their energy becomes very important, and at times our spiritual work may require periods of celibacy, whether for several days or several weeks, or on occasion, longer, when they have a reason or need of greater energy to direct elsewhere.

Men and women alike need to remember that sexual energy is a form of the serpent power and that it is creative energy. It can be channeled into many other forms of expression besides sex and procreation. In the spiritual life it is important that we learn to master the Fire Snake and to consciously direct it and channel it in various ways. When the serpent power stirs in our bellies and awakens, quite naturally we will experience a radical increase in our desire-energy, far greater desire than can ever be satisfied by sex alone, or by anything else in this world for that matter.

If we are not prepared for this, desire-energy could overcome us like a wildfire and we could become sorely intoxicated. How often do we hear of radical levels of greed and lust with men who come into positions of power, moving just a little bit more of the Fire Snake than others, or would-be "enlightened gurus" who awaken something of the serpent power, falling into scandals of mismanaged desire-energy with everyone around them. The third enemy on the path—power—which we have discussed previously, relates directly to this radical influx of desire-energy, and though men might be somewhat more susceptible to intoxication by desire, the phenomena is not isolate to men but can occur with women as well.

With regards to men, it is important that they are aware that when they wish to have more energy for a larger theurgic, spiritual, or other creative work, they will need to generate and store up energy rather than releasing it in a sexual encounter. Likewise, in general, it is important that men are conscious of how often they discharge their lightning, for they will want to make sure that their full power is present when they need to use it. Sometimes there is little or no forewarning as to when it may be needed, and it will either be there or it won't be there.

Essentially, the great talent of men is their capacity for a very swift and intense delivery of power, and their ability to direct a flow of power like a laser beam. Women tend to matrix and radiate power in a spherical way, while men tend to a very focused linear transmission, like lightning. Naturally, when men and women are carrying power together in sacred ceremony, as in life, this becomes extremely dynamic, particularly in spiritual workings and theurgic movements. Assuming the full charge of his energy is present, a man can have the power to bring about very radical shifts in energy, and thus to enact some pretty spectacular magic or wonders on short notice very swiftly.

Until the Fire Snake is awakened, there are other benefits of health and longevity for men who intentionally maintain the full charge of energy for the sake of spiritual works and other creative affairs. By paying attention to their energy and to when they discharge or withhold sexual energy, men can improve their health, boosting their immune system, and increasing their length of life. In truth, when men discharge their energy a vast amount of vital energy and life-force goes out from them, which is why from a relatively brief encounter with a woman they can cause the conception of a child. That power of conception, whether it takes hold or not, requires an incredible amount of energy from the man, his offering of himself to conception. Thus, too frequent a discharge can deplete his energy and can cause serious health issues, as well as shorten his life. The same depletion is also typically true with prolonged periods of celibacy, as it, too, can cause serious health issues, aside from the potential psychological consequences. Truly, men need a middle way that is conscious and balanced. That middle way is a central practice for men in the Mystical Path of Guadalupe, a true awareness, conscious use, and direction of energy.

Now here we must emphasize that one of the most central practices in the Mystical Path of the Celestial Maiden is respect—respect for ourselves, respect for one another, and respect for all life, all our relations. We seek to walk in a respectful manner and to be respectful in all our relationships. We seek to stay connected with our heart and our bellies, truly in touch with one another, seeing, hearing, being present with one another, and honoring each other. In the Mystical Path of Guadalupe, from a man's perspective, every woman is as the Noblewoman, the Holy Mother-Bride. From a woman's perspective, every man is an emanation of the Holy One. Likewise, every child is the Holy Child of the Father-Mother; all are emanations of the Human One of Light. This view is a central practice of the Mystical Path of Guadalupe. All exist equally in the Divine Mother; all are the emanation of Mother God, Father God, the Holy One. This view is integral to the play of sacred sexuality and to the full integration of our spirituality into life, in a seamless weave of the sacred and the ordinary, which is the Mother's Way.

Here we must say that spirituality surrounding moon time and lightning strikes, and sacred sexuality, is not isolate to heterosexual individuals, but includes gay, lesbian, and transgender individuals as well, all in the Divine Mother. Sophian Tradition insists that people of all orientations are welcomed and embraced by this mystery, finding and practicing these principles in their life experience as ordained by Divine Mother. In so doing gay, lesbian, and transgender children of the Divine Mother gather in the sparks of their unique life experience as an offering of hope and an affirmation for themselves and all their relations. All are in the folds of her garment.

Having addressed the play of energy in women's and men's bodies, and the awareness of the moon cycle with women and the lightning strike with men, next we can speak of some of the mysteries and practices of sacred sexuality in the Mystical Path of Guadalupe: the love-play between two lovers in worship of the Divine Mother.

The Pollen Path: Sacred Sexuality

We often speak of embodying the Spiritual Sun—something of the Divine Presence and Power and higher consciousness—and we often speak of the reintegration of our energetic and material being. Naturally this assumes a positive view and relationship with our body and desires. To embody the Light-Presence and Light-Power, we must accept our body and our life in this world, understanding the body and this life as a vehicle of the actualization and realization of our soul and its purpose.

Integral to a positive view and relationship with our body and the play of desire, is the development of a positive view and relationship with sexuality and sex, as well as the creative fantasy world that is integral to sex. There is no such thing as "sacred sexuality" unless we can truly hold a positive view of our sexuality and sex, and can recognize the innate blessedness and sacredness of sex just as it is, apart from any spiritual practice we might join to it.

It is interesting to note the very imbalanced and strange views surrounding sexuality and sex in the dominant culture, and the tendency to consider sex as unspeakable and somehow ungodly. The extremes of this repression and distortion lead to radical self-denial and self-loathing on one hand, or radical, hedonistic self-indulgence, and perversion on the other. This reflects a deep need for healing with so many of us surrounding our sexuality, sexual desire, and sex, for neither too little nor too much are healthy for us. And neither is too much healthy either. Our energetic and psychological balance and harmony lies in the middle, in a more relaxed and conscious approach to sexuality and sex that goes to neither extreme.

At the outset of taking up the spiritual alchemy of sacred sexuality, given all of the false religious morality that encrusts sexuality and sex, as well as all of the strange philosophies that have arisen in reaction, it is important that we look to see the issues that have arisen for us around our sexuality and sex life, looking to see our thoughts and feelings surrounding sex, and seeking to address and heal any distortions and wounds that we find. The aim of sacred sexuality is to heal and transform ourselves, and to reintegrate our energetic and material being, to actualize and realize our soul being. Ultimately, the aim is to invoke, hold, and ground Divine Energy, and to fully embody something of the Divine. Our intention is not to ignore or plaster over psychological and energetic issues, but to experience our healing and to recognize our innate wholeness in an integral self-realization. We are here to be as the Forever Whole and Perfect Maiden with the Light of the Spiritual Sun shining from within us.

Thus, seeking to take up the play of sacred sexuality, we will want to pray and meditate, to look and see whatever initial healing we might need, as well as look and see things that may need to be healed over time, specifically asking the Divine Mother and powers to show us how to bring about our healing. We will seek self-knowledge and enact self-purification, letting go of negative thoughts and feelings around our sexuality and sex, and invoking the power of the Divine Mother to heal any wounds, psychological and energetic.

Just like other practices of healing and wonderworking arts, the full power of this spiritual alchemy is something that can take years or even decades to actually access; weekend seminars and workshops are not going to teach and initiate us into these mysteries, nor will they empower us to actually perform them.

The true power of this spiritual alchemy isn't going to come by force, or by the use of special "tantric techniques" that awaken the power more swiftly. Such techniques can cause severe consequences. No, indeed, the power of this spiritual alchemy opens to us over time through a spiritual life and practice of which sacred sexuality is a part, coming through the experience of the sacredness of sex in and of itself, the natural experience of connectedness and devotion that occurs in true love-play, naturally and spontaneously, without being contrived.

When embracing sexuality and sex as innately blessed and sacred in our spiritual life, we remember this is a precious gift from the Creator, knowing that we can rejoice in the presence of God through music, song, and dance as surely as through our love-play. We give praise and thanks for this sensual gift, and in offering it up as worship, with no effort on our part, we will access the great power of this spiritual alchemy. This spiritual alchemy isn't about being some champion or expert in bed, or about stunning a lover by being the best ever at sex. It is about two people between whom there is passion and love, coming together to express their desires and fantasies with one another. It is about two people joining together in awareness of the profound energetic exchange that occurs in a sexual encounter, and in awareness of the innate presence and power of the Creator in it. Sexual alchemy is about two lovers taking up their love-play as a blessing from God and as passionate worship of God, the One Life-Power.

Taking some time then for self-knowledge and purification in preparation, we will look into any issues we might have about our sexuality and sex, and call upon the Divine Mother to help in our healing process. The very first practice of sacred sexuality is simply having sex, actively engaging in love play and enjoying ourselves and our lover, aware of the blessedness and sacredness of sex in and of itself, and offering our sexual play and enjoyment as a movement of devotion, worship of the Divine Mother.

This simple practice itself can be very powerful and can bring about significant healing for those who may have deep wounds surrounding sexuality and sex. Life and body affirming, the practice is to simply recognize what sex is and to take it up with the awareness that it is a blessing from God as it is, sacred and holy. Shedding all false religious moralities, and yielding to our passion and fantasies, our only rule will be mutual respect, openness, honesty, and harmlessness. Everyone involved must be a willing participant and aware of what they are doing, and whatever is transpiring in our love-play must cause no harm. In this way we can take up the play of sensuality and sexuality in a sacred manner, free from unnecessary entanglements, and we may know that our enjoyment is, in truth, godly, completely righteous. When we can engage in love-play, aware of sex itself as blessed and sacred, and aware of the enjoyment of sex as a form of worship, we can then take up various spiritual practices of sacred sexuality, practices that help us further draw out the energetic and spiritual power of sex.

First and foremost sacred sexuality is all a question of awareness and enjoyment, awareness of the great power in desire-energy and sex, and awareness of the deeply mystical and magical nature of sensuality and sex. Life giving power is in it. All life, you, me, everybody, has come into being through womanhood, the womb of life. In the Guadalupe Path, womanhood and all women are sacred, so also are all men sacred. Whether a person is a believer or not, faithful or not, this is how we view and relate with them, and how we view and relate with ourselves. Likewise, the play of attraction and desire, and the play of sensuality and sexuality are sacred, powerful, mysterious, and magical. If we approach our partners with this awareness, and hold the intention of offering our enjoyment up as worship of the Divine Mother, knowing our joy as her joy, our life as her life, then, indeed, inwardly we worship as we embrace our partner, regardless of their belief or unbelief. Uplifting our energy in this way, cultivating true enjoyment, will uplift and benefit our partner too, for if nothing else they will receive more enjoyment and be happier in the play of love with us.

Now sex is a creative affair and is a very magical play of fantasy. Let it be that and cultivate your creativity. Even a fantasy of sex becomes a sacred adventure, as does the play of attraction. Let sexual fantasy and the play of attraction energize and uplift you, and as you behold beauty and experience attraction, and the play of fantasy unfolds from it, know it as the beauty and good of the Divine Mother. Offer it up to her, praise her and give thanks to her for it. Enjoy, and in your enjoyment worship the Holy Mother-Bride.

Let beauty and desire have its full effect, and with holy awe and wonder embrace it, loving the Mother, loving life. In noticing beauty and the play of your desire, notice and love without shame; abide in the awareness of the original blessing in which all is conceived. The key is an open and loving heart, one filled with gratitude and appreciation for all of the innate good life offers, all of the innate blessings and good the Divine gives to us. Taking up sexual play as a way of worship isn't about making sex a burden, rather it is letting sex be what it naturally is, and it is freeing us to enjoy this delightful gift of life. Rather than getting into your head with it, get into your heart and belly, into your body and senses, and let yourself feel and experience what's happening and enjoy it deeply.

A person alone, in a play of sexual fantasy, can offer up their enjoyment in the same way as with a partner, and they can generate and send Light Power in the same way. It is all a matter of the sacred intention within the play. Offer up the play to the Mother with a heart-wish for the health and happiness of all beings, the healing of all beings, and fullness of life in their experience.

In the play of sexual fantasy we can intend a blessing and good fortune for others, likewise, in the visualization of sexual fantasies, with subtle bodies on the astral, charging them with the desire-energy of our play, we can generate luminous spirits that carry blessings of positive energy. We need only dispel shades and shadows surrounding our play and engage in our play with an awareness of the Divine Presence and Power, the *Holy Shekinah*.

Along a similar line, in wonderworking arts associated with sexual play, we can "feed the spirits" attracted to the subtle environment of our play and they may extend their power or energy to us in return, "smiling" upon us, as it were. Our awareness of the sacred dimension of sexual play and our view of this as a gift from the Mother, surrounds it with completely positive energy.

In this regard, we may comment upon the play of angels and spirits surrounding the birth of a child and the moment of death. Many luminous spirits and angels attend these events of life, as we have witnessed in our own experience of being present at times of birth and death; the same is true during times of sexual play and times of conception. When sexual play occurs with true affection, passion, and love, luminous spirits and angels gather with us in the company of the *Holy Shekinah*.

What is affirmed and envisioned in the moment of the full release of our vital energy is a very powerful prayer or invocation. Affirmation and creative visualization joined to the release of our energy is extremely powerful, and what is affirmed and envisioned tends to manifest. This is the essential key to sacred sex and the wonderworking art or magical art. Many powerful blessings can be sent in this way.

A Practice: Union with the Beloved

The first practice is called Union with the Beloved. Two lovers prepare to enter into love-play, each envisioning a union with Partzuf, a personification of the Divine, and they enter into their love-play as the embodiment of that holy emanation of the Divine. As they embrace, the two view one another as their Divine Consort, and as Divine Consorts they take up their love-play. When two lovers make love in this way, they invoke, hold, and ground Divine Energy for themselves and for the people. Embodying something of the Divine, their love-play becomes a prayer and blessing for the people and the land. This naturally attracts divine and holy beings and luminous spirits into the environment of love-play, and light and blessings extend from the place of love-play as a Heaven Earth Place where the Divine has "touched down."

This practice can be completely internal, held in heart and mind, and externalized only as the love-play itself, but it can also be extended through the creation of an altar or shrine in that place, the creative adornment of that sacred space, and through active prayers, meditation, and sacred ceremony before and after the love-play. This can include worship in music, song, and dance, as well as sacred ceremony invoking magical movements. Along a similar line, as both lovers are embodying something of the Divine, direct offerings of worship to the Divine-become-physical in the person of one's lover can be given, offerings of praise and thanks, food and drink, flower essences, incense, and such, as well as the pleasure of the love-play itself and all that it involves. Truly, this is a very dynamic, creative and powerful form of worship through sacred sexuality, profoundly mystical and magical.

This theme of becoming Divine Consorts and experiencing Union with the Beloved is the central practice of sacred sexuality. Naturally, this extends to viewing every man and every woman as an emanation of the Divine Masculine or Divine Feminine, the Groom or Bride in the Bridal Chamber, and to viewing all beings as the luminous hosts gathered in that Holy of Holies. This spiritual practice begins surrounding times of love-play, but then, progressively, gradually, it is extended throughout the relationship, taking up the relationship as a divine play between spiritual consorts, as with Lord Yeshua and Lady Miryam in our Gospel.

Now, as we know, there are many different faces of the Beloved—male, female, and angelic—and so as we become skilled in this practice we can take up various Divine Personifications, invoking different spiritual influxes for the people, and performing different spiritual works for the people, all as the Mother Spirit inspires.

Often both consorts will be mutually active in their worship in love-play, the love-play assuming the tone and texture of the Divine Personifications being embodied. At times one or the other might take a more passive role, becoming the "altar of worship," "palace of worship," or "matrix of worship," while their partner becomes the active worshipper or invoker of forces.

Naturally in this way of sacred sexuality, awareness of the interior stars, radiant holy breath, serpent power and body of light comes into play. In every case, sex is a radical exchange on an energetic level, and the more we are conscious of our energetic being and the energetic dimension, the greater the extent to which we can carry our worship and spiritual work in our love-play. As much as a sensual play with the physical body, we can engage an energetic play with the body of light. This happens naturally and spontaneously in the practice of sacred sexuality, but as in everything, with awareness and knowledge we can draw out greater power and wisdom.

What has been shared above, along with spiritual practices corresponding with the moon cycles of women and thunder strikes of men, form the basic foundation of the practice of sacred sexuality in the Mystical Path of Guadalupe. Next, expanding upon this, we can share examples of some of the practices that can be done, as well as discuss some basic teachings about how couples seeking to conceive a child might draw in a more luminous soul or a soul from among the elder races through the practice of sacred sexuality.

Sacred Sex & the Wonderworking Art

There are both mystical and magical dimensions to sacred sexuality. On the mystical level it is a way of devotion and worship, and may lead to deep spiritual and mystical experiences, knowledge of the Divine and unification with the Divine. On the magical level we can invoke spiritual powers and perform spiritual work for people through sacred sexuality, using the energy of sex in wonderworking or magical ceremony.

There is a basic formula to a wonderworking or magical ceremony:

First, we will arrange the sacred space according to our intention, and we will purify or banish, making that space sacred on an energetic level, clearing out all energies not in harmony with our intention. When arranged and purified, we will then clearly state the intention of the sacred ceremony.

Then, the Holy One and the Powers of Sacred Circle are invoked; praise and thanks are given, and offerings are made.

Once the Sacred Circle is invoked, we invoke the Divine Powers and spirits that correspond to the wonderworking we intend, opening the appropriate gates and invoking the movement of their spiritual powers.

When we have called in the spiritual powers needed for the work, we "feed the spirits," making offerings, and we ask the Divine Powers and spirits to take up the work we need accomplished, "charging and sending the spirit." At this point we speak exactly what we wish to have transpire, and as we speak we include symbolic movements or gestures that correspond to our intention, setting our energy into motion with the Divine Powers and spirits.

Then, in the Christian tradition, we will perform a Wedding Feast, a Holy Eucharist, praying for all our relations and sending blessings to all our relations. We will speak a special blessing upon the Divine Powers and spirits helping us in our spiritual work, and give praise and thanks to the Holy One, the Creator, our Mother-Father.

At the fruition of the ceremony we will thank and bless the angels and spirits, and bid them to return to their abodes in peace, bearing the Light of the True Cross into their realms. As we did at the beginning, we will perform a purification and banishing ceremony, clearing the space.

Naturally, sacred sex can be joined to this, and when sacred sex is joined to a wonderworking or magical ceremony it can be very powerful, for there is a great manifesting power between two human lovers, grounding or earthing intense influxes of psychic and spiritual energy into the physical or material dimension. When a wonder is to be performed, bringing about a radical change on a physical or material level, the use of sacred sexuality can be most powerful. Amazingly so!

When a woman is brought into a peak of her energy in a sensual and sexual exchange, as she climaxes and receives the influx of the thunder strike of the man, she naturally and spontaneously merges with Earth Mother, becoming as the Great Matrix receiving the influx of the psychic and spiritual power, integrating it with the physical or material dimension. Likewise, as the man releases his thunder strike, climaxing, what is invoked, and what is held in mind and heart, becomes imprinted in his body and the Matrix of Earth Mother, the woman. This is the energetic dimension within and behind the conception of children, drawing souls and spirits into incarnation. If and when this manifesting power is directed towards the manifestation of a wonder or magic, needless to say what transpires can be incredible.

Just as the focus of desire for a child in love-play can bring about conception, so the focus of desire to bring about a wonder or magical movement can bring about that wonder. It is a time of an influx of great power. In this regard, we are wise to understand that even apart from a wonderworking or magical ceremony we want to be very conscious and careful about our thoughts and emotions, and the power of our speech, during love-play, and most especially at the time of the climax of love-play and the period immediately following, for we are in a deep mystical experience: There, in that moment, is great manifesting, magical power. Conscious of it or not, things may manifest as we envision and speak them, for our good or ill.

When we wish to take up sacred sex joined to a wonderworking or magical ceremony, flirtation and foreplay may be joined to the invocations, and actual love-play may be joined to the "charge and sending of the spirits." Essentially, invoking the spiritual powers corresponding with the wonder that we intend, as we take up our love-play we hold this conscious intention in mind and heart, as surely as if we were intending to conceive a child, and at the very instant of the climax of our love-play, this intention becomes our sole focus.

When a woman climaxes she becomes Earth Mother, completely present in her body, the environment and the earth, and as she receives the influx she envisions what is to be manifest in complete and clear detail. When a man climaxes he becomes Sky Father, going up and out the top of the head, through a portal that opens into another dimension. As the woman is envisioning what is to manifest, he abides where he is, speaking into being what will come to pass. In this period of envisioning and speaking, the woman and man abide open and sensitive to the Mother Spirit and Powers, and they follow the inspirations that come to them. When they have run and returned in this way, the movement is blessed and sealed with the Wedding Feast, celebrating the mystery of the Bridal Chamber.

In this we may know and understand that the conception of a sacred child can occur on a psychic, spiritual, and physical level, that a "magical child" can be conceived, representing a wonderworking presence that can be conceived and birthed through a sacred relationship. In this, we may also know and understand that the "conception of a sacred child" is not isolate to a heterosexual relationship, for all forms of love-play have the potential for the generation of a sacred or magical child on psychic and spiritual levels. Only the matrix and way will be different, corresponding with the natural power of the gender involved. This, naturally, becomes very powerful when joined to the practice of Union with the Beloved, for then it is the Divine Presence and Power envisioning and speaking, the Divine touching down to direct the Powers and spirits.

The more the serpent power is awakened, refined, and uplifted in two lovers, the greater the manifesting power or wonderworking power between two lovers. The power of this practice is directly connected to the Fire Snake, and sacred sexuality is, perhaps, among the most natural and spontaneous ways to awaken this Divine Power. Now, it must be shared that when the intention is a manifestation of power in the physical or material dimension it is good for men to release their thunder strike outwardly, but when the intention is a manifestation on a more subtle level, a psychic or spiritual level, then it can be more powerful for a man to engage in the love-play but withhold himself from ejaculating, instead turning that great force inward and upward, shifting it into another dimension corresponding with the intention of the work. As an example, if a couple were to take up a spiritual work for someone, praying for their reception of the Holy Spirit and the opening of their sight into the World of the Holy Spirit, then the man would withhold his emission. He would merge with the person in body of light and draw the power up to the brow, holding it there with this sacred intention in mind. Conversely, if spiritual work was being done for a person in need of a job, then an outward release would be ideal, manifesting something in the physical or material world.

Previously, in our discussion of the moon cycles of women and the thunder strikes of men, we spoke of the need for men to be conscious of their energy and the need for men to generate a greater charge of energy for some forms of spiritual work. Naturally, if a significant spiritual working is to be done in this way, seeking a greater movement of energy and wonder, then a man will wish to generate a larger charge of energy and bring the fullest possible charge into the spiritual work. When he has a full charge, he will be more powerful and effective. In a similar way for women, any time of peak fertility, or three days before and three days following their moon time, are especially powerful times for the wonderworking art joined to sacred sex. If a man has generated a full charge of energy and these times are used, then a wonderworking or magical ceremony joined to sacred sex may be especially powerful.

In this, perhaps, you may understand how the practice of sacred sexuality is extended through the wonderworking art. All manner of wonderworking ceremonies may be done in this way. Here, no doubt, it would be good to mention that there are ways to use sexual energy without a partner, for sacred sexuality is not isolate to those with committed partners. Likewise, it would be good to mention that in the Mystical Path of Guadalupe not all practitioners necessarily engage in sacred sexuality. When individuals are not inclined to it, it certainly does not preclude their practice of this Mystical Path. Sacred sexuality is part of this Mystical Path because sexuality and sex is such a significant part of our lives, such a driving force in life. In the Divine Mother all of life is sacred and is included, all activities in our lives are potential vehicles of our spirituality and realization.

Sacred sexuality is simply a natural extension of the cultivation and refinement of desire, which is at the very heart of the Mystical Path of the Holy Mother-Bride. Whether a focus on actual sex is involved or not, our life and path is all about a spiritual alchemy with desire energy, and in one way or another we work with desire energy, seeking to master it. For those called to integrate sexuality and sex into their spiritual life, teachings on the practice of sacred sexuality are part of this Mystical Path.

The Pollen Path: Conception of a Sacred Child

In the original image of the Celestial Maiden we see the appearance of an angelito or a child-angel beneath her. This indicates a prophecy in the Guadalupe tradition. As the time of the new era that is coming draws near, the Age of the Holy Spirit or Sun of Flowering, there will be an influx of incarnations of more luminous souls or souls of higher grades. Specifically, these souls will incarnate from among the "star people" and "spirit people," realized souls from among the elder races.

These sacred children will bring with them an innate knowledge and understanding of the Way, the Path to Enlightenment, and they will carry great spiritual power and wisdom. They will incarnate in humankind on earth to help facilitate the time of the Second Coming and Age of the Holy Spirit, helping to balance the great influx of dark and hostile forces by invoking, holding, and anchoring the Supernal Influx, the Supernal Light.

This, of course, is always transpiring in every generation; there are always incarnations of divine and holy beings, or "star people" and "spirit people" among us. But during this time, as the force of darkness increases and the dawn of a new era approaches, there will be a far greater influx of these holy souls than ever before in human history, an influx equal to the play of the dark and hostile forces that will also be embodied among us.

The revelation of the Celestial Maiden happened in the early sixteenth century, nearly five hundred years ago, just as the very first influences of the Age of Aquarius began to enter, heralding the beginning of the thousand-year transition between the Piscean Age and the Aquarian Age. Now we are in the midst of that period of transition, that great in-between. Thus we are now in the time of this influx of souls from among the elder races, the time of these sacred children. Many would say that beginning in the 1960's, the great influx of these luminous souls began and that it continues increasing to this today.

Quite apart from what humankind does or does not do to facilitate this influx of souls, it will transpire through the Divine Grace of the Holy Mother-Bride, as reflected in the portent of the Woman of Light in chapter 12 of the Revelation and in the appearance of Our Lady of Guadalupe to Juan Diego. But as we know, the more we act as conscious agents and actively participate in the movements of the Mother Spirit, the greater becomes the manifestation of the Divine Presence and Power, the mercy and grace of the *Shekinah* of the Supreme, *El Elyon*.

For these reasons, a central practice among initiates of the Mystical Path of Guadalupe is not only prayer and sacred ceremony to invoke a greater influx of souls from among the elder races, but more, to live as these holy ones, taking up the spiritual labor of these holy ones and supporting the spiritual labor of *tzaddikim* and *maggidim* in the Holy Kabbalah.

As Sophian Tradition follows the Path of the Sun through the year, the focus of invoking the manifestation of light is on Winter Solstice, the Feast of the Mother and Child. This prayer for the incarnation of righteous souls is remembered and held on May Day, the Feast of the Holy Bride. In Winter Solstice, we pray for the light of an intention for the year to be seeded in its darkest day. In the Feast of the Holy Bride, we pray for the incarnation of holy souls, as we're surrounded by the height of springtime with its flowering, blooming, bursting into flame.

In the Mystical Path of Guadalupe, specifically the practice of sacred sexuality, there are spiritual practices for attracting a luminous soul while a couple attempts to conceive a child. There are also practices to invoke the wisdom and knowledge to raise and educate children as spiritual or authentic human beings. The prophecy of an influx of many holy souls before the Age of Flowering becomes something of a vision or noble ideal for parents generating family, the vision of a spiritual family.

Thus, when a couple wishes to conceive a child on the Mystical Path of Guadalupe, naturally they will take up a continuum of prayer and sacred ceremony, praying to the Celestial Maiden to help them conceive a child with a soul of a higher grade, a soul from among the elder races, and they will invoke the Spirit and Powers into their love-play. Taking up the practice of Union with the Beloved, embodying something of the Divine in their love-play, they will seek to bring in something of the Divine through the conception and birth of a sacred child.

At the outset, when two spiritual practitioners choose to conceive a child, they will take up a continuum of prayer and meditation, and they will seek to purify themselves and prepare themselves, and they will begin their invocations of *Ha-Shem* and the Divine Powers, the Mother and her Holy Emanations. Along with this, they might seek out and visit a person of knowledge and power, a seer and wonderworker, or a shaman, to bless them in their aspiration and to pray for them and perform sacred ceremony for them, and they may ask friends in Sacred Circle to pray with them for the conception of their child. Likewise, they might take up something of a continuum seeking vision, seeking guidance from the Divine Mother and Powers on what to do in order to draw in a soul from among the elder races, the conception of a noble-born daughter or son becoming the central focus of their spiritual life and practice during this time.

In cases where parents come to the Mystical Path already having children they might take up a similar continuum seeking a blessing upon their children and seeking guidance and empowerment on how to raise and educate their children in a sacred manner. Remembering Kabbalistic teachings on *ivurim*—the impregnation of souls with the sparks of souls of higher grades—an *ivur* may very well be invoked this way into the soul of their child.

Now, in a continuum to invoke the incarnation of a soul from among the elder races, the teachings of perfect success must be applied, and in the labor to conceive the child the prospective parents will seek to keep their thoughts, emotions, words, and actions completely positive. As much as possible, they will avoid all negativity, especially that of giving way to fear and anger, as they tend this continuum. Likewise, throughout this time, they will seek to deepen their continuum of spiritual practice, both together and individually, seeking to generate as much merit or Light Power as possible, uplifting their energy and vibration as much as possible, seeking to create an energetic matrix that might attract a more luminous soul. This is especially true surrounding their attempts to conceive. The aim is to create completely positive and luminous conditions surrounding the conception and gestation of the sacred child. After the birth, the parents will continue to generate a positive and luminous energetic matrix in which to nurture and raise this sacred child.

During the process of conception, it is entirely possible for parents to invoke Divine Powers to draw in a soul that might especially resonate with the family unit, as taught in the mysteries of the *Arayot* in the Holy Kabbalah. The essences or roots of souls are drawn from the *Holy Sefirot* of *Atzilut*, the Supernal World. Thus, during the conception of a child, if a couple embodies the energy of a particular *Partzuf*, and invokes corresponding Divine Names, archangels, angels, and spirits, they may call in a soul that carries the corresponding essence or root. This is especially true when the essence or root invoked parallels that of the parents, for the principle of energetic affinity applies. However, it is also possible to invoke other essences or roots as the Holy Spirit inspires, and as the *Shekinah* of the Supreme ordains.

Essentially, this is the very same way two lovers may invoke various influxes of spiritual power for the people and the land, but in this case the intention is the conception of a physical sacred child. The more experienced a couple is in the practice of sacred sexuality, the greater their capacity for this invocation.

There is something to be said regarding magical talismans when a couple is invoking the Divine Mother and Powers to bless their conception of a sacred child. First, it can be good to make a fetish representing the weave of energies of the soul being invoked and to burn incense corresponding to that weave of energies during love-play. Secondly, as flowers, and especially roses, are sacred to the Holy Mother-Bride, it is good to offer flowers to her in the sacred space of conception. In fact, love making on rose petals can be very good when attempting to conceive a sacred child.

Once a child is conceived, a similar continuum is kept during the cycles of gestation while the child is in the womb, and when the child is born, a sacred ceremony is performed for the "reception of the soul" and for the blessing of the child, a ceremony of anointing.

Naturally, the conception and birth of a sacred child is only the beginning of the process; the greater part of the process, as every good parent knows and understands, is the raising and education of the child, helping them embody and draw out the full knowledge and power of their soul, their energetic being. Integral to this is the exposure of children from an early age to the mystical path, the spiritual life and practice, and to people of knowledge and power, and to spiritual community. Tending to the spiritual education of the child, as to every other area of their education, is essential in the generation of sacred children, or true spiritual or authentic human beings. Our children should be taught how to walk in beauty and holiness.

In this way, conceiving and raising children, our labor in family becomes a spiritual practice in the Mystical Path of Guadalupe. Regardless of whether we are actually able draw in a soul from among the elder races into a child or not, this spiritual practice is the same. We labor to co-create with the Divine Mother a generation of more luminous and empowered youth, generating hope for the future. Indeed, we are called to this spiritual labor with the Divine Mother by Our Lady of Guadalupe, if we feel the impulse to have a family. Then we are called to the creation of as positive and spiritual a family as possible, all in the Divine Mother.

The intention in the Holy Mother-Bride, of course, is not to create an atmosphere of judgment surrounding our conception and raising of children, or to create undue tension or stress in families. It is to inspire us and encourage us in our efforts, giving us a noble ideal as parents and as spiritual communities. Likewise, the intention is to clearly speak of the integration of family duties into our spiritual life and practice. Having children does not preclude our involvement with the Mystical or Gnostic Path, but may represent a way on the Mystical Path, corresponding to the Way of Work and Way of Devotion.

These are the basic teachings for the conception of a sacred child. And we must say that, truly, all children are sacred, and it is good to teach all our children to walk lightly upon this earth in a sacred manner, aware of all life as sacred and holy. Be praised, Mother of the Great Energy-Truth, Mother of the Giver of Life, Mother of the Inventor of Humanity, Mother of the Lord of the Far and Close By, Mother of the Lord of Heaven and the Earth!

Kabbalistic Tree of Life

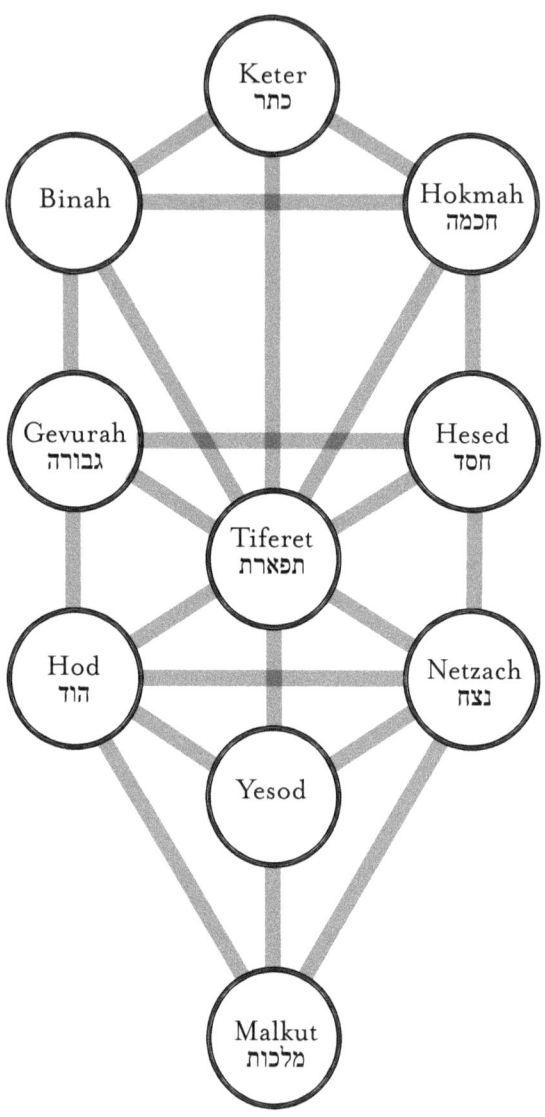

Keter (Crown): The First Sefirah of the Infinite One corresponds with the Will of the Divine. The Divine Names attributed here are *Eheieh* (I Am) and *El Elyon* (God Most High).

Da'at (Knowledge, or Gnosis): *Keter* in truth never appears on the Tree of Life. What appears is Da'at, which is what is revealed of *Keter*. This corresponds with the Knowledge of the Mysteries of God, or Revelation of the Divine. The Name *Yahweh Elohim* (LORD God) is often attributed here.

Hokmah (Wisdom): The Second Sefirah of the Infinite One is called Reshit, "the point of the beginning," beyond which nothing is knowable, because *Keter* beyond is ever-concealed. The wisdom of God corresponds with the most subtle and sublime awareness in the Mind of God. This corresponds with *Abba* (Father) and the Divine Name *Yah*.

Binah (Understanding): This is the Third Sefirah of the Infinite One, which corresponds with Thought in the Mind of God and the generation of the Supernal patterns or forms of all things. This corresponds with *Imma* (Mother) and the Divine Name *Elohim* (God).

Hesed (Mercy, or Loving Kindness): The Fourth Sefirah of the Infinite One corresponds with the sphere of all blessings, the love of God, and the principle of expansion. This corresponds with the Divine Name *El* (God).

Gevurah (Severity), or Din (Judgment): This is the Fifth Sefirah of the Infinite One, which corresponds to the principle of restriction and Laws upon which Creation is founded. Representing the principle of restriction, it is understood as a sphere of measured blessing. This corresponds with the Divine Name *Elohim Gibor* (Mighty God).

Tiferet (Beauty), or Rehamim (Compassion): This is the Sixth Sefirah of the Infinite One and is set at the center of the Tree of Life; it is understood as the Sefirah of the Messiah, the Anointed of God. This corresponds with the Divine Name *Yahweh* (LORD) and Yeshua Messiah (Jesus Christ).

Netzach (Victory, or Dominion): This is the Seventh Sefirah of the Infinite One, corresponding with the Dominion of the Divine throughout Creation. This corresponds with the Divine Name *Yahweh Tzavaot* (LORD of Hosts).

Hod (Glory, or Submission): This is the Eighth Sefirah, corresponding with the Glory of God that pervades all of Creation. This corresponds with the Divine Name *Elohim Tzavaot* (God of Hosts)

Yesod (Foundation, or Reciprocity): This is the Ninth Sefirah of the Infinite One, corresponding with God as the source and foundation of all Creation, sustenance of all things. This corresponds with the Divine Name *Shaddai*, (Almighty), or *El Shaddai* (Almighty God), or *Shaddai El Hai* (Almighty Living God). While *Shaddai* is translated as Almighty throughout scripture, in Hebrew it may also be translated as God of the Mountain or Breasted One.

Malkut (Divine sovereignty, or "Kingdom"): The Tenth Sefirah of the Infinite One corresponds with the manifestation of the Living Presence of the One in Creation, as well as the principle of the embodiment of the Divine. *Malkut* is also called *Holy Shekinah* (Indweller), the Feminine Presence of the Divine. This corresponds with the Divine Name *Adonai* (My Lord).

Giving and Receiving Practices

Giving and Receiving Practice is the central method through which Sophian practitioners generate the Sacred Heart of Love and Compassion. This reflects the Holy Mother's weave of teachings on the Mystery of the Crucifixion, the essence of which is Giving and Receiving. According to the Kabbalah, we must receive something in order to give it, and in order to fully receive something we must share it with others. Thus, first we must receive the love and compassion of the Light-Presence within us, and in giving it to others we fully receive the blessing of the Sacred Heart. For this reason, the development of Giving and Receiving must naturally begin with oneself and gradually extend over many steps to others, even the whole of this good earth.

Remembrance of Being Loved: Consider a time when you have felt loved and the person who loved you. Recreate and envision that situation in your mind in as detailed a way as possible—a love someone showed you that truly moved you. For many people this might be their mother or their father, a grandmother or grandfather, or anyone who showed us love and kindness. Sometimes, this might even be an animal friend. Other times some of us might be able to connect with Lord Yeshua or Lady Mary whose love brought us the Light Transmission, or perhaps our Root Tzaddik. Anyone can be used who has brought forth love from within us, with whom we experienced being loved. Envisioning this and letting it fill your mind completely, allow the feeling of love to arise in your heart again and pervade you with thanksgiving and gratitude. When you do this your love will naturally flow to whomever or whatever evoked it. Your heart will open, and though you may not always feel that you have enough love or may have forgotten your capacity for compassion, you will remember your love and compassion, for it will be present with you. Abide with this holy awareness as long as you can.

Others the Same as Oneself: The truth is that we all desire the same fundamental thing: We all want to be happy and to be free from suffering. We want to be prosperous, successful, healthy, and happy, however we might express it. This is true of all living spirits and souls. Essentially, if we can remember our basic sameness as human beings—living beings—we can open our heart to others. Bringing this to mind, see your own desire for prosperity, success, health, and happiness, and see the desire of others the same as your own. Let your heart open and genuinely wish for the prosperity, success, health, and happiness of yourself and others all together. This will naturally help you open up in your relationship with others and become more aware of both your own and others' needs and desires. Just imagine a world in which people considered one another in this way. Happiness would be on the rise and suffering diminished!

Exchanging Places: If you know of someone who is suffering but have no clue how you might help that person, put yourself without reservation in that person's place. Imagine yourself as that person, having that person's experience, as fully and vividly as you can. Look and see how you would feel, and all of the fears and grief and suffering that would arise. Be that person in your mind and open your heart completely to his or her experience. Any time we exchange places with someone we are naturally shifting away from our habitual self-grasping, and opening our heart to the experience and needs of others. If we make a habit of such a practice we will find that more and more a powerful empathy and affinity with others will arise, and that our heart will naturally open to others in our daily lives. We will find that we are healthier and happier in just doing this, and when we can engage in active compassion, rendering whatever help or support we can, we will discover a certain radiance of the Sacred Heart spontaneously coming from us.

Envisioning a Friend: Sometimes we find we can't so easily put ourselves in the place of someone who is suffering who we are not all that close to. When this is the case all we need to do is imagine someone we love, a friend or loved one, in that situation. The natural result of this is that one's heart will swiftly open and one will experience an outpouring of love and compassion. Some may fear that doing this with a friend might cause their friend harm, as though a psychic assault. However, nothing could be further from the truth. In doing this, the love and compassion one generates goes out to one's friend or loved one, as well as to the actual person who is suffering and in need, and it generates positive energy and karma for one's friend. Essentially, one is drawing one's friend into the Light Continuum and invoking a blessing upon him or her, for he or she has facilitated the Light Transmission by way of their love.

Opening to Compassion: Every day presents opportunities to open our heart and to experience love and compassion. Perhaps we pass a street person, or see someone with a lonely or angry face, or we see someone who is physically or mentally or emotionally challenged, or we see an animal dead on the roadside. Perhaps we hear of the plight of peoples in other countries or people experiencing ill fortune or suffering while watching the news. In life we see many people who are suffering and in need, and every time we see such things represents an opportunity to open our heart. In the face of the immeasurable suffering in the world, do not allow the opportunity for love and the sorrow it invokes to slip by you, but let the suffering and sorrow give birth to love and compassion in you. Then the great sorrow and suffering is not without purpose and meaning, but facilitates the manifestation of the Christ Presence within oneself and others. Let life itself invoke love and compassion. In these ways we can open our heart and remember our capacity for love and compassion. Undoubtedly, one can find many other ways as well. The point is very simple: In any way you can, access the love and compassion that is innate to you as a human being. This will bring you more satisfaction and happiness, and it will empower your Giving and Receiving.

Extending the Light of the Cross of Love and Compassion: In the process of generating spiritual love and compassion we are not alone. Though every person must work out his or her own salvation—their enlightenment and liberation—taking sanctuary in the Holy Mother, we receive blessings and grace from the Risen Christ. Likewise, we receive blessings and grace from the Holy Mother-Bride, and from all of the Apostles of Light who have gone before us. In truth there is a Great Luminous Assembly of *Tzaddikim* and *maggidim* ready and willing to help us in the Great Work. Thus, we are not alone in any part of our divine labor, for the Divine Grace of the *Holy Shekinah* and the Luminous Assembly is ever present to empower us in the Mother's work. We need only invoke the *Shekinah* and the *Tzaddikim* and *maggidim* to receive Divine assistance. When we have generated the Sacred Heart and wish to extend the force of our love and compassion to other living souls, we can pray to the Holy Mother to help us do so. We merely need to invoke her and pray from the depths of our being that everything we think, feel, envision, speak, and enact might serve to extend the Light-Presence in the world and be a blessing upon all living spirits and souls.

Giving and Receiving in the Environment: This method of Giving and Receiving focuses upon the atmosphere of one's own consciousness and one's immediate environment. As we are all aware, our moods and state of mind have a very powerful influence upon us. The ordinary person is essentially bound by whatever moods and mental states arise. According to our mood and state of mind we influence our environment and, in that we are part of the environment of other beings, our moods and mental states influence others. Thus, transforming our own moods and mental states, and uplifting our own consciousness, liberates us from the downward pull of negativity and helps uplift others in our environment as well.

Sit with your mind, heart, and body, and let yourself tune in to how the body feels, your mood, thoughts, emotions, and general atmosphere of your consciousness. Envision the Spiritual Sun in your heart and shift your focus to this Light-Center. If you feel uneasy, or notice any form of tension or stress, or any negativity or darkness however subtle it might be, imagine that your breath is linked to the Spiritual Sun and that your breath becomes light. When you inhale, breathe in whatever darkness or negativity is present and breathe out light into your body-mind. Envision the negativity and darkness instantly transforming into light by the Spiritual Sun in the center of your being. Breathing out, envision your whole body-mind becoming filled with light. It is as though your whole body and consciousness becomes the Light-Presence of the Spiritual Sun in the material dimension. When your body and consciousness have become the Spiritual Sun, envision the Light extending into your immediate environment, shining upon everything around you and transforming the environment into light. Once you have transformed yourself into the Light-Presence and your immediate environment into an abode of light, you can conclude the meditation with a prayer to extend the light.

Giving and Receiving with Oneself: In this method one envisions the Spiritual Sun in the heart and oneself instantly transformed into the Light-Presence. Then one envisions a shadow image of oneself magically appearing before oneself. The Light Self is the aspect of yourself that is whole and complete, warm, loving, understanding, and Spirit-filled: a Living Presence and Power of Light that is a good friend, willing to be there for you without judgment, regardless of whatever your faults or shortcomings might be. The shadow self is that aspect of yourself that feels wounded or hurt, rejected, unworthy, misunderstood, betrayed, frustrated, grief-filled, resentful, angry, or bound to all kinds of negativity.

When the Light Self and shadow self are present in your visualization, as the Light-Self, open your heart to the shadowy image of yourself, and smile upon the shadow self with love and kindness. Breathe in the negativity and darkness of the shadow self and breathe out Light and love upon it. Envision the darkness as reddish brown sooty smoke or black inky smoke, and as you breathe it into the Spiritual Sun see it transformed into Fiery-Light. Drawing off the negativity and darkness, and breathing light into the shadow self, envision the shadow self gradually transforming into a Light Self, until it shines as brightly as you. Then envision these two Light Selves breathing light upon one another, so that there is light upon light, filling the whole environment. Once the surrounding environment is transformed into a Light Womb, embrace this other aspect of yourself, envisioning it merging into you so that you form One Light-Presence, whole and complete. When the meditation is complete, pray that the Light of the Cross is extended to all beings.

Giving and Receiving in an Actual Life Situation: In this method bring to mind a situation in which you have behaved poorly and that is a cause of grief to you: Merely thinking about might make you feel quite badly. Envision the situation completely, exactly what you said or did, and the harm it brought to others and the darkness it released into the world. Feel it deeply and let it penetrate your heart. Then, envision the Spiritual Sun in your heart, and as you breathe in, accept full responsibility for what you have done in that specific situation, without any attempt to justify or minimize your actions or words, or dodging responsibility in any way. Look and see exactly what you have done and the harm it has caused, and from the depths of your being ask for forgiveness. Breathing in, receive forgiveness and breathing out, give forgiveness and reconciliation. Pray those who might have been harmed are healed and blessed, and that understanding might uplift one and all. Essentially, you breathe in responsibility and blame, and you breathe out blessing, healing, and the undoing of injury. As you do this, envision yourself filled with the Light-Presence, as though the Spiritual Sun expands to pervade your whole body, and envision everyone involved filled with Light and restored to wholeness of being.

Giving and Receiving for Others: Begin as you did in the method for oneself, but in place of the shadow image of yourself, envision someone you know who is suffering and in pain.

Envision the Spiritual Sun in your heart and your whole body filled with the Light-Presence. As you breathe in, breathe in the suffering and pain of this person, and all of the negativity and darkness that plagues him or her, seeing it transformed by the Spiritual Sun into Light. As you breathe out, breathe out Light upon this person. Just as in Giving and Receiving with Oneself, gradually envision the person growing more and more self-luminous, until they shine with brilliant Light. When the person is healed and made whole and filled with Light in your visualization, be confident that he or she is healthy and happy, completely liberated from the cause of suffering and pain, and envision the person exchanging light with you, so that there is light upon light and the whole environment is filled with light. Then see the person go his or her own way in the company of luminous beings, and close your practice with the extension of the Light of the Cross. When practitioners have become familiar with this essential method of Giving and Receiving for Others, they will be prepared to practice the Complete Method of Giving and Receiving.

The Complete Giving and Receiving Meditation: Through the Divine Power of the Sacred Heart, we take on the sorrow and suffering of all beings—their negativity and darkness, fear, grief, frustration, anger, guilt, doubt, bitterness, rage, and hatred—and we give them all of our good and happiness, our light and love, healing power, well-being, peace of mind, and fulfillment. Essentially, we make ourselves a holy sanctuary for others, and a vehicle through which others might be uplifted into the Light Continuum. Begin the practice by calling upon the Mother and abiding in Primordial Meditation. Let yourself become empty, so that you might be Spirit-filled. Take up the practice in chapter 2 called "Union with Our Lady" and open your mind and heart fully to her Divine Presence. Feel her filling you with love and compassion and empowering the Light-Presence and Sacred Heart in you.

Engage the practice of Giving and Receiving for Others. In its climax, extend the awareness of the liberation of yourself and the person you are practicing for into the Christ Presence within the Light Continuum. Contemplate the complete dissolution of your own self-grasping, and the unity of the Soul of Light and Messiah in you with the Holy Soul and Messiah of the person you are practicing for, aware of your complete interconnectedness and interdependence. Become aware of your unity with all that lives and your innate unity with the Messiah. Let your soul be the Soul of Messiah, your mind be the Mind of Messiah, your heart be the Sacred Heart of Messiah, and your body be the Mystical Body of Messiah. In this state of mystical union, listen and hear the invocation of blessing the Anointed One speaks for this person and let it be spoken through you.

Envision yourself becoming a Great Light-Presence shining upon the earth and all who dwell in it. Imagine the negativity and darkness of the whole world gathered up into a great mass of smoke-like substance, just the same as when you worked with the person in need. As when you performed Giving and Receiving for a person, so now perform it for the world. Breathe into the Spiritual Sun all negativity and darkness of the world, and breathe out Light and Love upon the world. Envision the whole world becoming as the World of Supernal Light: the Mystical Body of the Messiah. Then envision that the world dissolves into fluid flowing Light and pours into your Sacred Heart, remanifesting there as though the whole earth is in your heart, the Sacred Heart of Christ. Abide with this holy awareness as long as you can. When the heart moves or the mind is distracted, return them to their place, and when you are finished, close with a prayer to extend the Light of the Cross into all realms, worlds, and universes. This concludes the Complete Method of Giving and Receiving. May the Light of the Mother God be extended unto all beings! Amen.

Glossary

Abba: "Father" is a personfication of the Divine indicating the transcendental and changeless aspect of the Divine. This Divine personfication corresponds with the *Sefirah Hokmah* and the Universe of *Atzilut*.

Adonai: Hebrew for Lord, a name of God often spoken in place of the Name *Yahweh* in the Jewish faith; this Divine Name corresponds with *Malkut*. In the Christian Kabbalah, this Name may indicate an individual who embodies divinity or enlightenment, as in the case of Adonai Yeshua (Lord Jesus).

Aeon: Greek for Age, a cycle of time, a period of evolution, a consciousness or orientation held by people. In Christian Gnosticism this is also a term for spiritual powers and spiritual realms formed by them. It is also a term frequently indicating an angelic being or influence of a specific order, i.e. the Order of Aeons.

Age of the Holy Spirit: This is another term for the Second Coming of Christ in Glory, or Age of Flowering, the Dawn of Christ Consciousness in a larger segment of collective humanity. In the Book of Joel, a prophesy of this Age is proclaimed, *I will pour out my spirit on all flesh; your sons and your daughters shall prophesy, your old men shall dream dreams, and your young men shall see visions. Even on the male and female slaves, in those days, I will pour out my spirit* (2:28-29).

Arayot: A Kabbalistic teaching and practice of sexual mysticism, intended to help couples transform their shared sexual life into a vehicle of spiritual realization, as well as for the drawing in of luminous and righteous souls into incarnation. This practice is very similar to that of Tantra Yogas in the East.

Archon: "Ruler," a common Gnostic term for spiritual beings-forces that are neither Divine nor demonic, but rather are forces of an admixture of light and darkness, good and evil. These are spiritual forces that most often serve their own self-interest, and as such, frequently enter into direct opposition to the Divine sovereignty. In Gnostic thought, these are the forces that dominate the world and unenlightened society.

Asiyah: "Universe of Making," this corresponds with the manifestation of the Divine Powers as the material universe and world.

Astral earth: This indicates the appearance of the earth in the astral plane or universe, hence, an inner, subtle manifestation of the earth within the astral.

Atzilut: "Universe of Nearness," this corresponds with the Supernal universe and the World of Sefirot.

Aura: The radiant, energetic field that surrounds objects appearing in this world, seen through inner sight.

Ayatl: The mantle in which Juan Diego carried the miraculous flowers from Guadalupe to the Bishop to prove her revelation to him. On this same mantle, her image miraculously appeared and is said to remain upon it to this day.

Beriyah: "Universe of Creation," this corresponds with the spiritual universe and great cosmic powers within it.

Body of Vision: This is a term that indicates the body of teachings and practices a spiritual adept or master gives that form a vehicle of spiritual realization. On the other hand, this may also refer to the appearance of a Body of Light in light realms beheld in the visionary dimension, which become visualizations for prayer and meditation.

Bridegroom: See Son.

Chrism: "Anointing," a Christian term for the ceremonial anointing with oil during initiation or blessing. Spiritually, it indicates an experience of an energetic transmission or the reception of the Christ Spirit.

Clear Light: The simple, uncreated, primordial light, the very essence and nature of consciousness. It refers to the Primordial Foundation of All, the Essence of the Supernal Light, the Bornless Nature of souls.

Comity of Stars: This is a poetic term in Sophian Gnostic teachings for the Universal Order of Enlightenment; this indicates the dawn of enlightenment through countless world systems.

Continuum or Light Continuum: This indicates the ongoing revelation of the Divine. It also indicates the reality of the Infinite One within and behind all that appears and all that transpires. All reality is within the Continuum, yet the Continuum also indicates the Eternal Realm. In the Christian Kabbalah, this term is often synonymous with the Divine Name *Yahweh* (LORD), a Name that means, "That Which Was, Is, and Forever Shall Be."

Daughter: A Divine personfication in the Kabbalah corresponding with the Sefirah *Malkut* and *Holy Shekinah*.

Demiurge: A Gnostic personification of the cosmic ego, or cosmic ignorance, which in classical Gnostic Creation stories is depicted as a false-creator, a half-maker, who in pride and arrogance puts itself off as the True God. The Demiurge in effect is the cause of the bondage of souls, the sorrow and suffering of souls, and the generation of all evil that must be overcome. As ignorance, the Demiurge is understood as the illusion of separation and the self-grasping and self-will, desire, and fear that arises within it.

Devekut: A Hebrew word meaning "cleaving" or "attachment," this is a principle of energized enthusiasm, zeal, or joy in prayer and meditation and worship; this indicates a unification of heart, soul, mind, and life with the Infinite One through awe and love.

Divine I Am: In Hebrew, this corresponds with the Name *Eheieh*, "I Am" or "I Shall Be," the Name revealed to the prophet Moses at the Burning Bush. This is also the Name in which Yeshua Messiah speaks the most lofty revelations of the Truth of Messiah. This Name corresponds to the truth of the inmost being of each and every one of us and its realization.

Elder: This is a term for a spiritual adept in the tradition, a lineage-holder, who is a teacher and guide and embodies the Living Presence; this is an initiate who has the capacity to impart Light Transmission that facilitates the Gnostic experience with others.

Elder Races: In Sophian Gnostic teachings, this term indicates souls that have become realized in other world systems; it also indicates angels that are elder siblings to us.

Elohim: This is the Divine Name mentioned in the story of Creation in Genesis thirty-two times, a Name associated with all of Creation. It is the Name corresponding with the matrix of Creation in which the Infinite One manifests as countless many, and yet abides as one, a sacred unity. This name is specifically associated with God the Mother, and it is a Name corresponding with the Immanence of God, the All-in-All.

Emanation Body: This is the appearance of a realized being, a true spiritual adept or master among us; it is more though, than their physical, material appearance, for this indicates the energy of enlightenment and the field of enlightened energy surrounding them.

Energetic Body or Subtle Body: This is the energetic dimension within and behind the physical or material body; in the process of awakening, this subtle body becomes transformed into a Body of Light filled with the glory of the Infinite One.

Fiery Intelligence: This is synonymous with the Holy Spirit. When there is a true reception of the Holy Spirit, there will be an intelligence gazing into mysteries, into God, generating

Knowledge, Understanding, Wisdom, and Love. In this, you may understand that this fiery intelligence is love, a power of unification with others and the Infinite One.

Fire Snake: This is a Divine power in us that in the East has been called "Kundalini." This power is an evolutionary force within us and, it may be said, it is the power of the Holy Spirit in us, which, when we are touched by the Holy Spirit, is awakened. This power is also called the serpent power in our tradition.

Gematria: In the Hebrew alphabet letters are also numbers, so every word also equals a certain sum. In Gematria it is understood that words that share the same number represent the same spiritual force.

Gilgulim: This is the transmigration of souls, or the principle of reincarnation through which souls awaken and become realized; this is also a term that indicates the bondage of souls moving in ignorance, self-grasping, desire, and fear, that at some point must be brought into cessation.

Glory Body: The body of light, or radiant appearance of realized beings in the visionary dimension akin to Yeshua (Jesus) in the Transfiguration when Moses and Elijah appeared with him.

Gnosis: Greek indicating spiritual knowledge, knowledge acquired through direct, spiritual, and mystical experience.

Habad: This is an acronym for *Hokmah-Binah-Da'at*, or Wisdom-Understanding-Knowledge. This indicates various gradations of higher consciousness and greater intelligence that arise in a progressive enlightenment experience.

Ha-Shem: This means The Name: *Yahweh*. This is said in reverence in place of the Great Name.

Hashmal: A Hebrew word for the experience of a speaking-silence or an angel from the order of *Hashmalim*.

Hayyah: Hebrew for "living," in the sense of life-force and also an inner-aspect of the soul in Kabbalah.

Imma: Hebrew for "mother," a personification of the Divine as the Feminine corresponding with the Sefirah *Binah* on the Tree of Life.

Imma-Gadol: Hebrew for "Great Mother."

Ivur or Ivurim: Hebrew for "impregnation," this is a term in the Kabbalah indicating the ability of holy souls to implant sparks of their soul into other souls, blessing and uplifting them.

Kabbalah: A Hebrew word for "receiving" or "revelation," the mystical tradition within Judaism and Christianity.

Kallah: Hebrew for "bride," this a personfication of the Divine associated with the Sefirah *Malkut* on the Tree of Life. Also a term for St. Mary Magdalene.

Kavvanah: A Hebrew word with several meanings, the most principle being focus and concentration, as well as intention. With *kavannah* one restrains the mind from wandering and internal reverie so the guidance and inspiration of the Holy One may be heard.

Klippah or Klippot: A Kabbalistic term meaning "husk" or "shell" or "barrier," impure or adverse manifestations of the sefirot. According to the Kabbalah, sparks of the Infinite Light are bound up in these husks and need to be drawn out and liberated.

Kodesh Imma-Kallah: A chant in Hebrew for "Holy Mother-Bride."

Kundalini Yoga: Sanskrit, an ancient Hindu practice for the awakening of a spiritual energy within us.

Light-Power: A Sophian term for the manifestation of the Holy Spirit with us.

Light-Presence: A Sophian term for the Indwelling Christ.

Logos: Greek for "word," as well as the understanding of anything spoken, nature becoming conscious of itself, the embodiment of enlightenment.

Maggid or Maggidim: Hebrew for "angel" or "angels," this term is used for all manner of angelic beings in the Christian Kabbalah; it can also be utilized to indicate an inner, spiritual guide.

Makom: Hebrew for "dwelling place"; this is also understood as a name of God corresponding with *Shekinah* in the Kabbalah.

Messianic Consciousness: A term for enlightenment in the Messiah, the experience of Supernal or Supramental consciousness; this self-realization is the aim of Sophian Gnostics.

Mochin: Hebrew for "mind," "intelligence," or "mentality," usually indicating the higher mind or the experience of expanded states of consciousness; also a cognomen for *Hokmah* and *Binah* on the Tree of Life.

Moonwise: A counter-clockwise movement in Sacred Circle, this direction is often associated with dissolution and banishing; it is also attributed to the Divine Feminine.

Mother-Bride: In the Christian Kabbalah this indicates the unification of the Mother and Daughter, or Upper and *Lower Shekinah*.

Nahautl: The indigenous language of the Aztecs.

Neshamah: In the Kabbalah this indicates the Supernal, or heavenly, aspect of the soul; it is understood to mean "Divine" or "Enlightened Nature."

Partzuf or Partzufim: The principle of personifications of the

Divine in the Kabbalah, such as the aspect of the Holy One as Father, Mother, Son, or Daughter; this is also a term used for holy and enlightened ones who embody something of the Divine among us.

Perfect Success: A common spiritual practice in the Sophian Gnostic tradition as taught by Tau Malachi in *Living Gnosis*.

Pleroma of Light: Literally "Fullness of Light," a Gnostic term indicating the Eternal Realm; this corresponds with *Atzilut* or the World of the Sefirot, often synonymous with the term "Light Realm" and "Light Continuum."

Primordial Tradition: The principle of primordial enlightenment or truth from which all authentic wisdom traditions of the world arise.

Ruach: Hebrew for "Spirit" or "Intelligence," this is a significant aspect of the soul in Kabbalah; this aspect of the soul is said to be rooted in the heart.

Ruhaniyot: Essences or radiant breaths associated with the sefirot.

Second Coming: Sophians believe we are living in the Second Coming of Christ, a time of the dawn of a new and higher consciousness within the human collective. From a Sophian perspective, Guadalupe heralds the dawn of the Second Coming.

Sefirah or Sefirot: Emanations or Attributes of the Divine; it is through the sefirot that souls are able to unify with the Holy One. Sefirot is plural of a singular Sefirah.

Shefa: This indicates the spiritual influxes or spiritual powers of the sefirot; shefa is also understood to convey the ruhaniyot.

Solar Being: This is among the terms for the state of holy and enlightened being in the Sophian tradition.

Son: A personification of the Divine as *Tiferet* and the Messiah.

Sophia: Greek for "wisdom," created and uncreated, often personified in the feminine; in Sophian tradition she is Mother Wisdom and Daughter Wisdom.

Sophian: An initiate of the Sophian tradition of Gnostic Christianity.

Spiritual Sun: A term for Christ among Sophians.

Sun of Flowering: A term in Aztec tradition indicating a time of the dawn of a new and higher consciousness; in Sophian Gnostic tradition it is synonymous with the Second Coming.

Sunwise: A clockwise movement in Sacred Circle associated with formation and invocation; it is attributed to the Divine Masculine.

Supernal or Supramental Consciousness: A state of consciousness transcending cosmic consciousness, synonymous with Messianic consciousness.

Supernal Shekinah: In the Kabbalah, this term indicates the *Upper Shekinah*, or *Mother Shekinah*; at times, it may also indicate *Malkut* of *Atzilut*.

Tau: Literally, a cross, synonymous with the Greek "Omega," it is a term for a spiritual master or *holy tzaddik* among Sophians.

Teotl: A Nahuatl principle for the energetic Presence of Awareness pervading all of nature, terrestrial and celestial; consider Teotl synonymous with the Greek "Logos."

Thunder Beings: In many Native American traditions it is said that Thunder Beings believed themselves to be equal with Creator; for their pride Creator bound them to momentary forms of fiery lightning without substance. In view of their volatile and sometimes wrathful displays of power, one is wise to be humble before Creator.

Tikkune or Tikkunim: The principle of mending, healing, or completing Creation as an active co-creator with the Infinite One; this is also a term for the progressive healing and illumination of the soul.

Tree of Life: A glyph depicting the metaphysical structure of Creation, or the array of Divine attributes. See Appendix I.

Truth Body: This is the principle of enlightenment or enlightened being; it corresponds with pure, radiant awareness, or non-dual, Gnostic awareness.

Tzaddik or Tzaddikim: Hebrew for "Righteous One," this is a term for spiritual adepts or masters in the Jewish and Christian Kabbalah; it is also used to indicate a spiritual or righteous person.

Wedding Feast: A Sophian Gnostic term for the Holy Eucharist.

White father seed and red mother seed: The energetic essence of one's father and mother imparted at the moment of conception and held within the subtle body; this is a common teaching within Jewish Kabbalah as well as Tibetan Buddhism.

Winds: A term for the spiritual power of the directions of Sacred Circle; it is also an expression for internal, subtle energies within the spiritual body.

Woman of Light: The appearance of God the Mother beheld by St. John the Beloved in his Revelation 12:1-3.

World of the Holy Spirit: Synonymous with "Pleroma of Light."

Yahweh: Hebrew for "That Which Was, Is, and Forever Shall Be," it is the Light Continuum and the proper name of God translated as LORD in the Old Testament. In the Kabbalah this is understood as the Great Name of God YHVH.

Yeshua: Aramaic for the Greek name "Jesus," which literally means, "*Yahweh* delivers."

Yetzirah: "Universe of Formation" in the Kabbalah associated with the world of angels.

Zohar: Hebrew for "radiance," this is also the title of a multi-volume source of Kabbalah containing mystical commentary on the Old Testament. The hard copy of this mystical, magical journey of many famous 1st-century rabbis emerged in the thirteenth century written by the hand of Moses de León. Legends say de León received his inspiration directly from the rabbis about whom he wrote.

Bibliography

Audlin, James David (Distant Eagle). *Circle of Life: Traditional Teachings of Native American Elders*. **Sante Fe, NM: Clear Light Publishing, 2005.**

Brading, D.A. *Mexican Phoenix: Our Lady of Guadalupe: Image and Tradition Across Five Centuries*. **Cambridge: Cambridge University Press, 2001.**

Castillo, Ana, ed. *La Diosa de las Américas: Escritos sobre la Virgen de Guadulpe*. **New York: Vintage Español, 2000.**

de la Torre Villar, Ernesto and Ramiro Navarro de Anda. *Testimonios Históricos Guadalupanos*. **México City: Fondo de Cultura Económica. 1982.**

Escalada, Xavier. *San Juan Diego. El gran milagro de México*. **Miami: Santillana USA Publishing Company, 2003.**

Malachi, Tau. *Gnosis of the Cosmic Christ: A Gnostic Christian Kabbalah*. **Woodbury, MN: Llewellyn, 2005.**

———. *The Gnostic Gospel of St. Thomas: Meditations on the Mystical Teachings*. **Woodbury, MN: Llewellyn, 2004.**

———. *Living Gnosis: A Practical Guide to Gnostic Christianity*. **Woodbury, MN: Llewellyn, 2005.**

———. *St. Mary Magdalene: The Gnostic Tradition of the Holy Bride*. **Woodbury, MN: Llewellyn, 2006.**

———. *Gnostic Healing: Revealing the Hidden Power of God*. **Woodbury, MN: Llewellyn, 2010.**

Matthews, Caitlín. *Sophia, Goddess of Wisdom: The Divine Feminine from the Black Goddess to World-Soul*. **London: Mandala Publishers, 1991.**

Meyer, Marvin, and Willis Barnstone, eds. *The Gnostic Bible.* Boston: New Seeds Books, 2003.

Mini, John. *The Aztec Virgin: The Secret Mystical Tradition of Our Lady of Guadalupe.* Sausalito, CA: Trans-Hypoborean Institute of Science, 2000.

Pagels, Elaine. *The Gnostic Gospels.* New York: Random House, 2004.

Patai, Raphael. *The Hebrew Goddess.* Detroit: Wayne State University Press, 1990.

Pinchbeck, Daniel. *2012: The Return of Quetzalcoatl.* New York: Penguin Group, Inc., 2006.

Robinson, James M., ed. *The Nag Hammadi Library.* New York: Harper-One, 1990.

Rodriguez, Jeanette. *Our Lady of Guadalupe: Faith and Empowerment among Mexican-American Women.* Austin: University of Texas Press, 1994.

Sanchez, Victor. *The Toltec Path of Recapitulation: Healing Your Past to Free Your Soul.* Santa Fe, NM: Bear & Co., Inc., 2001.

———. *Toltecs of the New Millenium.* Santa Fe, NM: Bear & Co., Inc., 1996.

Schipflinger, Thomas. *Sophia-Maria: A Holistic Vision of Creation.* York Beach, ME: Samuel Weiser, Inc., 1998.

Tuck, Jim. *The Quetzalcoatl "Trinity".* Mexconnect. Web. (accessed 15 June 2010).

Winkler, Gershon. *Magic of the Ordinary: Recovering the Shamanic in Judaism.* Berkeley: North Atlantic Books, 2003.

Ywahoo, Dhyani. *Voices of our Ancestors.* Boston: Shambhala Publications, Inc., 1987.

Index

A

altar 1, 61–63, 78, 159, 168, 188, 190-195, 206, 241
angelito 162, 304
angels 10, 35, 37, 38, 39, 43, 47, 65, 80, 103, 107-109, 116, 123, 126, 127, 130, 137, 140, 141, 143, 164, 171, 183, 193, 196, 198, 204, 205, 207, 208, 210, 218, 233, 235, 238, 252, 254, 261, 277, 297, 300, 307, 331
arayot 182, 307
archon 25, 41, 90, 111, 117-119, 130, 170
Asiyah 149
astral earth 108
Atzilut 193, 307
aura 219
Aztec 2, 25, 30, 31, 33, 34, 45, 76, 102, 103, 112, 118, 119, 123, 133, 134, 137, 143, 152, 161, 200, 209, 223, 276

B

belly cords 217, 218
Beriyah 149
Binah 36, 233
Body of Vision 43, 100, 110, 114, 129, 160, 230, 231, 243, 258, 287
Bride 1-5, 76, 81, 85, 86, 97, 98, 99, 100, 101, 102, 105, 114, 116, 119, 129, 145-148, 153-155, 157, 167, 177, 181, 183-185, 187-192, 194, 195, 196, 197, 201, 202, 203, 210, 214, 215, 217, 219, 221, 222, 224, 232, 234, 236, 238, 239, 241, 242, 243, 244, 248, 249, 250, 251, 258, 264, 266, 267, 272, 278, 280, 291, 296, 298, 304, 305, 307, 308

C

candle magic 192
chakras 123, 233
Christ 1-9, 14, 25, 31-34,

92, 102, 112, 116, 117, 127, 134, 141, 149, 174, 176, 188, 192, 278
Christian 4, 33, 55, 67, 78, 112, 118, 124, 132, 133, 134, 153, 157, 161, 163, 187, 201, 204, 223, 277, 300, 332
Clear Light 85, 131, 176, 232, 276
Comity of Stars 182, 185, 265
conception 5, 26, 67, 72, 75, 86, 87, 162, 173, 183, 283, 291, 297, 301, 302, 304, 306-309
Continuum 30, 42, 46, 73, 116, 138, 143, 173, 176, 195, 215, 243, 287, 315, 319, 320
Cosmic Christ 4, 9, 102
crone 206

D

Daughter 75, 85, 136, 162, 244, 323
demiurge 28, 41, 49, 50, 111, 117, 118, 119, 130, 170, 172, 230

desire-energy 39, 54, 163, 214, 225, 279, 280-282, 290, 295, 296
Divine Feminine 46, 76, 183, 185, 298
Divine I Am 91, 93, 218, 225, 231, 232, 244
Divine Masculine 123, 183, 185, 298
dream 22, 43, 44, 51, 54, 56, 57, 59, 60, 62, 64, 65, 66, 76, 88, 92, 119, 131, 132, 135, 138, 158, 160, 163, 180, 186, 196, 206, 210, 216, 218, 227, 321
dream altar 60-62
dreamcatcher 86, 196
dream union 60, 66
drum 193, 197, 200, 207, 208, 219, 257, 259, 265, 267

E

eagle 101, 151
Eagle Woman 15, 46, 109, 146, 147, 150, 200, 201, 241, 266
Earth Mother 10, 28, 35,

45-48, 50, 51, 63, 70,
80, 81, 86, 87, 98,
105, 107, 108, 111, 113,
114, 123, 125, 146, 151,
152, 164, 196, 197,
206, 211, 216, 217,
218, 219, 222, 243,
250, 254, 256, 259,
261, 262, 263, 264,
265, 267, 269, 270,
284, 300, 301
Eheieh 84, 85, 93, 121
elder 75, 132
elder races 182, 183, 242,
282, 299, 304, 305,
306, 308
Elohim 5, 46, 47, 55, 70,
77, 84, 85, 125, 175,
226, 230, 241, 244,
262
energetic body 29, 123, 131,
163, 187, 217, 218,
232, 234, 240, 254,
255, 256

F

feathers 164, 190, 194, 196,
200, 201
Fiery Intelligence 26, 52,
53, 82, 116, 151, 154,
214, 215, 216, 277,
278, 324
fire 254, 258, 262, 265,
269, 273
Fire Snake 52, 54, 82, 88,
113, 157, 163, 216, 218-
222, 225, 226, 229,
236-238, 277-279,
289, 290, 302
Four Enemies 37, 49, 95,
242
full moon 146, 148, 184,
185, 186, 265, 266

G

Gevurah 24, 233
Glory Body 149, 150, 163,
191, 325
gnosis 4, 9, 42, 98, 152,
187, 231, 232, 278
gospel 189, 298
Grandfather Fire 197, 210,
220
Grandmother 11, 76, 81, 82,
86, 87, 88, 136, 146,
147, 200, 220, 241,
265, 276

H

Habad 41, 83, 97, 98, 232
Hashmal 68, 71, 191
Hayyah 77, 80, 89
heart womb 66, 121, 144, 148, 193
Hesed 233
Hod 233
Holy Hill 11, 12, 13, 14, 15, 16, 19, 35, 44, 67, 70, 77, 100, 101, 106, 115, 117, 122, 140, 142, 156, 170
Holy Spirit 2, 3, 5, 23, 26, 32, 33-35, 53, 55, 70, 72, 78, 79, 81, 90, 102, 103, 105, 106, 119, 125, 128, 134, 136, 145, 157, 159, 162, 171, 181, 182, 192, 206, 209, 213, 218, 224, 225, 227, 231, 232, 240, 242, 251, 252, 258, 268, 277, 278, 302, 304, 307
hummingbird 200

I

Imma 36, 76, 84-86, 88, 89, 148, 165, 175, 176, 183, 186, 188, 195, 241, 242, 244, 262
Infernal Woman 16, 46, 109, 146, 147, 148, 150, 151, 200, 206, 242
Inquisition 14, 25, 94, 122, 130, 133, 161
interior stars 3, 6, 123, 163, 218, 219, 224-236, 240, 253, 271, 298
ivur 306

J

Juan Bernadino 15, 133, 136, 137, 138, 139, 149

K

Kabbalah 22, 24, 43, 46, 56, 61, 65, 80, 94, 125, 139, 182, 193, 208, 223, 233, 277, 305, 307, 332
Kallah 242, 244, 326
kavvanah 37, 69, 219
klippah 92, 176, 228
klippot 109, 231
Kundalini Yoga 163, 278

L

lightning strike 217, 292
Light-Presence 28, 30, 52, 82, 99, 110, 121, 141, 166, 176, 232, 292, 327
Lodge 272, 273
Logos 188, 230, 276

M

maggidim 305, 316
Maiden 11, 12, 13, 14, 15, 16, 18, 19, 26, 43, 82, 85, 89, 105, 106, 114, 115, 117, 118, 119, 122, 123, 132, 136, 140, 141, 142, 145, 146, 147, 148, 152, 156, 158, 160, 163, 165, 166, 170, 172, 180, 184, 186, 190, 191, 193, 195, 198, 201, 202, 203, 208, 210, 217, 219, 223, 235, 241, 242, 243, 248, 253, 273, 279, 280, 291, 293, 304, 306
Makom 90
Malkut 36, 85, 233
Messiah 4-7, 27, 31-34, 44, 46, 80, 85, 86, 87, 94, 99, 108, 116, 118, 119, 121, 145, 151, 157, 171, 172, 176, 177, 187, 200, 223, 229, 232, 238, 248, 249, 266, 282
Mexico 12, 16, 24, 25, 31, 76, 93, 94, 106, 117, 123, 134, 148, 161, 165
moon cycle 3, 184, 185, 217, 281, 283, 285-288, 292, 303

N

Nahautl 214
neshamah 44
Netzach 233
New Jerusalem 95
new moon 184, 185, 186, 259, 283, 283, 286

O

oral tradition 1, 2, 6, 23, 76, 102, 132, 145, 175, 187, 199, 240

P

Partzuf 36, 297, 307
Path of the Moon 125, 126
Path of the Sun 81, 125, 126, 267, 305
perfect success 73, 306
Pleroma of Light 138, 167, 186
prayer 28, 69, 80, 91, 125, 126, 158, 160, 163, 164, 165, 174, 180, 183, 187, 190, 192, 193, 195, 200, 203, 204, 208, 209, 212, 213, 216, 230, 239, 244, 248, 251, 252, 257, 259, 263, 267, 268, 269, 273, 276, 283, 297, 306
flower bundle 2, 158, 159, 172, 174, 175, 194
prayer ties 158, 159, 167, 272
prayer tree 159, 167
Primordial Mother 81, 86, 90, 232
Primordial Tradition 68
purification 48, 69, 117, 168, 193, 203, 204, 207, 210, 222, 257, 265, 268, 273, 285, 293, 294, 300

R

rattles 3, 199, 212, 244
red mother seed 236
revelation 1-4, 11, 21, 22, 24-27, 31, 33, 36, 43, 45-47, 50, 51, 59, 67, 68, 72, 78, 83, 84, 86, 88-90, 92, 96, 97, 101, 102, 109, 136, 137, 146, 158, 172, 175, 181, 185, 188, 189, 193, 228, 278, 304, 305, 311
Roman Church 25, 127, 128
Ruach Ha-Kodesh 5, 79, 106

S

Sacred Circle 28, 42, 59, 67, 69, 70, 80, 105, 107, 125, 137, 145-150, 152, 158, 164, 166, 186, 188, 191, 193, 195, 197, 201, 204, 206, 207, 210, 211, 214, 226-231,

233, 238-240, 241,
263, 267, 276, 288,
299, 300, 306
Second Coming 1,3, 6, 7,
33, 90, 116, 127, 134,
136, 181, 185, 278,
304
Sefirah 36, 80
Sefirot 65, 193, 233, 307,
322
serpent power 3, 52, 54,
151, 186, 199, 200,
214-218, 220-223,
225, 226, 232, 234-
238, 240, 241, 277,
278, 279, 280, 281,
282, 289, 290, 302
Serpent Woman 46, 109,
146, 147, 151, 186,
235, 241, 276, 280
sexual mysticism 182
Shabbat 36, 132
shaman 27, 30, 31, 32, 33,
34, 37, 40, 43, 48,
50, 53, 68, 69, 79,
102, 105, 107, 124,
131, 133, 141, 142,
159, 166, 168, 180,
183, 199, 202, 203,

209, 241, 248, 262,
268, 272, 306
shamanism 32
shefa 80
shrine 2, 88, 90, 91, 123,
124, 159, 168, 191,
192, 195, 196, 298
silence 50, 67, 72, 73, 74,
181, 187
Sixth Sun 33, 134, 181
smudging 147, 164, 167,
192, 201, 203, 205,
207, 212, 223, 252,
258, 267, 272
Solar Being 116, 117, 121,
154, 172, 186-188, 217,
232, 236, 253
Son 76, 86, 162, 243
Sophia 8, 87, 97, 136, 152,
277
Sophian 1-6, 25, 42, 88,
105, 216, 236, 241,
248, 277, 283, 287,
291, 305, 315
Spider Woman 46, 109,
146, 147, 150, 152,
186, 196, 197, 235, 241

spirit catcher 196-198
Spiritual Sun 14, 29, 30, 44, 51, 55, 66, 70, 76, 78-82, 85, 86, 88, 89, 97, 99, 100, 101, 103, 108-110, 112, 116, 121, 122, 126, 127, 129, 130, 136, 145, 166, 168, 171, 172, 174, 186, 187, 188, 192, 193, 200-202, 206, 214, 216, 217, 222, 223, 237, 238, 243, 249, 250, 259, 263, 266, 270, 278, 279, 280, 282, 292, 293

staff 105, 147, 194, 199, 201, 202, 207, 219, 243, 259, 259, 266

stones 101, 103, 104, 161, 190, 194, 211, 212, 259, 262, 263, 265

subtle body 224, 235, 238, 266, 270, 288, 324

sun 11, 125, 207, 219, 236, 248, 253, 262, 264, 267

Sun of Flowering 33, 159, 162, 192, 242, 244, 278, 304

Supernal 26, 32, 34, 36, 41, 44, 46, 59, 63, 69, 89, 93, 97, 98, 101, 109, 110, 116, 135, 137, 138, 144, 152, 154, 181, 182, 185, 193, 200, 218, 226, 231, 232, 235, 242, 243, 262, 304, 307

Supernal Shekinah 36, 236

Supramental 76, 93, 218, 231, 232, 235, 327

T

Tau 135, 248

Teotl-Dios 10, 13, 18, 24, 25, 28, 115, 170

Tepeyacac 10, 13, 17, 19, 22, 35, 45-47, 77, 90, 91, 96, 106, 123, 156, 170, 174, 175, 180

Thunder Beings 151, 221

Tiferet 80, 193

tikkune 42, 65, 139, 167, 204

Tlatelolco 76

Toltec 24, 30, 31, 33, 37, 45, 95, 103, 112, 133, 134, 162, 187, 200, 209, 223, 276, 333

Tonantzin 44
Torah 133, 139
Tree of Life 233
Truth Body 191
Tzaddik 139, 165, 168, 305
tzaddikim 125, 139, 305

W

walk of power 48, 50, 105, 106, 195
War Woman 16, 46, 109, 146, 147, 150, 151, 206, 242
waters 113, 193, 204, 257, 258, 259, 261, 268
Wedding Feast 148, 164, 241, 242, 244, 259, 300, 302
white father seed 236
Winds 50, 59, 67, 70, 164, 173, 205, 211, 238, 243, 263
Woman of Light 10, 24, 46, 88, 89, 96, 101, 116, 137, 146, 151, 152, 176, 181, 185, 186, 243, 282, 305,

Y

Yahweh 42, 46, 55, 68, 70, 73, 84, 85, 125, 262, 276
Yeshua 4, 5, 7, 14, 22, 27, 32, 33, 34, 46, 64, 77, 80, 87, 89, 92, 94, 95, 100, 101, 116, 118, 119, 221, 127, 130, 134, 153, 223, 238, 240, 248, 257, 268, 269, 298, 312, 313
Yetzirah 149

Z

Zumárraga 12, 106

www.ingramcontent.com/pod-product-compliance
Lightning Source LLC
Chambersburg PA
CBHW071650160426
43195CB00012B/1419